CONSUMING SCHOOLS:
COMMERCIALISM AND THE END OF POLITICS

The increasing prevalence of consumerism in contemporary society often equates happiness with the acquisition of material objects. *Consuming Schools* describes the impact of consumerism on politics and education and charts the increasing presence of commercialism in the educational sphere through an examination of issues such as school–business partnerships, advertising in schools, and corporate-sponsored curriculum.

First linking the origins of consumerism to important political and philosophical thinkers, Trevor Norris goes on to examine the distinction between the public and private spheres through the lens of twentieth-century intellectuals Hannah Arendt and Jean Baudrillard. Through Arendt's account of the human activities of labour, work, and action, and the ensuing eclipse of the public realm, and Baudrillard's consideration of the visual character of consumerism, Norris examines how school commercialism has been critically engaged by in-class activities such as media literacy programs and educational policies regulating school–business partnerships.

TREVOR NORRIS is an assistant professor of philosophy of education at the Ontario Institute for Studies in Education, University of Toronto.

TREVOR NORRIS

Consuming Schools

Commercialism and the End of Politics

UNIVERSITY OF TORONTO PRESS
Toronto Buffalo London

© University of Toronto Press 2011
Toronto Buffalo London
www.utppublishing.com
Printed in the U.S.A.
Reprinted 2012

ISBN 978-1-4426-4205-8 (cloth)
ISBN 978-1-4426-1107-8 (paper)

Printed on acid-free paper.

Library and Archives Canada Cataloguing in Publication

Norris, Trevor, 1971–
   Consuming schools : commercialism and the end of politics / Trevor Norris.

   Includes bibliographical references and index.
   ISBN 978-1-4426-4205-8 (bound). – ISBN 978-1-4426-1107-8 (pbk.)

   1. Commercialism in schools.   2. Business and education.
   3. Consumption (Economics) – Political aspects.   4. Consumption
   (Economics) – Social aspects.   I. Title.

   LC1085.N672 2011   371.19′5   C2010-906082-2

This book has been published with the help of a grant from the Canadian
Federation for the Humanities and Social Sciences, through the Aid to
Scholarly Publications Program, using funds provided by the Social
Sciences and Humanities Research Council of Canada.

University of Toronto Press acknowledges the financial assistance to its
publishing program of the Canada Council for the Arts and the Ontario
Arts Council.

 Canada Council   Conseil des Arts    ONTARIO ARTS COUNCIL
for the Arts   du Canada   CONSEIL DES ARTS DE L'ONTARIO

University of Toronto Press acknowledges the financial support of the
Government of Canada through the Canada Book Fund for its publishing
activities.

For Carly, who inspires and begins

The miracle that saves the world, the realm of human affairs, from its normal, 'natural' ruin is ultimately the fact of natality.

– Hannah Arendt, The Human Condition, 247

Contents

Key to References

Arendt, Hannah. *The Human Condition*. Chicago: University of Chicago Press, 1958 (HC)

Barber, Benjamin. *Consumed: How Markets Corrupt Children, Infantilize Adults, and Swallow Citizens Whole*. New York: W.W. Norton, 2007 (CN)

Barber, Benjamin. *Jihad vs McWorld: Terrorism's Challenge to Democracy*. New York: Ballantine Books, 2001 (JM)

Baudrillard, Jean. *The Consumer Society: Myths and Structures*. London: Sage, 1970 (CS)

Baudrillard, Jean. *Simulacra and Simulation*. Ann Arbor: University of Michigan Press, 1994 (1981) (SS)

Baudrillard, Jean. *The System of Objects*. London: Verso, 1996 (1968) (SO)

Kenway, Jane, and Elizabeth Bullen. *Consuming Children: Education-Entertainment-Advertising*. Philadelphia: Open University Press, 2001 (CC)

Marx, Karl. *Das Kapital: A Critique of Political Economy*. New York: Modern Library, 1906 (1867), (DC)

Molnar, Alex. *School Commercialism: From Democratic Ideal to Market Commodity*. New York: Routledge, 2005 (SC)

Foreword

BENJAMIN R. BARBER

For over a century, critics of capitalism have complained about hyper-consumerism: the economy of overspending driven by the manipulation of wants and needs by marketers and advertisers aiming to sustain consumer demand long after real needs and wants have been met. The object is to allow capitalism to survive after the era of productivist activity has diminished and spending has become far more important than saving. The formula: how much easier to sell to those who have the means, whether or not they have the needs, than to sell to those who have the needs but may lack the means to satisfy them. How much simpler to accumulate profits through merger and acquisitions and buying on credit than increasing the real goods economy.

The story of consumerism is an old one. From Herbert Marcuse in *One-Dimensional Man* to John Kenneth Galbraith in *The Affluent Society*, from Walter Benjamin's critique of the age of mechanical production to David Riesman's critique of the lonely crowd and Thorstein Veblen's critical exploration of conspicuous consumption in his *The Theory of the Leisure Class*, commentators have been focusing less on capitalism per se than on the ills and abuses of consumer society and commercial culture. The historical inevitability of capitalism was already a component in Karl Marx's materialist analysis, and history itself has now made clear that capitalism is not only an inevitable form of social organization but possibly the only viable form that economic organization can take in the modern world. Its rival ideologies rooted in the command economy – statist notions of socialism or communism or fascist corporatism – have not survived their application in the real world. So the question of the new millennium is not so much '*whether* capitalism' as '*what kind* of capitalism?'

If early critics of capitalism were focused on predatory producers stealing the labour power of exploited workers, more recent critics of consumerism have targeted predatory marketers manipulating
compulsive shoppers and addictive consumers. For these critics, the
fundamental insight has been to notice how much more efficient the
exploitation of people can be if they can be made willing enactors of
the behaviour that exploiters once had to coerce them to undertake. In
the eighteenth century, Jean-Jacques Rousseau was already remark-
ing on the way in which the unnecessary amplification of psychological wants could outrun the physical capacity of humans to satisfy them.
Ironically, more power could unleash more wants and thus produce relative unhappiness, even (especially!) among those who were relatively
well off. Unhappiness, Rousseau wrote, is a function of the distance between our perceived wants and the power we have to satisfy them. The
paradox is that imagination and social pressure constantly cause wants
to outrun power, even if power grows.

Alexis de Tocqueville took Rousseau's insights further, noting that
the chains inside the human head could be far more binding than those
placed on the body. His logic is evident in a notorious African monkey
trap that captures greedy simians by allowing them to put their paws
into an anchored box through a small hole and grasp a nut. The trouble
is, they cannot withdraw the paw without unclasping the fist, but to do
so means relinquishing the nut. This they assiduously refuse to do, and
so they remain captive by virtue of their own imprudent desire.

Modern consumers sometimes seem to imitate the monkey: although
in no way 'forced' to consume, they remain manacled to the mall by
desire – by manipulated will and shopaholic addiction. No producer
or vendor puts a gun to their heads and forces them to buy. Indeed,
producers insist they merely 'give customers what they want.' They
even talk about 'empowering' consumers, enabling children to become
consumers. In reality, the new consumerism corrupts children while
dumbing down adults in a new ethos of infantilization. If once, in Max
Weber's image, early productivist capitalism was driven by Protestant
values like hard work, saving, and deferred gratification (the rise of
capitalism and the Protestant ethic), today in a consumerist economy
what is required is an infantilist ethic that encourages leisure rather
than work, spending rather than saving, and impulsive self-gratifica-
tion rather than a prudent deferral of needs. This new 'infantilist ethos'
has a delusionary quality, however. 'Empowered' consumers no more
possess real power than trapped monkeys possess real freedom, for

neither monkeys nor consumers can be regarded as autonomous moral persons or free citizens. Infantilization erodes autonomy and undermines the virtues that once sustained a capitalism of investment and productivity.

As a consequence, in our consumerist era, courtesy of the infantilist ethos, commerce has become omnipresent, a kind of totalizing ether that envelopes society and penetrates every domain. How paradoxical! For when society is dominated by religion in every sector and domain, we call it theocracy and protest it as a form of tyranny. And when it is dominated by politics so that neither private life nor economics nor religion is safe from politicization, we call it totalitarianism and deem it the very negation of all liberty. Yet when commerce dominates our life world in every aspect, we call it liberty and celebrate our putative empowerment.

This paradox goes to the heart of the challenge of consumerism in today's world of fiscal crisis and economic uncertainty, for unending credit afforded to impulsive consumers who spend more than they have and want more than they need has precipitated a global financial crisis in which banks find themselves over-leveraged and saddled with endless bad debt whose value cannot even be calculated. Consumers find themselves swamped in debt, home foreclosures and credit card insolvency have ballooned, and the underlying social capital and civic trust on which the entire capitalist economy rests are radically diminished. Hyper-consumerism's chickens come home to roost, as it were.

These daunting considerations make Trevor Norris's important new study of consumerism a timely and relevant contribution to the literature of our commercialized, over-consuming society. Norris brings both a theoretical and an empirical sensibility to the crisis, allowing him both to explore the sources and mechanisms of modern consumer capitalism and to reckon their costs – not just for democratic culture but for capitalism itself. He updates and deepens the themes laid on the table over the last hundred years by Marcuse, Galbraith, Veblen, Riesman, Benjamin, and others, and does so with imagination and conviction.

Norris properly locates the debate over consumerism in the political theory of classical liberalism as it unfolds in Thomas Hobbes, John Locke, and Adam Smith, and then traces its course through classical Marxism down to modern thinkers like Hannah Arendt and Jean Baudrillard, who are attentive to its democratic and symbolic entailments. But Norris has done more than follow the trajectory of liberal thought through consumerist space. He understands that the debate today turns on the role of education, for as once upon a time education and democracy stood in a vital relationship to one another, the second resting crucially on the first, with civic pedagogy as the key to robust citizenship, today education and consumerism stand in a similarly crucial relationship. Can the classroom become a site of resistance to commercial culture or will it turn into its willing ally? Is consumerism itself a new pedagogy, with advertising and marketing tools that offer the young an alternative tutor that reinforces rather than challenges its dominion? Or will commercialist corruptions be cured by the application of a civic curriculum to consumer thinking?

Norris treats these questions not simply as provocative issues for public debate but as determiners of classroom behaviour and curriculum. His message is clear: if education cannot restore democracy to a place of autonomy and independence, the wall separating commerce and pedagogy is likely to grow porous and the future of democracy will be left to the dubious whims of ever intrepid marketers.

Benjamin R. Barber is a Distinguished Senior Fellow at the think tank DEMOS in New York and Walt Whitman Professor Emeritus at Rutgers University. His seventeen books include *Strong Democracy*, *Jihad vs McWorld*, and *Consumed: How Markets Corrupt Children, Infantilize Adults, and Swallow Citizens Whole*.

CONSUMING SCHOOLS:
COMMERCIALISM AND THE END OF POLITICS

Introduction:
Consumerism in Our Own Schoolyards

Of wealth, no boundary lies known to man.

– Solon[1]

Great Orators

In the days after the attacks of 11 September 2001, George W. Bush sought to provide reassurance, strength, and direction to a disoriented American people. Joining a long tradition of great orators in times of struggle, his inspiring words galvanized a nation and reflected what has become the defining spirit of the American people: he called upon the American people to go shopping.

Amid the tumult and distress of those shocking days, the peculiarity of this conflation of grieving and consuming was easily overlooked and forgotten. That it would be the responsibility of a democratically elected leader to call upon the people to shop is surely a perversion of the meaning of political leadership. Had Bush himself not raised the topic, it might otherwise seem offensive or inappropriate to bring up shopping in the context of war. Indeed, Benjamin Barber wonders if it is proper to criticize consumerism in a time of war, asking, 'How much should we care? In an age when terrorism stalks the planet, when fear of Jihad is as prevalent as the infringement of liberties to which fear gives rise, when AIDS and tsunamis and war and genocide put democracy at risk in both the developing and the developed world, it may seem self-indulgent to fret about the dangers of hyperconsumerism' (CN, 4).

Yet dramatic and provocative images of war and violence might otherwise conceal the quiet and gradual spread of consumerism. A month later, Bush reiterated the same message: 'We cannot let the terrorists achieve the objective of frightening our nation to the point where we don't conduct business, where people don't shop.'[2] This thoroughgoing equation of America's strength as a nation with 'consumer confidence' perhaps was intended simply to reassure the populace by conveying a sense of normalcy. Yet it is radically unlike the words spoken by other great political leaders in times of turmoil, and radically different from the slogans of the Second World War about the importance of courage, frugality, and investing in war bonds. Consider, for example, Winston Churchill's profound and inspirational speech to the British people on 4 June 1940, in which he passionately declared, 'We will fight them in the beaches, we shall fight on the landing grounds, we shall fight in the fields and in the streets, we shall fight in the hills; we shall never surrender.'[3] Today a trip to Walmart is said to perform the same political function and express equivalent love of country.

In the weeks that followed, many American cities coast to coast participated in 'America: Open for Business,' an initiative intended to help encourage consumption and 'boost consumer confidence.'[4] Numerous corporations also tapped into patriotic shopping, and some began selling 'Patriotic Shopping Totes.'[5] Florida governor Jeb Bush agreed with his brother about the importance of shopping as a patriotic duty: 'We need to respond quickly so people regain confidence and consider it their patriotic duty to go shopping.'[6] Vice-president Dick Cheney claimed that shopping was not only an act of patriotism but also an act of military aggression, describing shopping as a way for ordinary citizens to 'stick their thumbs in the eye of the terrorists.'[7] Ironically, a few months later Bush insisted, 'Too many have the wrong ideas of Americans as shallow, materialist consumers ... But this isn't the America I know.'[8] Yet five years later at a press conference he restated his original solution: 'I encourage you all to go shopping more.'[9]

Concerns about the prevalence of consumerism have even emerged from economists, who worry that the spread of consumerism in the Western world has led to exceptionally low savings rates: Whereas twenty years ago savings rates were 20 per cent of annual income and by ten years ago had declined to 10 per cent, savings rates were recently measured at 0.5 per cent in Canada and -0.6 per cent in the United States, 'the lowest level on record.'[10] Perhaps it is no coincidence that 'the country that spends the most per capita on advertising has the lowest savings rates among advanced economies.'[11] While economists warned for years that this decline was cause for concern, economic events of fall 2008 are a direct result of this pattern.

Yet low consumption rates are said to be equally problematic as dramatic differences in consumption and savings rates between the West and China are construed as a major source of global economic instability. A 2008 IMF report stated that 'gross domestic savings in China have surged since 2000, climbing to over 50 percent of GDP in 2005,' and that perhaps most remarkably this increase occurred even as interest rates on savings remained low.[12] A *Globe and Mail* article noted that American and Chinese central bankers Alan Greenspan and Zhou Xiaochuan were addressing similar but opposite crises: the world economic system would be destabilized if the Chinese did not reduce their savings rates and increase their spending by adopting Western consumer habits. Xiaochuan noted, '"This means we need to reform our social security system to give households more confidence to spend money."' Traditional Confucian religious values were construed as impediments to consumption and were therefore to be undermined: '"We have a very big challenge: We have too much investment in our economy and relatively weak domestic consumption,"' Mr Zhou said. '"Probably it's related to the Chinese tradition, the Confucian tradition ... they save the money for old people; they save too much money. It's the contradiction of the situation in the United States."' In an example of Orwellian doublespeak, Greenspan responded by emphasizing the need for the Chinese to 'reduce dissaving.'[13] To increase consumption, the Western world exerted diplomatic and economic pressure on China to encourage its citizens to adopt global consumption habits: 'What is most pressing for the Chinese is the need to increase general domestic consumption, something the International Monetary Fund has touched upon.'[14] Chinese 'oversaving' was held up as one reason for the global economic crisis during the fall of 2008, and it was suggested that U.S. bank bailouts could be supplemented by increased consumer spending in China: 'Most everyone agrees that to put the global economy right, Americans must stop borrowing so much and start producing more. But the flip side, crisis watchers say, is that China needs to save less and spend more ... over-saving can be as much of an economic vice as overspending.'[15] Global economic stability requires the thorough integration of all countries and cultures into consumer society.

Shopping itself has now become a news story, and several large newspapers such as the *New York Times* and *Toronto Star* include a separate 'Shopping' section, full not only of advertisements but also helpful suggestions and elaborate stories of exciting shopping experiences. The *Economist* published a special supplement titled 'The Consumer as King' detailing ways that consumption can be more widely embraced.[16] There are now several entire television channels dedicated to shopping: ShopTV, Planet Shopping, and the Shopping Channel. A new genre of fiction has emerged celebrating the joys of shopping, including the series titled 'Confessions of a Shopaholic' in which the female protagonist struggles with and celebrates her shopping habits, now made into a feature movie.[17]

In 2006 *Advertising Age* broke from its tradition of awarding the prize for the 'most successful advertiser' to an advertising agency, and instead awarded the prize to 'The Consumer': 'The marketing world leaders took to the stage and declared that it's time to give up control and accept that consumers now control their brands.' The magazine editors claimed this coup occurred because consumers are increasingly making their own commercials and posting them online. 'Consumers [today] have lots of ways of communicating, and trust each other's views above marketers' overt sales pitches.' Thus it appears that consumerism has now taken on the character of populist, grassroots activism as a way to wrest control away from marketers. Asked if this is a threat to advertising agencies, the author suggests that this is yet another opportunity for advertisers: 'The question for 2007 will be whether marketers and agencies find ways to harness that consumer-bred creativity – so unpolished and unaccountable – and deploy it in the service of brands.'[18]

In an insightful survey of the 'education-entertainment-advertising' cultural matrix, Jane Kenway and Elizabeth Bullen assert that 'consumerism is now recognized as a defining characteristic of the lifestyle of the Western world' (CC, 8). A wide variety of contemporary developments support this notion: protestors in anti-globalization movements have increasingly targeted sites of consumption such as shopping malls, storefronts, and commercial logos; the expenditure by corporations on advertisements and image creation has grown exponentially and now often far outstrips the costs of the physical production of commodities.

While international politics increasingly takes on the tone of apocalyptic fervour, some have argued that the centrality of consumerism to the American way of life is itself responsible for widespread anti-Western resentment. In *Jihad vs McWorld*, political theorist Benjamin Barber asserts that the proliferation of Western consumerism constitutes a new 'soft' power of 'McWorld's assiduously commercialized and ambitiously secularist materialism,' and 'inadvertently contribute[s] to the causes of terrorism' (JM, xxvi, xi). All too often the West has been more successful at spreading consumer goods and values than the institutions and practices of democracy: 'McWorld in tandem with the global market economy has globalized many of our vices and almost none of our virtues' (JM, xxvii). For Barber, consumerism is 'a kind of soft imperialism in which those who are colonized are said to "choose" their commercial indenture. But real choice demands real diversity and civic freedom' (JM, xxxi). And yet Barber notes, 'The war against Jihad will not, in other words, succeed unless McWorld is also addressed' (JM, xiv). More recently Barber noted, 'The victory of consumers is not the same as victory of citizens. McWorld can prevail and liberty still lose' (CN, 4).

Cultural theorists Robert Goldman and Stephen Papson agree that the signs of consumption breed violent reactions by disrupting meaning and identity: 'The same conditions of semiotic weightlessness breed fundamentalist political backlashes as people once again search for the security and moral certitude of fixed meaning that will see them through an epoch of bewildering changes.'[19] Sociologist Manuel Castells agrees that fundamentalism is often a reaction against consumerism and identity disruptions because dramatic global changes lead to reactionary identity formations and extreme political movements that become the central markers of the self: 'In such a world of uncontrolled, confusing change, people tend to regroup around primary identities: religious, ethnic, territorial, national. Religions fundamentalism, Christian, Islamic, Jewish, Hindu, and even Buddhist, is probably the most formidable force of personal security and collective mobilization in these troubled years. In a world of global flows of wealth, power, and images, the search for identity, collective or individual, ascribed or constructed, becomes the fundamental source of social meaning.'[20]

In its quest to establish new markets and satiate our own consumer society, the Western world extends its reach globally and draws all nations into its orbit. What theorists have called the McDonaldization, Disneyfication, and Coca-colonization[21] of society is not only a new force in the evolving international system but a colonial force in our own backyard – or rather, in our schoolyards. The inroads made by advertisers into the school environment in order to gain access to the student body are possibly the most compelling evidence that our society has become a consumer society. Today's youth market is worth billions, and advertisers are aggressively pursuing this target audience through 'school–business partnerships,' by which schools become an opportunity to secure a new market of consumers. Ideally, education is considered a means of critically engaging students in social and political issues, constructively enabling the development of a robust democracy and active citizenry. Consumerism, however, undermines the critical task of education, reducing it to a process by which students become increasingly acquisitive yet decreasingly inquisitive. When corporations go to school, what they learn is how to undo schooling. Yet education must be preserved as the location for the development of the reflective capacity to critique these same dominant social practices through the cultivation of civic responsibility for the renewal of a vibrant public realm.

As unprecedented historical developments point towards the emergence of a new form of political order with consumption at its centre, and as this new order is reflected in our own subjective experience and self-understanding, its problematic features are becoming increasingly apparent, perhaps most accurately conveyed through the equation of consumerism with our very existence in an update of the famous Cartesian *cogito ergo sum*: 'The original quest for salvation has been transformed into one for consumption ... "I consume therefore I am."'[22] The central issue is that we are not only consuming products but that something fundamental within ourselves and essential to our political existence is compromised. Today even time itself is being consumed; we often speak of activities as being 'time consuming.' We are colonized by consumerism, which seems to spread of its own accord.

Consumerism's institutionalized production of need and relentless invention of new desires entails the systematic inculcation of inadequacy and yearning for completion through material gratification such that consumerism becomes conflated with happiness and personal fulfilment. *Oniomania*, the compulsive desire to shop more widely known as 'shopaholism,' has entered the vernacular and is now recognized as the medical condition 'compulsive shopping disorder,' a *DSM-IV* 'impulse control disorder.' An organization called Shopaholics Anonymous has formed an online support group, Loose Change.[23] Perhaps appropriately for an age of commodities and quick fixes, there is a pill solution for oniomania called Citalopram.[24]

What several cultural theorists have called the 'malling of America'[25] is evident in the fact that 'shopping center space has increased by a factor of 12 in the last 40 years ... By 2000, there were more than 45,000 shopping malls in the United States, with 5.47 billion square feet of gross leasable space.'[26] The group DeadMalls[27] documents the decline of malls throughout North America as they are replaced by large 'box stores.' Yet consumption entails more than the mere fiscal transaction of physical acquisition. I will critique but not stop at this common understanding of the term, and will instead examine consumerism as an archetypal activity of contemporary society. As Frank Trentmann puts it, the 'tendency to reduce consumption to a materialist acquisition of goods by individuals makes it difficult to explore the multi-faced workings of consumption in society and politics.'[28] The model of consumerism extends itself into all aspects of human life, including the teacher–student relationship, the nature of knowledge, and the experience of citizenship. In this sense, consumerism constitutes a process that expands beyond the purchasing of a product to include the transformation of all things in the world into objects for human consumption. This trend parallels the decline of active political citizenship and participation in the public realm – we are asked to shop as a means of supporting our country in a time of need – and the transformation of human relations into consumer relations. We experience ourselves as consumers before and above other forms of self-understanding, such as political animals and democratic citizens. The consumer replaces – or rather even 'consumes' – the citizen.

Consumerism is important to study because it is a concept that illuminates the defining features of our lives and calls us to rethink our faith in progress and democracy itself. That said, I will not attempt to develop a final or all-encompassing theory of consumerism but rather explore its philosophical underpinnings, cultural manifestations, and political and pedagogical implications with a deep concern for how education can better serve democracy and public life. In doing so, I implicitly appeal to the democratic theories of thinkers like John Dewey, who in *Democracy and Education* defines democracy as more than a form of government, set of institutions, or periodic elections, but rather a 'mode of associated living, of conjoined communicated experience,' even a 'way of life.'[29] More recently, Benjamin Barber emphasized the centrality of the democratic function of education by stating that democracy and education are 'inextricably linked and that in a free society the link is severed only at our peril. Education must be both public and democratic if we wish to preserve our democracy's public spaces.'[30] This link is fundamental to the emergence of a global citizenship: 'Citizenship is nurtured first of all in democratic civil society. A global citizenship demands a domain parallel to McWorld's in which communities of cooperation do consciously and for the public good what markets currently do inadvertently on behalf of aggregated private interests. This is no easy task' (JM, 277).

This book begins by exploring the historical origin and nature of

consumerism through recent centuries, culminating in the conflict between capitalism and communism in the twentieth century. The second
chapter considers its problematic pedagogical implications such as the
inroads made by corporations and advertisers into the educational environment. I ask why corporations might want access to schools, and
then provide several examples of this dynamic, arguing that consumerism's penetration into education must be tempered as it negates education's critical and democratic possibilities. Chapter 3 demonstrates
the relevance of Hannah Arendt's account of human activities and the
impact of consumerism on the public realm. The semiotic character of
consumerism is not fully explored by Arendt, but is carried forward
more recently by Jean Baudrillard. Thus, the fourth chapter outlines
his semiotic analysis of consumerism as a discourse or 'code' that separates the commodity from its sign and results in the death of the real
behind the image. The similarities and differences between Arendt and
Baudrillard help prepare new ground upon which to advance our understanding of this fundamental political and pedagogical challenge
of our times. However, Baudrillard leaves us at an impasse regarding
the possibilities of resisting consumerism. Therefore, to forefront how
education can better serve democracy, the final chapter considers how
the impact of consumerism on education can and has been critically
engaged, beginning with policies regulating school–business partnerships and moving on to more effective in-class activities such as media
literacy and culture jamming, strategies for subverting the intended
meanings of media and advertisements. I address the tension between
education as the reproduction of consumerism and as a site for its critical resistance by considering how consumerism can be explicitly engaged in the classroom.

As a last point, it is important to explain the use of the words *we, our,*
and *us* as it relates to consumerism. While to some extent these words
do not describe the majority of the world's population because they
refer more specifically to North Americans of particular class and
social status, consumerism as an ideology affects everyone, even at
the furthest corners of the world. The accelerating flow of globalization and export of culture demonstrates that, despite economic, racial,
cultural, religious, or linguistic differences, it is almost impossible to
escape consumerism.

1 The Origins and Nature of Consumerism

I will offer one thousand gold pieces to any man who can show me a new pleasure.

– Xerxes[1]

In the modern world the production of consumption becomes more important than the consumption of production.

– John Lukacs[2]

What are the central characteristics of consumerism, and what evidence indicates its prevalence? What are the implications of the rise of consumerism when it becomes a way of relating to the world and others, and a way of engaging in politics and education? Are there alternative modes of politics and schooling less based on consumerism? The longings of the ancient Persian king Xerxes 2500 years ago have now become the central feature of contemporary times. Yet ironically the very pervasiveness of consumerism constitutes a significant impediment to thinking about and understanding consumerism. Sut Jhally notes that 'because we live inside the consumer culture, and most of us have done so for most of our lives, it is sometimes difficult to locate the origins of our most cherished values and assumptions.'[3] Consumerism is so pervasive that, like fish in water, we don't even notice it anymore.

This chapter explores the origins and nature of consumerism while avoiding simplistic good/bad Manichean categories and without expressing nostalgia for pre-capitalist societies or idealized notions of the past. Nevertheless, because wariness towards a good/bad approach has the potential to lead to a tacit acceptance of consumerism, the approach taken is highly critical. This tacit acceptance is a common position taken by marketers when they insist that consumers are increasingly 'savvy,' and that the popularity of consumerism demonstrates that there is nothing wrong with consumerism and that its critics are elitist. Marketers use such arguments to justify the growing presence of ads ('adcreep,'[4] 'the advertization of society'[5]) as a necessary response to savvy consumers.[6]

Rather than argue against all acts of consumption, a more fruitful approach is to explore what happens when consumption intrudes into the political and pedagogical realms and becomes a dominant ideology, for consumerism is not only about shopping or meeting our needs. As Kenway and Bullen note, 'Shopping is no longer limited by time and space' (CC, 12). As an ideological force, consumerism is not simply a habit of shopping but an entire way of being in the world, as it 'involves much more than simply purchasing, obtaining, and using goods and services.'[7] It is necessary to extend the meaning of consuming beyond shopping in order to explore how it shapes politics and schooling.

An initial understanding of consumption can be acquired through an etymological account. Hannah Arendt often explores the original meanings of terms that we take for granted so as to 'distill from [words] their original spirit' (HC, 38). According to the *Oxford English Dictionary*, the word *consume* first appeared in early English towards the end of the fourteenth century, when it meant 'to cause to disappear' or 'to evaporate.'[8] Consumption later became associated with the self-degenerative wasting disease of the Middle Ages, now known as pulmonary tuberculosis, which seemed to consume people from within.[9] However, the word *consumer* did not appear until well into the 1700s at the height of the Industrial Revolution. Cultural theorist Raymond Williams notes that although the word was originally understood in a pejorative sense, it slowly took on a neutral, abstract meaning in twentieth-century political economy – even as consumerism became more ubiquitous.[10]

In English, *consume* can be derived from two distinct Latin verbs:

- *consumere*, from *con sumere*, means to take in, to devour, to incorporate; To make an end of, or put to an end to, by doing away with. It implies to use up, wear out, and reduce to nothing, as in 'the fire consumed the building.'
- *consummare*, from *con summa*, means to sum up, bring to completion, fully accomplish, make perfect, or fulfill in a teleological culmination, as in 'to consummate.'[11]

This semantic ambivalence and paradoxical character of consumption apparent in its Latin origins implies that consumption is both a creative act of completion and consummation, and a destructive act of negation. We can speak of being consumed by anger, swept up and compelled towards action. But it also implies that it has overtaken us and undermined our freedom or agency. We could say that we are consumed by consuming. Perhaps it is this semantic ambivalence that is part of the seductive power of consumption: we can both create and destroy, both release our aggressive impulses and comfort and satiate ourselves, 'destroy something and obtain pleasure from it at the same time.'[12]

The Productivist Bias

A key theme in this brief historical account is the displacement of production by consumption: whereas early thinkers like Smith, Marx, and Weber emphasized the importance of commodity production, consumerism has now taken a dominant place in modern society.

Many thinkers have argued that politics is challenged by the prevalence of industrial production and its accompanying mechanical and instrumental world view. The emphasis on production promotes a tendency to view the world as composed of mere raw material, and promotes corresponding types of thought oriented towards subduing it for human use. While this focus on production is important, it has resulted in a comparative neglect of the importance of consumerism. Consumer theorist Jean-Christopher Agnew notes that unfortunately the 'history of consumer cultures scarcely compares in breadth or depth to the written history of industrial cultures; it is, if anything, a conspicuous absence.'[13] Anthony Giddens suggests that traditional analysis has therefore suffered from a 'productivist bias' due to the 'primacy of industry.'[14]

The gradual shift from the importance of the production of goods to the importance of production of needs, from a prevalent self-understanding as workers and producers to one of consumers, significantly affects the formation of human values: 'As we move through the circuit of capital in contemporary society, from the phase in which human labor is embodied in commodities available for exchange (production) to the phase in which surplus value is realized by those who own and sell them (consumption), quite different beliefs, values, and meanings, will accompany the process.'[15] Agnew asks, 'What were the processes by which a nineteenth-century "producer ethic" – a value system based on work, sacrifice, and saving – evolve into a dominant twentieth-century "consumer ethic"? ... How did consumption become a cultural ideal, a hegemonic "way of seeing" in twentieth-century America?'[16] Consumer theorists such as Aldridge, Bocock, and Clarke suggest that because the experience of production is alienating, we seek fulfillment in consumption, and that therefore the modern subject is experiencing a shift in identity and its expression from the workplace to consumption.[17] Douglas Kellner and Steve Best describe this as the shift from the union hall to the shopping mall: 'In consumer capitalism, the working classes abandon the union hall for the shopping mall and celebrate the system that fuels the desires it ultimately cannot satisfy.'[18]

Evidence of the increased cultural and political importance of consumerism can be observed in the changing character of political protests. In the 'Battle-of-Seattle' of 1999, anti-globalization activists protested sites of consumption such as corporate logos and storefronts.[19] Factors such as the decline of the 'life-long career,' widespread large-scale layoffs, and the growing sense of job insecurity resulting from 'outsourcing' or 'offshoring' led to a corresponding decline in the cultural importance of the workplace, unions, and labour. People decreasingly identify themselves with traditional work-based social groupings and more so with consumer products and the messages and meanings conveyed about them. As Henry Giroux says, there has been 'a shift away from the old forces and values of industrial production to a new emphasis on the "immaterial" production in the information industries.'[20]

Consuming is thus construed as an affirmation of self, a way of acting in the world, of expressing one's identity and difference and participating in something larger than oneself. It is driven by the conflicting impulse to both belong and be different, to identify with and differentiate from. As personal identity is in flux and decreasingly bound by rigid traditions and permanent constellations of meaning derived from work, consumption provides the opportunity for the development of a sense of self and cultivation of identity. This increasingly affects the notion of a cultural hero, as consumerism displaces the captains of industry and 'heroes of production' with Hollywood icons characterized simply by their consumption habits and lifestyles of excess: 'Self-images are increasingly taken from the world of consumption rather than from the world of work, modeled on the "heroes of consumption," the movie stars and the jet set, rather than on the "heroes of production," people like Andrew Carnegie, Henry Ford, and Bill Gates.'[21]

Consumerism has also been portrayed as an effective way to control and subdue populations by preventing the emergence of 'class consciousness.' In *Captains of Consciousness* Stewart Ewen argues that advertising and consumerism emerged because other forms of social control failed to restrain opposition to industrialization and the growing mechanization of human life. Growing working-class resentment could be simultaneously reduced and redirected through advertising and consumption. Early founders of public relations and advertising, such as Edward Bernays, embraced these possibilities: 'If we understand the mechanism and motives of the group mind, it is now possible to control and regiment the masses according to our will without their knowing it. Mass psychology is as yet far from being an exact science and the mysteries of human motivation are by no means revealed. But at least theory and practice have combined with sufficient success to permit us to know that in certain cases we can effect some change in public opinion by operating certain mechanisms.'[22] Thus, consumption became a means of '*buying* compliance from workers [because] the worker no longer needed to be enforced by discipline, but was ensured by the seductive rewards on offer in the sphere of consumption.'[23]

Consumer society entails a shift from the production of physical goods to the production of cultural signs and their meanings and the production of human needs – even the production of the consumer itself. Not only have we moved from an industrial to a post-industrial society, but the social and cultural importance of production has been overtaken by consumerism.[24] Galbraith and Larkin argue that more efficient productive technologies and therefore increased productive capacity result in an excess or overproduction of goods. Thus we live in a 'post-scarcity'[25] or 'affluent society.'[26]

The field of economics studies principles of consumer demand under the assumption that the market is guided by natural laws and driven by economic agents who are characterized primarily by rational self-interest. Economists assume that through access to objective information regarding products and their intrinsic qualities consumers are able to rationally deliberate and calculate and 'maximize utility.' However, in its self-characterization as the objective study of natural laws, classical economics minimizes the importance of factors that are fundamental to understanding consumerism, such as 'irrational' or emotional impulses ranging from desire and hedonism to anger and grief (we are encouraged to shop after 9/11). Thus, a deeper understanding of consumerism must be pursued beyond the productivist perspective of classical political economy in order to fully grasp its character and implications.

Consumerism as an Ideology: The End of History and the Nylon War

How did consumerism become so dominant in modern Western society? It could be argued that as the nation-state retreats in the face of commercial forces it has not been replaced by new forms of citizenship or political movements but instead by the rise of global capitalism and the international spread of consumerism. Rolling back the state has not necessarily transferred power to individual citizens but instead to unaccountable and unregulated market forces. Benjamin Barber aptly calls this 'market totalism' or 'consumer totalism,' and asks why we believe that a free market linked with consumerism will invariably lead to freedom and liberty. He notes that 'when religion colonizes every sector of what should be our multidimensional lives, we call the result theocracy; and when politics colonizes every sector of what should be our multidimensional lives, we call the result tyranny. So why, it might be asked, when the marketplace – with its insistent ideology of consumption and its dogged orthodoxy of spending – colonizes every sector of what should be our multidimensional lives, do we call the result liberty?' (CN 219–22).

Yet consumption has always been an integral part of human existence – our very physical survival depends on consuming. Regardless how aware we are of our consuming habits, or the extent to which we practise deliberate self-restraint or pursue alternative choices, we all remain consumers in some form. However, there is an important difference between consumption as a function of biological survival, and consumerism as an 'ism' or ideology. As British consumer theorist Frank Trentmann argues, 'By nature all human beings are consumers, but the political meaning and identity attached to consumption varies in history.'[27] In this book the word *consumerism* refers more broadly to the larger ideological framework, while *consumption* refers to more specific individual acts, either before or outside ideology.

What does it mean to say that consumerism is an ideology? Ideology has been a key political concept, beginning with Karl Marx. Arendt notes that ideologies are 'isms which to the satisfaction of their adherents can explain everything and every occurrence by deducing it from a single premise, [and] are known for their scientific character; they combine the scientific approach with results of philosophical relevance and pretend to be scientific philosophy.'[28] Consumerism is an ideology insofar as it is a hegemonic world view that is normalized, naturalized, and socially pervasive, yet often invisible and unquestioned, even as it is adhered to vigorously and even dogmatically.

Although consumerism displays these dimensions of ideologies, it stands apart from extreme ideologies such as fascism and communism in several important ways: there is no 'Consumers Party' that represents the will of consumers (though there are agencies that lobby on their behalf); there is no formal spokesperson or charismatic leader who inspires political guidance (though it is promoted by famous celebrity representatives drawn from the entertainment industry); there is no cohesive written or unwritten doctrine or founding text that can provide theoretical orientation (though there are countless marketing and advertising textbooks and guides that defend key presuppositions that promote consumerism).

Despite the defeat of the extreme ideologies driving two world wars, the story of the twentieth century may be more about the rise of consumerism than the deepening and broadening reach of democratic institutions and practices. The prevalence of consumerism brings into question the celebratory arguments about historical progress made by neo-conservative thinkers such as Francis Fukuyama, who suggests that there is a historical movement towards the emergence of liberal democratic institutions and values as the result of technological progress and the opening of economic markets, culminating in what he calls the 'end of history' in the realization of the liberal-democratic capitalist state.[29] He claims that 'there is a fundamental process at work that dictates a common evolutionary pattern for all human societies – in short, something like a Universal History of mankind in the direction of liberal democracy.' Fukuyama argues that with the end of such major ideological movements as fascism and communism we have entered a concluding stage of world history culminating in the global convergence of political systems around liberal democracy, because 'earlier forms of government were characterized by grave defects and irrationalities that led to their eventual collapse.' The failure of earlier forms of government demonstrates both the success and universal character of the underlying principles of Western capitalist societies. There can be no alternative to the present configuration of political life because 'we cannot picture to ourselves a world that is essentially different from the present one, and at the same time better.'[30] However, I argue that the Western world has proven much more successful at cultivating and spreading consumerism around the world than it has at cultivating and spreading the institutions and practices of democracy. In fact, the global spread of what Benjamin Barber calls 'McWorld' may help explain why the West is often reviled worldwide.[31]

Another celebrator of historical progress is *New York Times* columnist Thomas L. Friedman, who contends that the global spread of consumerism will invariably lead to the global spread of peace and democracy. Arguing that McDonald's exemplifies this trend, Friedman asserts that 'no two countries that both had McDonald's had fought a war against each other since each got its McDonald's.'[32] This notion came to be known as his 'Golden Arches theory of conflict prevention,' which asserts that peace and democracy will surely follow if consumerism is allowed to spread throughout the world.[33]

American cultural historian Lizabeth Cohen argues that in addition to its identification with progress and democracy, consumerism has become synonymous with the American dream itself, because 'material goods came to embody the promise of America' and demonstrated the superiority of the American dream over Soviet communism. She argues that 'not only would American products appeal in their own right, but their obvious superiority to shoddy Soviet manufacturers would dramatize the superiority of capitalism over communism.'[34] Social historian Gary Cross agrees, tracing how consumer goods and values became weapons in the Cold War through their equation with freedom and the American way of life.[35] Consumerism functioned as an essential component in the battle between capitalism and communism as the comparative lack of consumer goods among communist countries indicated the failure of any political system but capitalism.

Both of these American cultural theorists described how President Nixon responded to the Communist Russian superiority in the space race, following the launch of the Sputnik satellite, by asserting the superiority of Capitalist America at producing consumer goods. The famous 'kitchen debate' took place between Nikita Khrushchev and Richard Nixon in 1959 in a model home filled with consumer items demonstrating the comforts and labour-saving fruits of capitalism. These goods provided evidence of the superiority of the American way of life by emphasizing the affordability and accessibility of new homes and household appliances.[36] Nixon claimed that consumer goods were more important than military equipment to any victory in the Cold War. Khrushchev fatefully announced, 'Let us compete. The system that will give the people more goods will be the better system, and victorious.'[37] The debate between two world leaders ended very amicably with an agreement that both countries should become more open to each other.[38]

In the 1960s, American sociologist David Reisman parodied this conflict between communism and capitalism in a fictional 'Nylon War.' In this absurd war, America 'bombed' the USSR with consumer goods, such as nylons and ovens, believing that 'if allowed to sample the riches of America, the Russian people would not long tolerate masters who gave them tanks and spies instead of vacuum cleaners and beauty parlors.'[39] In Reisman's story, the Soviets at first believed that 'American capitalism had reached so critical a point that only through forcible gifts overseas could the Wall Street ruling clique hope to maintain its profits and dominance.'[40] The Soviet authorities changed their story and claimed that these consumer goods had been deliberately contaminated with atomic radiation and must be immediately turned in to the authorities. These 'bombings' created roaming tribes of Soviets, trekking across the Siberian wastelands and through Moscow streets, endlessly searching for the next air drop. The story concludes with Soviets planes dropping cans of caviar and fur coats over America, unsuccessful in converting new followers.

While there may be many reasons why communism eventually collapsed, examples from the kitchen debates to the nylon wars show how consumerism gradually took its place as a dominant political ideology. As the Berlin Wall fell, Gloria Steinem aptly described the emergence of consumerism within former communist countries: 'First we have a revolution, then we go shopping.'[41] Gorbachev would seem to agree, having now appeared in commercials for Pizza Hut.[42]

Origins of Consumerism

While there have been many attempts to characterize our own age, from the information age to the knowledge economy, or more recently the 'intangible economy,'[43] recent historical developments point towards the emergence of a new form of political order with consumerism at its centre. These developments highlight the distinction between humanity's requirements for survival, and the growth of an ideologically based consumerism whose proclivity is consumption for consumption's sake. I am concerned with the particular form that consumerism has taken in modern Western society insofar as it has become central to our entire way of life, permeating our experience of politics and pedagogy. While the 'consumer' is an economic category insofar as it is based on market relations, rather than political identification such as 'British subject' or 'Canadian citizen,' it is important to investigate its political implications and philosophical origins. While it may be best to 'avoid pinpointing one single "consumer revolution," and to accept that today's consumer society was brought about by a number of intersecting and overlapping changes,'[44] it is important to identify key historical changes in order to determine its distinguishing features. Hannah Arendt herself insists on the importance of making distinctions, arguing that without recognizing the importance of distinctions, we would be unable to discern the unique characteristics of modern society.[45] It is only by noticing what is new and different that we can understand the topic at hand.

Because some aspects of consumerism predate modernity, it is helpful to review several key thinkers and texts throughout Western history and offer an interpretation that highlights their treatment of consumerism. In considering the 'origins,' I am not looking for causes that logically follow from one to another and set into motion a chain of historical events that inevitably lead to a particular or predetermined outcome. I am not implying historical determinism but rather investigating key aspects and influences that suggest some earlier recognition of the character and consequences of consumerism.

The relative neglect of consumerism is apparent in the key works of some of the most influential Enlightenment thinkers, including Adam Smith (1723–90), Karl Marx (1818–83), and Max Weber (1864–1920). Each thinker was revolutionary in his own way: each wrote foundational texts (*The Wealth of Nations; Das Kapital; The Protestant Work Ethic and the Spirit of Capitalism*), founded entire disciplines, and expounded ideologies still with us today: political economy, Marxism, and sociology.

At the early stages of the Industrial Revolution Adam Smith wrote his *Inquiry into the Nature and Causes of the Wealth of Nations* in 1776, a book he humbly called 'the dawn of a new science and the opening of a new era in Europe.'[46] Smith hoped that his work would give 'order and meaning to the newly emerged world of commerce and the newly emerging world of industry.'[47] In doing so he 'was one of the first to recognize that the world had changed fundamentally with the advent of modernity – that henceforth the *economic* sphere (the "invisible hand" of the market) rather than the *political* sphere (the heavy-handed authority of the state) would be the determinant factor in shaping the overall life of society.'[48]

With great enthusiasm Smith celebrated the 'many advantages' that can be gained through the division of labour, arguing that an increase in labour power and production, and therefore wealth itself, would follow specialization. He emphasized how labour and the human propensity to trade goods can contribute to a general improvement in economic efficiency. However, the issue of consumption arose only briefly in his analysis when he critiqued mercantilism, the dominant economic paradigm of his time. Smith argued that 'consumption is the sole end and purpose of all production; and the interest of the producer ought to be attended to, only so far as it may be necessary for promoting that of the consumer ... But in the mercantile system, the interest of the consumer is almost constantly sacrificed to that of the producer; and it seems to consider production, and not consumption, as the ultimate end and object of all industry and commerce.'[49] While it is noteworthy that consumption surfaces at all, this excerpt marks the sole discussion of consumption in its approximately nine hundred pages; Smith gave only marginal consideration to the nature of consumption or its political implications.

Western scholars and historians suggest that distinctive features associated with the emergence of modern capitalism became increasingly apparent as the Industrial Revolution advanced. For example, some suggest that consumption was a response to the homogenizing forces of mechanization and technology caused by industrialization and growing urbanization.[50] People began to react against the crowding caused by growing urbanization and the increasing mechanization of daily life by embracing the values and habits of consumerism. Thus, consumption became a principal mode of self-expression, a common language through which we communicate and interpret shared cultural signs and meanings, and engage in the twin processes of identity formation and expression (DC, 36).

In the mid-1800s, almost a century after Adam Smith, Karl Marx also investigated problems arising from the process of industrialization – though with considerably less triumphalism. Like Smith, Marx focused his analysis of capitalism and political economy primarily on the political importance of human labour, arguing that the material conditions of production were the primary determinants of human consciousness and political order. Marx argued that we produce ourselves through our labour because human consciousness and political structures are determined by the ownership of the modes of production. His analysis focused on the central place of the commodity as the primary object of consumption, and what he termed the 'commodity fetish' as the driving force behind consumption in capitalist societies. However, like Smith's, his analysis is limited insofar as it emphasizes the importance of labour and production rather than consumption.

Whereas Smith opened *The Wealth of Nations* with a discussion of the division of labour, Marx opened *Das Kapital* with the first extensive analysis of the commodity and its political implications in terms of its use-value and exchange-value. *Use-value* refers to the function or utility of a commodity and is based on its inherent physical properties and specific function (for example, corn can be eaten). While the use-value of a commodity is fixed by its specific function, *exchange-values* are interchangeable depositories of use-value. The exchange value of a commodity is derived only when placed in relation to other commodities. Exchange-value is based on a variable relationship in which use-values are exchanged for other use-values, and their value is determined by their exchangeability: 'the proportion in which values in use of one sort are exchanged for those of another sort, a relation constantly changing with time and place. Hence exchange value appears to be something accidental and purely relative' (DC, 43).

An important part of Marx's understanding of the commodity is not only this distinction between use-value and exchange-value, but also his analysis of how it leads to the fetishistic character of commodities. 'At first glance, a commodity seems a commonplace sort of thing, one easily understood. Analysis shows, however, that it is a very queer thing indeed, full of metaphysical subtleties and theological whimsies' (DC, 81). Marx went on to outline how the commodity acquires a life of its own by being endowed with particular characteristics beyond its immediate use – its metaphysical subtleties and theological whimsies – when its exchange-value overcomes and eclipses its use-value and the commodity becomes valued primarily for exchange. The word *fetish* not only contrasts the rationality and instrumentalism prevalent in labour and production, but also suggests the residue of religion still present in commodity relations, in the belief that inanimate things have human characteristics. Thus, the idea of a 'commodity fetish' suggests that the commodity becomes mystified and animated with magical properties, turned into what Baudrillard calls a 'sign.' Consistent with his critique of the political function of religion as the 'opium of the masses' that undermines the possibility of social transformation, so too does the commodity itself take on a religious character.

Ironically, the commodity becomes animated and personalized at the same time that social forces and patterns become depersonalized and construed as objective, unchanging, and unchangeable. Marxist political theorist Joachim Israel says that as a result of fetishistic commodity relations, 'individuals feel that they are no longer affected by or subjugated to personal, human influences but to impersonal, objective, thing-like conditions, which they cannot change. Thus the transformation of interpersonal processes into "objective" processes carries with it a feeling of being a powerless object directed by forces outside human control.'[51] Even as the commodity becomes animated and personalized, the social world we create around us becomes construed as concrete and absolute. We feel helpless before forces that are larger than we are when human relations become depersonalized and we encounter others and society in an objectifying way; humans are able to bring commodities 'to life' yet unable to transform their own political conditions. Israel argues that for Marx this is a thoroughly inhospitable and inhuman environment for human life, in which we 'become a mechanical part of a mechanical system.'[52]

While *Das Kapital* marks an important early attempt at understanding modern industrial societies, several problems arise from Marx's account of the commodity. These problems are important because, although Marx is of course very well known as a profound critic of modern capitalism, his analysis is remarkably consistent with several key components of consumerism: nature is construed as 'raw material,' human needs are seen as insatiable, and we are construed as economic creatures first and foremost. I explore each in this order.

First, Marx emphasized the importance of labour to such an extent that he saw nature as mere raw material at our disposal to be used up in the productive process. Nature was simply available for human use, and without inherent value: 'To what extent some economists are misled by the Fetishism inherent in commodities ... is shown by the dull and tedious quarrel over the part played by Nature in the formation of exchange value. Since exchange value is a definite social manner of expressing the amount of labour bestowed upon an object, Nature has no more to do with it than it has in fixing the course of exchange' (DC, 94). Because the value of commodities comes only from the labour that went into them, Marx disregarded the inherent value of anything outside of the economic system of production and consumption.

The second limit of Marx's analysis is that he didn't question how we come to develop certain needs, whether there is a limit to our needs, or the extent to which human needs might be socially constructed. In doing so, he overemphasized the uniform or common characteristics of need. For example, on the first page of *Das Kapital* he asserted that a commodity is 'a thing that by its properties satisfies human wants of some sort or another. The nature of such wants, whether they spring from the stomach or from fancy, makes no difference' (DC, 41). In suggesting this, Marx overlooked the infinity of wants that spring from 'fancy.' Furthermore, in consumer society there is a conflation of necessity and luxury such that luxury becomes construed as a necessity. Last, those wants that emerge from 'fancy' may be more readily manipulated than those that emerge from the stomach. As I discuss in chapters 3 and 4, it is primarily our fancy rather than need that allows us to be influenced by consumerism.

The third limit of Marx's reasoning is his overemphasis on our status as economic beings. Marx's aim in *Das Kapital* was 'to examine the capitalist mode of production, and the conditions of production and exchange corresponding to that mode' (DC, 13). For Marx as much as for Smith, people were primarily creatures of production and exchange, the 'guardians' of commodities. He argued that people 'exist for one another merely as representatives of, and therefore, as owners of, commodities ... and the personifications of the economical relations that exist between them' (DC, 97). What dignifies us as humans is that we are capable of production and exchange, and he very narrowly focused on *Homo economicus*, on the determinative character of our economic activities of production and exchange. Traditional or orthodox Marxist analysis therefore suffers from what could be called a 'productivist bias.'

In sum, 150 years ago political economy did not include a significant consideration of consumerism. Marx did not consider the problematic implications of the ascent of economic concerns to a position of political dominance, as Arendt expressed. Nor did his analysis consider the communication of symbolic meaning through commodities, and was therefore unable to consider the extent to which signs and symbols could become commodities themselves, as is so central to the work of Jean Baudrillard. However, control over the mode of consumption is as important as control over the mode of production, and the production of signs is as important as the production of commodities.

Moving to the beginning of the twentieth century, German sociologist Max Weber (1864–1920) investigated the religious and ethical origins of capitalism in his famous *Protestant Work Ethic and the Spirit of Capitalism* of 1905.[53] Weber argued that the rise of capitalism was driven primarily by shifting religious values, specifically those that encouraged the application of rationalism towards the pursuit of economic gain. Coupled with this rationalism, moral worth could be affirmed through divinely sanctioned values such as hard work and thrift, while avoiding sinful luxury or self-indulgence. Work was construed as a moral and religious duty in itself, rather than driven by the desire to consume.

Weber's account of capitalism emphasized a combination of rationalization, the role of puritanical self-restraint, and the moral commandment to reinvest capital into business rather than spend on consumption. As Weber puts it, 'The peculiarity of this philosophy of avarice appears to be the ideal of the honest man of recognized credit, and above all the idea of a duty of the individual toward the increase of his capital, which is assumed as an end in itself.' He goes on to argue, 'The *summum bonum* of this ethic, the earning of more and more money, combined with the strict avoidance of all spontaneous enjoyment of life, is above all completely devoid of any eudaemonistic [happiness], not to say hedonistic, admixture. It is thought of so purely as an end in itself, that from the point of view of the happiness of, or utility to, the single individual, it appears entirely transcendental and absolutely irrational. Man is dominated by the making of money, by acquisition as the ultimate purpose of his life.'[54] The comments on savings mentioned in the introduction indicated that spending has become more important than saving, indicating a significant shift away from this puritanical basis of capitalism.

Although these values may have characterized the early stages of modern capitalism several centuries ago, consumerism is advanced by unleashing the desire to spend; consumerism must advocate hedonistic self-indulgence, not puritanical self-denial. Therefore, capitalism is not necessarily driven by a pervasive rationalization of all aspects of human life and social existence, but often by irrationality and desire. In fact, it could be said that if humans were as rational as Weber – and most economists – suggest, then advertising and marketing would have very limited effect.

However, the decline of puritanism has not stopped consumerism but in fact provides a new source of legitimacy and impetus for its survival. Benjamin Barber rightly criticizes Daniel Bell's assertion that while the passing of puritanism has left capitalism 'with no moral or transcendental ethic,' it has instead 'acquired a new and different ethic which has both secular and religious overtones and which legitimates the tendencies that consumer capitalism today requires in order to survive' (CN, 40). Consumerism has come to replace puritanism and the Protestant work ethic upon which Weber focused.

Moving from these three political economists and sociologists who emphasized the importance of trade, production, and saving as the foundations of modernity, let us turn to a parallel historical development that helps account for the emergence of consumerism.

Consumerism and Liberalism: Individualism, Privacy, and Possessiveness

Although consumerism became dominant only within recent decades, some theorists argue that because of its emphasis on freedom, choice, and property, the roots of consumerism can be found in the birth of liberal political thought in the early stages of the Enlightenment. Ironically, consumerism emerged in the liberal account of politics and subjectivity even as Smith, Marx, and Weber emphasized the political importance of labour and production. In *The Political Theory of Possessive Individualism*[55] Canadian political philosopher C.B. Macpherson argues that while liberalism claims to work towards consensus between rational subjects, it often conceals other more problematic and insidious dynamics. While possession and private property were originally construed as a way to protect oneself against the power of the state and other citizens, liberalism in fact has radically different implications.

Macpherson asserts that 'the original 17th century individualism contained [a] central difficulty, which lay in its possessive quality.'[56] For Macpherson, the birth of modern liberalism in the early British social contract theorists John Locke and Thomas Hobbes was based primarily on the drive towards private acquisition, which made liberalism a 'political theory of appropriation.'[57] For Hobbes and Locke, humans are compelled to enter into civil society and submit to a social contract largely because the state of nature is characterized by tremendous uncertainty concerning the protection and security of one's possessions. Hobbes argues that humans are driven primarily by their innate and incessant appetites and desires, and that 'all men must seek incessantly to attain satisfaction of their desires.'[58] The Lockean theory of politics is intended primarily to safeguard the private sphere of the possessing individual, to ensure security and enable individuals to maximize their self-interest. Locke argues that in the state of nature one can 'dispose of their possessions and persons as they think fit,'[59] because 'God, who hath given the world to men in common, hath also given them reason to make use of it to the best advantage of life and convenience. The earth and all that is therein is given to men for the support and comfort of their being.'[60]

This liberal emphasis on privacy and possessiveness is also associated with the capacity to autonomously assess one's needs, deliberate rationally about one's desires, and make choices on the basis of that autonomous deliberation. It is primarily through the liberal political philosophers John Stuart Mill and Jeremy Bentham that the notion of utility maximization, so central to understanding 'consumer behaviour,' came into prominence.[61] Utilitarianism holds that people seek to produce the maximal balance of positive value over disvalue because each seeks to maximize personal wealth without limit. Utilitarianism envisions a society aiming to maximize 'the aggregate utility of the whole membership of the society, or [maintains] that ... the market [should]. Each individual [is] to count as one, and all utilities [are] as good as each other.'[62]

Autonomy and deliberation, desire and needs, are often construed by liberal theorists as existing prior to society, as inherent features of the individual preoccupied with choice and the maximum satisfaction of personal preferences. The philosopher of education Ruth Jonathan goes so far as to argue that liberalism is 'a social philosophy defined by the *priority given to preference satisfaction.*'[63] Like Macpherson, Jonathan argues that the freedoms offered by liberalism are in fact 'illusory.' When isolated into private units of possessiveness, we are less able to conceive of ourselves as members of a democratic political community with the capacity to engage in anything beyond our own self-interest and gratification. Once isolated, we are more readily swayed by consumerism as the only available outlet for political engagement. It is this private individual that advertising seeks to create, that is the primary 'product' of advertising. Arthur Brittan claims, 'Advertisers sell privatization – they sell the means whereby individuals isolate themselves from the demands and obligations of political and social relationships.'[64] Politics simply can't be understood in terms of choice because the language of rights and choice still speaks primarily to isolated individuals, as if they consisted exclusively of needs and desires.

Macpherson suggests that the liberal emphasis on individualism, privacy, and possessiveness reveals a compatibility with consumerism, and that they emerged through parallel historical processes. This trend continued into the twentieth century, as consumerism became increasingly prevalent and analysed, beginning with the first to extensively describe consumerism, Thorstein Veblen and his theory of 'conspicuous consumption.'

Theorists of the Twentieth Century

Theorists of consumerism such as Alan Aldridge and Robert Bocock argue that a shift occurred in the twentieth century from an emphasis on the importance of the production of goods to the importance of the production of needs, as people increasingly sought fulfillment in consumption because the experience of production is alienating.[65] As a result, the identity of the modern subject thus shifts from the workplace to consumption as people came to identify less and less with traditional work-related values and social groupings and increasingly with consumer products and the messages and meanings conveyed about them.[66] This trend is an important dimension of the work of American economist Thorstein Veblen at the turn of the twentieth century.

While we saw that Marx, Smith, and Weber emphasized productive processes, Thorstein Veblen (1857–1929) was perhaps the first to extensively explore several key aspects of consumerism and its cultural and political importance. In contrast to Weber, Veblen argued that capitalism is based on neither the importance of the productive processes nor the application of rational self-interest to maximize utility, but instead contains the residue and remnants of our primitive cultural practices. Although trained as an economist and employed as an economics professor, Veblen wrote primarily as an anthropologist and cultural theorist. In doing so, he was perhaps the first to extensively explore what could be called the 'irrational' dimensions of economic activity.

In *The Theory of the Leisure Class*, Veblen presents his now-famous notion of 'conspicuous consumption,' the attempt to display status through habits and symbols that allow people to emulate others from higher classes and rank themselves accordingly. Veblen argues that earlier 'barbaric' or 'primitive' stages in human history emphasized the importance of predatorial prizes acquired by seizure and conquest, such as the display of trophies of the hunt and plunder from foreign battles. He suggests that while a shift seemed to occur with the emergence of industrial organization and its emphasis on private property and accumulation, display and social recognition remain as important today as during 'primitive' eras. 'Gradually, as industrial activity further displaces predatory activity in the community's everyday life and in men's habits of thought, accumulated property more and more replaces trophies of predatory exploit as the conventional exponent of prepotence and success.'[67]

Conspicuous consumption is an attempt to mark oneself off as more refined than others so as to develop and express a distinct social identity, yet at the same time to emulate dominant patterns of consumption. Through this process, the primitive emphasis on the rites and rituals of display continued into modern capitalist society. The image of human beings that emerges through Veblen's analysis is of a tribalistic group of irrational creatures who emphasize social recognition over happiness, 'rational self-interest,' or even physical well-being. One commentator on Veblen argues that this runs against the emphasis on rationality and utility in economics: 'Contemporary economic theory was based on the assumption that an article was purchased because of its utility, whereas Veblen's investigations led him to the conclusion that goods were often purchased because of their futility.'[68] In some cases, people will compromise the basic necessities of life and experience tremendous discomfort in order to acquire objects that advance their status and recognition. Veblen describes how some goods become even more desirable and sell even better as their price increases, simply because they become more expensive.

For Veblen, as the meaning of consumption becomes increasingly complex, the skill with which one consumes is critically evaluated by others – a process requiring that extensive knowledge be acquired concerning the most conspicuous ways to consume: 'This cultivation of the aesthetic faculty requires time and application, and the demands made upon the gentleman in this direction therefore tend to change his life of leisure into a more or less arduous application to the business of learning how to live a life of ostensible leisure in a becoming way. Closely related to the requirement that the gentleman must consume freely and of the right kind of goods, there is the requirement that he must know how to consume them in a seemly manner. His life of leisure must be conducted in due form. Hence arise good manners and ways of living are items of conformity to the norm of conspicuous leisure and conspicuous consumption.'[69]

Veblen outlines how this 'life of leisure' and its conspicuous rewards deepened hostility towards manual labour and instead elevated the labour and expertise required for proper consumption. Habits of consumption become endlessly insatiable when based on comparison and relative measures of affluence: 'As fast as a person makes new acquisitions, and becomes accustomed to the resulting new standard of wealth, the new standard forthwith ceases to afford appreciably greater satisfaction than the earlier standard did. The tendency in any case is constantly to make the present pecuniary standard the point of departure for a fresh increase of wealth; and this in turn gives rise to a new standard of sufficiency and a new pecuniary classification of one's self as compared with one's neighbours. So far as concerns the present question, the end sought by accumulation is to rank high in comparison with the rest of the community in point of pecuniary strength.'[70]

In Veblen's view, we are always evaluating our own worth or lack of worth by relative measures with a view to rank and social status. Thus, we seek to emulate or mimic certain habits or symbols of rank in order to gain the adulation of others. A pithy restatement of this phenomenon by Australian consumer theorist Clive Thompson in his book *Growth Fetish* is that 'people buy things they don't want, with money they don't have, to impress people they don't like.'[71] The economist Robert Heilbroner notes that, in contrast to Marx's theory of class conflict, conspicuous consumption promotes emulation and identification such that 'the lower classes are not at sword's points with the upper; they are bound up with them by the intangible but steely bonds of common attitudes. The workers do not seek to displace their managers; they seek to emulate them.'[72]

A biting satirist, Veblen describes 'conspicuous consumption' as a form of neo-tribalism by drawing parallels between modern society and 'primitive' ways of life. By uncovering these vestiges of tribal life in modern consumer society, Veblen turned not only the idea of social progress on its head but the centrality of rationality and utility maximization.

While Veblen explored consumerism more generally, several decades later the philosopher and cultural theorist Walter Benjamin explored the distinct locations in which consumption took place, the 'creation of specific places and spaces geared towards the promotion of consumption and the temptation of the consumer.'[73] Benjamin describes a growing celebration of the commodity and its increasing cultural importance, culminating in the product exhibitions of the nineteenth century. These exhibitions promoted the latest technological innovations and consumer products, and brought their displays from city to city. These product exhibitions emerged around the same time as the celebration of the practice of shopping itself, apparent in the first 'arcades' of nineteenth-century Paris. The arcades were enclosed networks of shops where leisurely strolls allowed one to sample and admire commodities in passing within a 'primordial landscape of consumption.'[74] Benjamin describes the *flâneur* as the stroller or 'street reader' 'who walks long and aimlessly through the streets.'[75] These arcades involved not only the display of products but the display of people, as shoppers observed not only commodities but other shoppers as well; Benjamin explores not only the spatiality of consumption but the emergence of a corresponding 'person': the birth of the shopper.

In addition to the above accounts of consumerism, several contemporary theorists distinguish between the *consumer* and the *customer*. Pasi Falk claims that this distinction is 'a means of distinguishing "customers" of local shops, before the emergence of the consumer society, from "consumers" under conditions of mass consumption.'[76] According to consumer theorist Robert Bocock, the customer embraced a more personalized and intimate set of long-term relationships rooted in familial and communal contexts, while the consumer replaced such relations with more impersonal and anonymous relationships based on the mechanical act of purchasing mass-produced items.[77] The consumer inhabits a fragmented society where impersonal commercial transactions replace long-term kindred and intimate relationships. In observing this key transition, political scientist Robert Lane asks, 'Has shopping become less of a social experience, more solitary, impersonal, and friendless? The days are long gone when there were counter clerks instead of check-outs, when a neighborhood store was a social center and the storekeeper was everyone's friend ... Shopping is decreasingly a social experience.'[78] Humanized figures like Ronald McDonald and the Green Giant were developed as a response to this trend, to personalize consumption by reintroducing intimacy and familiarity into the relationship between consumers and commodities.[79]

For French philosopher and 'speed theorist' Paul Virillo, consumerism is evident in a growing love for change, innovation, and acceleration. Virillo coined the neologism *dromology*, derived from the Greek *dromos* ('to race'), the 'science of speed.'[80] Virillo writes about 'the acceleration of all reality,' and the erasure of difference between past and future – even spatiality itself – such that 'here no longer exists; everything is now.'[81] For Virillo, commodities and physical phenomena around us are no longer construed as lasting or durable fixtures but instead become quickly obsolete and disposed of. This trend is explored by theorist David Harvey in his notion of 'time-space compression.'[82] Harvey suggests that our changing relationship to time affects our relationship to space, because time-space compression is among the 'processes that so revolutionize the objective qualities of space and time that we are forced to alter, sometimes in quite radical ways, how we represent the world to ourselves. I use the word "compression" because a strong case can be made that the history of capitalism has been characterized by speed-up in the pace of life, while so overcoming spatial barriers that the world sometimes seems to collapse inwards upon us.'[83] The prevalence of speed is apparent in the accelerated experience of change in consumer goods: change happens so fast that, through 'built-in obsolesce' and the rapid redundancy of consumer goods, we increasingly experience vertigo and disorientation. In consumer society, shopping becomes so ubiquitous that it is liberated from both time and space itself; it becomes everywhere and always.

Contemporary sociologist Zygmunt Bauman describes the 'quick-fix' world view of consumerism in which there is a 'consumer solution' to every personal and political problem, when all human longings can be satiated through acquisition, 'trusting that for every problem, already known or as may still arise in the future, there is a solution – a special object or recipe, prepared by specialists, by people with superior know-how, and one's task is to find it.' The consumer attitude means 'translating the task of learning the art of living as the effort to acquire the skill of finding such objects and recipes, and gaining the power to possess them once found.'[84]

Having traced the historical rise of consumerism to its current dominant position, it is also evident that consumerism has taken a prominent place in the global political landscape.

Imperialism and Globalization: Consumerism on the International Scene

In its quest to establish new markets and satiate our own consumer society, the Western world extends its reach globally and draws all nations into its orbit – an essential force in the evolving international system. In contrast to Samuel Huntington's view of civilizational conflict along lines of religion and culture,[85] Benjamin Barber describes consumption as a form of 'neo-colonialism.' Barber provocatively argues that fundamentalism and violent extremism are a reaction against a global homogenous culture of a 'McWorld': 'The struggle of Jihad against McWorld is not a clash of civilizations but a dialectical expression of tensions built into a single global civilization as it emerges against a backdrop of traditional ethic and religious divisions, many of which are actually created by McWorld and its infotainment industries and technological innovations' (JM, xvi).   Barber notes that often the West has been more effective at spreading markets for consumer goods than democracy or public values, because 'a pervasive culture of fast food, fast computers, and fast music advanced by an infotainment industry rooted in the spread of brands tends to homogenize global markets and render taste not merely shallow but uniform. McWorld's culture represents a kind of soft imperialism in which those who are colonized are said to "choose" their commercial indenture' (JM, xxi). This is because, unfortunately, 'McWorld in tandem with the global market economy has globalized many of our vices and almost none of our virtues' (JM, xxvii).

While the language of nature and the divine pervades free-market discourse, creating a reverence for the market and a faith that it adheres to laws both natural and universal, Barber reveals that markets for consumer goods don't just fall from the heavens or grow from the earth. Instead, they are highly contingent and variable political and social creations, often as easily connected with authoritarian regimes as democratic ones: 'Market economies have shown a remarkable adaptability and have flourished in many tyrannical states ... Capitalism requires consumers with access to markets and a stable political climate in order to succeed: such conditions may or may not be fostered by democracy, which can be disorderly and even anarchic, especially in its early stages, and which often pursues public goods costly to or at odds with private-market imperatives. On the level of the individual, capitalism seeks consumers susceptible to the shaping of their needs and the manipulation of their wants while democracy needs citizens autonomous in their thoughts and independent in their deliberative judgments' (JM, 14–15).

Perhaps most provocatively, Barber claims that the clash between civilizations outlined by Huntington is increasingly between consumerism and militant fundamentalisms, both equally destructive of civilization and democracy: 'What we face is not a war between civilizations but a war within civilization' (JM, xvi). This is because McWorld is as anti-democratic as jihad:

> The encompassing practices of globalization we have nurtured under the arches of McWorld and the banner of global markets have in fact created a radical asymmetry: We have managed to globalize markets in goods, labor, currencies, and information without globalizing the civic and democratic institutions that have historically constituted the free market's in-

dispensable context. Put simply, we have removed capitalism from the institutional box that has domesticated it and given its sometimes harsh practices a human face … We have globalized the marketplace willy-nilly, because markets can bleed through porous national boundaries and are not constrained by the logic of sovereignty. But we have not even begun to globalize democracy, which – precisely because it is political and is defined by sovereignty – is trapped inside the nation-state box. (JM, xxvi)

This globalizing trend can also be understood through the lens of those who experience it most immediately and can observe it with deepest intimacy, those non-Western thinkers among the first to notice this trend. For the Iranian intellectual Ali Shari'ati, the excess productive capacity within the West meant that it was forced to 'step over its national boundary and push goods into foreign markets … Every single human on the face of the earth would be coerced into becoming a consumer for the produced merchandise. European markets became saturated rapidly; consequently the surplus goods had to go to Asia and Africa. Asians and Africans had to consume the surplus products.'[86] Imperialism for Shari'ati was thus a project that aimed to establish a market for surplus goods through which the West could spread consumerism and achieve domination and colonization. In place of national independence and global cultural diversity, the non-European is affected in such a way that 'his desires, his choices, his suffering, his sorrow, his tastes, his ideals, his sense of beauty, his tradition, his social relations, his amusements – all must be changed so that he is coerced into becoming a consumer of European industrial products.' As a result, non-Westerners adopted 'the feelings, desires, and behaviour resembling those of present-day Americans, English, or French.'[87] As argued by Barber, consumerism is therefore an imperial project of the global expansion of cultural uniformity.

Shari'ati argues that while consumerism functioned as a process of imperialism, it was advanced by the West as a process of civilizing and modernizing non-Western countries, that 'non-Europeans were modernized for the sake of consumption.'[88] Modernization thus dispenses with traditional cultural values and replaces them with Western consumer values. For Shari'ati, the result of this attempt at cultural assimilation is alienation and estrangement: 'Western societies have been able to impose their philosophy, their way of thinking, their desires, their ideas, their tastes and their manners upon non-European countries to the same extent that they have been able to force their symbols of civilization into these countries which consume new products and gadgets.'[89]

The production of consumers is also described by the Indian environmental activist Vandana Shiva in her *Monocultures of the Mind*.[90] In compelling and provocative terms, she describes how peasant farmers are transformed from preservers of seeds and self-sufficient independent growers to consumers of Western seed technology and chemical fertilizers. This market of new consumers is created by first undermining the farmers' ability to cultivate their own seeds, and then manufacturing seeds that cannot reproduce and must be purchased anew each year, a 'terminator technology' that Shiva calls 'the death of birth'[91] or 'thanotechnology.'[92] Shiva argues that, as a result, 'under globalization, the farmer is losing their social, cultural, economic identity as a producer. A farmer is now a "consumer" of costly seeds and costly chemicals sold by powerful global corporations through powerful landlords and money lenders locally.'[93] What is often construed in the West as innovation, entrepreneurialism, and ingenuity is in fact outright theft and appropriation disguised as discovery or invention, what Shiva calls 'biopiracy.'[94]

In the market for consumer goods, this trend is evident in Nike's successful entry into the Chinese market, where its shoes outsell local brands that are half the price. A *Time* article proudly announced that the success of Nike demonstrates that previous attempts to enter China, beginning with the earliest Western traders and missionaries, were not as successful as modern corporations and their sophisticated marketing agencies. 'Westerners have dreamed of penetrating the elusive Chinese market since traders began peddling opium to Chinese addicts in exchange for tea and spices in the 19th century ... Today, Nike is opening an average of 1.5 new stores a day in China.' Nike figured out how to access the Chinese market by undermining community values and replacing them with more individualistic ones: 'Nike unabashedly made American culture its selling point, with ads that challenge China's traditional, group-oriented ethos.' Children now influence their parents' shopping habits, in a reversal of traditional Confucian deference to elders. Schools have been instrumental in this success story: Terry Rhoads, director of sports marketing for Nike in China, 'donated equipment to Shanghai's high schools and paid them to open their basketball courts to the public after hours ... At games Rhoads blasted the recorded sound of cheering to encourage straitlaced fans to loosen up.'[95] It is also notable that, in contrast to Thomas Friedman's thesis about the democratizing potential of consumerism, this trend is occurring despite the lack of democracy in China; the flourishing of consumer values does not necessarily require a democracy to succeed, nor does it necessarily even promote democracy.

Consumption and the Corporation

To understand consumerism further, it is necessary to consider the modern institution with which it is closely linked, the multinational or transnational corporation. Political economists such as John Kenneth Galbraith have argued that consumerism is a phenomenon associated with the modern multinational corporation,[96] because, through advertising and marketing, corporations produce the commodities we consume and the brand meanings associated with them. Joachim Israel argues that corporations shape the character of consumerism by exerting considerable 'control over the process of consumption through the influencing and controlling of consumers and their behavior.'[97]

In his landmark book and documentary *The Corporation*, Canadian constitutional legal theorist Joel Bakan examined the extensive political implications of the modern corporation, arguing that the corporation has become the 'dominant institution of our time,' replacing such governing bodies as the church and monarchy.[98] By the latter half of the twentieth century, many corporations had grown to an unprecedented size, overshadowing most nations.[99] For example, in 2005 the annual revenue of Walmart surpassed the annual GDP of Sweden, and by 2009 exceeded it by $117 billion.[100] Canadian business ethics expert Wesley Cragg notes that 'the largest transnational corporations now have budgets that dwarf those of most of the world's nations. Of the 15 companies/governments with the largest budgets, six are governments and nine are companies. Of the 100 largest economies in the world, 51 are now global corporations and only 49 are countries.'[101] Cragg reports that 'the Global Policy Forum calculates that of the 25 corporations/ governments with the largest budgets, 13 are governments and 12 are corporations.'[102] Philosopher of education John Dewey himself anticipated this trend some eighty years ago when he said, 'The need of the present age is to apprehend the fact that, for better or worse, we are living in a corporate age.'[103]

The central argument of *The Corporation* is that as corporations assume a significant role in contemporary society, they secure for themselves the legal status of 'person.' And yet ironically the political categories of democracy, the public realm, and citizenship are being eroded even as the corporate institutions of global capitalism are gaining political status: corporations have been personalized as legal 'persons' and humanized as 'corporate citizens.' This humanization of the corporation parallels the transformation of human relations into consumer relations and erosion of active 'human' political citizenship – we are asked to shop as a means of supporting our country in a time of need. Corporations claim the status of citizen even as citizens become 'consumers' of governmental services and the consumer replaces or even 'consumes' the citizen.

In his book *The McDonaldization of Society*, American sociologist George Ritzer explored how consumerism becomes embodied within the modern monolithic corporation. Ritzer defines *McDonaldization* as 'the process by which the principles of the fast-food restaurant are coming to dominate more and more sectors of American society as well as of the rest of the world.'[104] He argues that this process has advanced to such an extent that 'no aspect of people's lives is immune to McDonaldization.'[105] Ritzer argues that perhaps what is most troubling about McDonaldization is that not only does it affect the character of commodities (i.e., hamburgers and fries), but it also promotes the intensification and proliferation of consumer values and ways of life.

McDonald's co-exists with contradictory tendencies, because 'rational systems inevitably spawn irrationalities … rational systems are often unreasonable.'[106] These systems of consumption are irrational because they are often false, unhealthy, dehumanizingly mechanical, and – contrary to their claims – remarkably inefficient (i.e., we wait in line for overpriced fast food). The 'rationality' of productive processes and their dehumanizing implications leads corporations towards a re-enchantment with commodities and even themselves (e.g., the McDonald's corporation presents itself to the public as 'fun' rather than 'efficient'). Ritzer suggests that 'there is a kind of magic of enchantment associated with such food and their settings.'[107] The corporation sets out to conceal both the rational and irrational dimensions of production with 'magic' or 'unreason,' which helps explain why consumerism is so irresistible. American sociologist Daniel Bell describes this contradictory character of the corporation as it is both rational and irrational, and the contradictory values of reason and unreason it promotes: 'On the one hand, the business corporation wants an individual to work hard, pursue a career, accept delayed gratification – to be, in the crude sense, an organization man. And yet, in its products and its advertisements, the corporation promotes pleasures, instant joy, relaxing and letting go. One is to be "straight" by day and a "swinger" by night.'[108]

McDonald's has become such a globally uniform icon that it is now used as an informal indicator for monetary policy. The *Economist*, a British weekly, developed a 'Big Mac Index,' which uses the price of a Big Mac sold in different countries as an informal measure of exchange rates.[109]

2 Consuming Schooling: Whose Schools Are They?

Any nation that spends almost three times as much on the purchase and operation of automobiles as it does on education has a problem in values, not in economic capability.

– Raymond Callahan[1]

In light of this account of the rise of consumerism to a place of political dominance, what can be said regarding its impact on schooling and youth?

The school is a key site where the consumer is produced in contemporary society, an institution that can either promote a society centred upon consumerism or resistance to it. Several important questions concerning education follow: What is the difference between educating students and acquiring new life-long consumers? When do schools become commercial spheres rather than educational environments and facilitate the transformation of our culture into a consumer culture? And, as noted educational thinker Neil Postman asks, 'Whose schools are they?'[2] These questions demand an exploration of the educational implications of the rise of consumerism. Before considering school commercialism itself, it is necessary to explore the impact of production on schooling, and then consider how it came to be displaced by consumerism.

Reproduction and the Productivist Bias

In the previous chapter we looked at several important thinkers who focused on the political importance of production in their time. This focus is also apparent in the field of education; many educational thinkers who are critical of the influence of commercial forces on education focus on the characterization of schools as sites for the production of workers, the application of managerial and business strategies to school policy and administration, and the notion that schools must serve the demand for economic expansion in measurable forms such as GDP growth.

In *Knowledge and Power in the Global Economy*, David Gabbard describes the *'economized* worldview that pervades the contemporary educational reform movement' and questions the widespread presupposition of a direct correlation between education and economic progress, that 'a people's economic development proceeds in direct proportion to their level of educational attainment.'[3] However, many important educational thinkers forefront the most common critiques of the influence of commercial forces on education by criticizing the impact of productivist expectations on education, yet overlook the influence of consumerism.

In *Cultural Reproduction and Social Reproduction*, Pierre Bourdieu explores how schooling reproduces and legitimates inegalitarian distributions of 'cultural capital,' by which he means the social relations that include the accumulated cultural knowledge that confers power and status. Bourdieu explores 'the laws that determine the tendency of structures to reproduce themselves by producing agents endowed with the system of predispositions which is capable of engendering practices adapted to the structures and thereby contributing to the reproduction of the structures.'[4]

According to Bowles and Gintis in their classic text *Schooling in Capitalist America*, schools reproduce social phenomena such as class structures and modes of production, and thereby impede social change.[5] In their classically Marxist work they claim that the primary function of schooling is the creation of workers, because implicit authoritarian structures in schools prepares students to become compliant workers as adults. They argue that 'the educational system does not add to or subtract from the overall degree of inequality and repressive personal development. Rather, it is best understood as an institution which serves to perpetuate the social relationship of economic life through which those patterns are set, by facilitating a smooth integration of youth into the labor force.' They assert that because 'work under capitalism is an alienated activity,' social change requires far-reaching economic transformation rather than educational reform. However, in emphasizing the production of workers, Bowles and Gintis overlook the challenges consumerism presents to schooling, arguing that social change can happen without 'sacrificing the conveniences of modern life.'[6]

In *Education and the Cult of Efficiency*, historian of education Raymond Callahan examines how the emergence of Frederick Taylor's discipline of 'scientific management' and the rise of the 'efficiency expert' affected education in the first decades of the twentieth century. Callahan argues, 'In this period as in the decades immediately preceding it, the most powerful force was industrialism – the application of mechanical power to the production of goods – and along with that the economic philosophy of the free enterprise, capitalistic system under which industrialism developed.'[7] The successes in applying the principles of scientific management to factories, coupled with its resulting growing popularity within society, invariably resulted in the attempt to apply the 'business-industry ideology' to education. This trend was fuelled by complaints that schools were much more wasteful and inefficient than factories, and was driven by hopes to 'yield commensurable returns on educational units.'[8] After all, if scientific management had proven so effective in factories, why wouldn't it be able to make education more efficient? 'Whatever its source, the influence was exerted in the form of suggestions or demands that the schools be organized and operated in a more businesslike way and that more emphasis be placed upon a practical and immediately useful education.'[9] Leaders in educational administration began to identify themselves increasingly with business leaders and captains of industry such as Carnegie, Rockefeller, and J.P. Morgan.

In *The Transformation of the School*, historian of education Lawrence Cremin examines the important changes in education over the course of a century, particularly the rise and influence of progressivism.[10] In a chapter titled 'Education and Industry,' Cremin examines the influence of science and technology on schooling driven by 'the voracious manpower demands of an expanding industrial economy.' Some of this pressure arose in response to international developments such as German unification and economic competition from Britain and Russia, and were promoted by such organizations as the National Association of Manufacturers that created a Committee on Industrial Education to ensure that education facilitates economic and scientific progress as efficiently as possible.[11]

Canadian philosopher of education Emery Hyslop-Margison explores how productivist assumptions influence various dimensions of schooling, including career preparedness programs, 'employability expectations' and the 'skills gap,' and the 'market economy discourse of the Conference Board of Canada.'[12] Heather-Jane Robertson describes how Canada faced similar fears early in the twentieth century when Mackenzie King established the Dominion of Canada Royal Commission on Industrial Training and Technical Education. 'Education reform had become a matter of some urgency, for it was feared that Canada's schools were adjusting inadequately to the new economy. The charge to the commissioners warned that "industrial efficiency is all-important to the development of the Dominion and to the promotion of the home and foreign trade of Canada in competition with other nations."'[13]

Ivan Illich was among the first educational theorists to contend with consumerism, though only briefly. In *Deschooling Society*,[14] Illich criticizes the unquestioned role of formal schooling in modern life, culminating in his radical call for a 'deschooling' of society. Illich is prescient in his anticipation of the prevalence of consumerism, stating that schools are the 'reproductive organ of a consumer society.' While Bowles and Gintis emphasize schooling as preparation for undemocratic economic relations, Illich acknowledges that schools also produce consumers: 'School is a ritual of initiation which introduces the neophyte to the sacred race of progressive consumption ... its purpose is to celebrate the myth of an earthly paradise of never-ending consumption.' Furthermore, he acknowledges the important role that consumerism performs on the international stage: 'The engineering of consumers has become the economy's principal growth sector. As production costs decrease in rich nations, there is an increasing concentration of both capital and labor in the vast enterprise of equipping man for disciplined consumption.'[15] While Illich was among the first to recognize the links between consumerism and formal schooling, the limitation of Illich's criticism of schooling should be noted in its failure to acknowledge the public and transformative possibilities of schooling.

Both the influence of productivist values (expectations of efficiency and human capital creation) and the influence of consumerism (advertising and school–business partnerships) are often legitimized as strategies for cost reduction. While the demand that education serves economic expansion has been an explicitly stated aim and administrative policy, few would explicitly state that the function of schools is to create consumers. Yet the examples I describe below confirm this growing trend. I want to extend the claim that schools reproduce problematic features of society, in order to draw attention to an emerging phenomenon in which schooling contributes to the reproduction of a society centred upon consumption.

From Nature to Consumption: When Corporations Go to School

Once a relatively protected and de-commodified public good, education is being swept up by neo-liberal forces, transformed into a commercial enterprise, and reoriented towards a more integrated relationship with commercial interests. Today the subjugation of schooling to consumerism has attained monumental proportions, and the capacity of education to perform its public responsibility and fulfill its liberatory possibilities is profoundly threatened. Instead, constructing markets of young consumers has become a central component of the educative project. When corporations go to school, what they learn is how to undo schooling, as children become subjected to unpredictable and unaccountable market forces. What the quotation at the opening of this chapter confirms is that this is a question not of economic capabilities, but of human values. We will begin with a concrete and contemporary description of the impact of commercial forces on education: the closure of a publicly funded environmental education centre and the emergence of a new for-profit corporation: Field Trip Factory.

The Leslie M. Frost Centre is located near Dorset, Ontario, on a small lake surrounded by wooded hills about two hours north of Toronto. Between the 1940s and the 1990s it hosted over 250,000 students on overnight retreats focused on environmental education designed to increase students' understanding of natural ecosystems. However, budget cuts initiated in the late 1990s placed the Frost Centre in financial peril. The minister of natural resources justified the closure by explaining that the Ontario government is 'using a results-based planning approach that focuses on the achievement of specific results in support of key priorities,' and that 'by building a strong and prosperous economy, we can provide our people a high-quality of life.'[16] Construed as frivolous and unaffordable, the centre was eventually closed, despite intensive lobbying and opposition by parents, students, and an active local group called Friends of the Frost Centre.[17] As vines grow up the sides of its abandoned buildings, nature is slowly reclaiming the site. Meanwhile, it is consumer culture that is claiming today's high school students.

The closure of the Frost Centre can be contrasted against the emergence of a new type of field trip, run by for-profit corporations with the aim of using schools to secure new consumers. In place of overnight environmentally oriented field trips, a new Chicago-based corporation called Field Trip Factory designs educational tours that take students to toy stores, pet stores, and sports stores. A fun drawing on their website shows hearts, stars, and apples coming out of smokestacks.[18] It claims to book '10,000 to 12,000 such excursions nationwide each year,' and to have 'served over 1 million classrooms over the last 10 years.' Its president proudly proclaims, 'We make it easy for the teacher and it's free,' while its vision statement asserts that 'Field Trip Factory is a learning protocol that turns communities into classrooms. Positive attitudes and behaviors are promoted through experience-based learning.'[19]

Students on trips with Field Trip Factory visit major financial institutions (Harrisbank), car makers (Saturn), or box stores (Walmart), where they learn the computerized retail process, nutritional eating habits, and ways to find good bargains.[20] 'As children explore the grocery aisles of their local Wal-Mart Supercenter, they will learn how to incorporate healthy behaviors into their daily lives ... Eating healthy, making smart choices and learning how to integrate exercise into daily living are the main messages of this hands-on field trip.'[21] All field-trip fees are paid for by corporate sponsors, and Field Trip Factory provides everything a teacher needs for the trip, including permission slips and school buses, as well as trained store personnel and tour guides. At the end of most trips students receive free bags with the company's logo on the side.

In *School Field Trips and Public Spaces*, educational theorist Jan Nespor explores the important function of school field trips in the creation of public spheres, arguing that field trips are important because they provide a rare opportunity for students to leave the school building, and 'because they are distillations of the relationships of schools to the worlds outside their walls.'[22] Thus, they have a significant function in the creation of public spheres: 'Educators need to recognize that [schools] are not just territories regulating movements within their borders: schools are *vehicles*. Field trips ... physically and symbolically transport young people through and across social and material landscapes. In the process, they help *produce* what people think of as "public" spaces – indeed, they are of singular importance in the performance of public space to the degree that they serve as the means by which children are introduced to the downtowns, museums, national parks, monuments and historical sites that symbolize the public sphere.'[23]

Field Trip Factory has a significant impact on students, because field trips help 'produce what people think of as "public spaces"' – though it is noteworthy that commercial spaces for shopping are not listed by

Nespor. While Nespor notes that field trips help produce what people think of as public spaces, Arendt will soon show that there is very little that is public about these spaces, because they are more of an introduction to private spaces of consumption.

The closure of the Frost Centre and expansion of Field Trip Factory indicate larger changes happening to education today under the influence of commercial forces and the prevalence of consumerism. Rather than learning conservation values, students learn consumer values; rather than gathering as a community of learners, they are gathered as a market of young consumers; rather than embarking on field trips designed to teach about the natural world, students take field trips to the local Walmart, where they do not have the opportunity to develop a learned connection to the natural environment around them. And, as we will see in the next chapter, rather than forming what Arendt calls a 'public realm,' these students are gathered as a collection of private consumers. Although the Field Trip Factory webpage proclaims that the trips are 'free,' what is their true or hidden cost? As Gary Ruskin of Commercial Alert puts it, 'Sometimes free is too expensive.'[24]

A report on school commercialism by the Commercialism in Education Research Unit notes, 'School commercialism is part of a trend of aggressive marketing to children and youth. In the United States, annual corporate spending on marketing to kids has grown substantially, from $100 million in 1983 to $15 billion (US) currently.'[25] This dynamic is apparent in such trends as the incursion of advertising into schools, the spread of school–business partnerships such as field trips, the selling of naming rights, and the managing of public schools for profit by corporations.

Ruth Jonathan aptly describes why it is important to study the impact of such trends on education: 'Education is the one social practice which both reflects and produces social circumstance and values, [and is therefore] a uniquely significant site for studying how our beliefs and commitments about human possibility and defensible social principles cash out in the real world. As the most fundamental of all social practices, its study is both a key component of, and a fruitful test-bed for, social theory.'[26] Public schools are fundamental institutions to democracy itself because, as teacher Larry Kuehn notes, 'Democracy requires public space, places where debate and discussion inform decision making. And it requires education that prepares people to participate as critical citizens in that public space. If we are to achieve the democratic ideal of equity, there must be a commons, and it must be accessible for all to participate effectively. Public education is an important part of that commons.'[27]

In contrast to numerous ever-changing trends in educational research and instructional strategies, school commercialism continues unabated. In fact, what is often construed as dramatic educational reform may in fact conceal deeper and more long-lasting neo-liberal trends. As dramatic events like school shootings gain widespread media attention, and as issues like discipline, class size, a crowded curriculum, and standardized testing demand teachers' attention, school commercialism can easily slip under the radar. My intention is not to minimize these other issues, nor to play down their urgency, but rather to explore an often overlooked trend. Although there has been growing work in recent decades on consumerism in a variety of disciplines, from anthropology and cultural studies to social and political theory, this topic remains generally under-theorized within educational thought. Witness a recent study undertaken by the Commercialism in Education Research Unit (CERU), run by Alex Molnar at Arizona State University. The 2006 CERU study laments the 'relative absence of coverage of schoolhouse commercialism in the education press,' and found that there is significantly greater interest in school commercialism in the business and marketing world than among academics and educators. In fact, 'the education press accounts for only 1 percent of all references to school commercialism. Business and advertising magazines account for the remaining 99 percent. Simply put, the topic has yet to become one that managed to get on the "radar screen" of education journals in any consistent and systematic way.'[28]

That said, occasional occurrences of school commercialism throughout the twentieth century can be noted. The advocacy group Consumer Alert notes, 'In the 1920s, Ivory Soap sponsored bar carving competitions; a decade later bankers forged alliances with students to buff up their Depression-battered images.'[29] In a *New York Times* article, Deborah Stead writes, 'In the late 1930's, the National Association of Manufacturers distributed a weekly gazette, *Young America Magazine*, to 70,000 schools,' which included such articles as 'Your Neighborhood Bank' and 'The Business of America's People Is Selling.'[30] However, these cases of school commercialism were comparatively rare and easily overlooked.

Yet while school commercialism is not entirely new, it has certainly grown to unprecedented proportions. Today schoolchildren are exposed to thousands of advertising images every day, and the educational environment is drawn into this trend as schools turn to corporate advertisers for revenue. Contributing to student empowerment is reduced to strengthening purchasing power, and the development of self-esteem is equated with the development of consumer confidence. Through these processes, schooling as a public undertaking is co-opted by private economic forces – yet still retains the image of legitimacy as a public activity.

The ascent of consumerism to a place of political dominance is increasingly apparent in the field of education, as school space is colonized by the images and logos of commercial discourse and youth receive more and more attention from advertisers. While there has long been a debate about the proper relationship between religion and schooling, the debate about the incursions by commercial interests into schools is comparatively recent but increasingly urgent. Atheists and secularists argue that because religion is a personal issue it is best kept out of schools, yet because we are all consumers it is harder to justify a separation between commercial interests and schooling. However, education is profoundly compromised when youth are viewed as consumers and not as future members of a public world, and when education is viewed as an opportunity to secure a new market of consumers rather than a preparation of citizens for public participation.

This is not to imply that schooling is the only possible site of learning. Learning in some form is constant and continuous. There are countless ways in which learning occurs outside the school walls, in the family, religious institutions, and popular culture. Any teacher or parent will marvel at the scope of knowledge that their children or students reveal about sports, fashion, music, and the daily lives of celebrities. The texts of popular culture are important pedagogical sites, and the field of cultural studies has explored the extent to which youth are affected by the 'pedagogy of advertising.'[31] However, what I am suggesting is that there is something unique and important about the public function of schooling.

The suggestion here is not that schooling should return to some mythical former glory by evoking a lost golden age when schooling was pure and uninfluenced by commercial demands. Nor is it my intention to suggest an idyllic era when education was fair and just and inclusive. Schools have long served as sorting devices and have long been places of systemic racism, sexism, and oppression. However, it is not necessary to return to what *was* in order to consider what *can be*.

Dystopian Days and Consuming Children

In 1952 General Motors president Charles Erwin Wilson famously rec-
ollected, 'For years I thought what was good for the country was good
for General Motors and vice versa.'[32] This outright equation of commercial institutions with national identity, of corporate good with the
American good, has shifted only slightly in the last half century. Many
corporations have grown to unprecedented size and now overshadow
most nations, and, as the quotation that opens this chapter notes, there
is now more spent on carmaking than educating. This equation of commercial good with national good has spread from carmaking to the field
of education. One industry group favouring corporate involvement in
schools reported in 2002 that schools receive $2.4 billion a year in the
United States from what the Council on Corporate and School Partnerships calls 'business relationships' with corporations.[33]

However, education is never neutral, never merely the acquisition of
technical knowledge and skills to be applied in a predictable manner
for instrumental purposes. It is always value-laden, reproducing hegemonic structures and economic paradigms, shaping democracy and
the public realm. If education is construed as neutral, then its political
implications remain concealed.

If there was any doubt concerning the extent to which marketers and
advertisers had gained access to schools, this trend can be observed
within the daily life of any and every student. Before even setting foot
in a school building, students in North America are surrounded by
advertising images, when boarding a school bus labelled with ads inside and out, driving to a school that's been named after a corporation,
just like their gymnasium, cafeteria, or other classrooms. In fact, one
Philadelphia school board president and self-proclaimed 'director of
corporate development' talks about 'peddling the naming rights to the
district's only school on eBay' and 'instituting a school uniform policy
and selling ads on the uniforms.'[34] As these already inundated students
enter the school building, posters in their bathrooms and hallways often
replace their artwork and class projects with more advertising. Before
their lessons begin, they are required to watch several minutes of Channel One, or in Canada the Youth News Network (YNN), an American
broadcaster that 'charges advertisers $200,000 per 30-second advertis-
ing spot.'[35] Once the lesson begins, some teachers may be 'sponsored'
by a candy company such as General Mills, which offered teachers $250
per month to act as 'freelance brand managers' for Reese Puffs.[36] Text-

book covers display advertisements provided by Cover Designs, and include math exercises that refer to consumer products, biology cases that favourably profile a large pharmaceutical corporation, or nutrition lessons sponsored by Hershey's Chocolate. Their online research habits are monitored for market researchers. Classroom activities include brainstorming to develop new product ideas, or completing surveys and market research studies, as outlined by Melissa Lickteig: 'Chips Ahoy gives schools a counting game where children count the number of chips in their cookies. Kellogg's sponsors an art project for children to make Rice Krispies sculptures. Campbell's Soups designed a science lesson comparing Prego sauce to Ragu to teach students about viscosity.'[37] Some students receive one doughnut for every A on their report card,[38] or free pizza for improved reading skills.[39] Upon leaving their classroom, they may find that their cafeteria serves unhealthy fast food and their sports teams wear uniforms dominated by corporate logos. While this would certainly be a dystopian day in the life of a student, and all these events might not necessarily occur at the same time, each of these activities has been well documented.[40]

If this description didn't provide an adequate indication of the extent to which commercial forces are present in schools, some schools have opened up directly in shopping malls. After all, if businesses and advertisers can't get into schools, then why not just put the schools in the mall? Since 1998, America's largest mall developer, the Simon Property Group, has been opening alternative public schools in malls through its non-profit Simon Youth Foundation in partnership with local public school systems. By 2004, Simon had opened nineteen such Education Resource Centers in eleven states.[41] The program has been described as 'an alternative to traditional approaches to school facility funding [that] relies on innovative programs in which the private sector provides the space for classrooms and the school districts provide the teachers and textbooks.'[42] While in the mall, parents can participate in a program called Shop and Support Fundraising Program, in which schools sell gift cards to parents whose shopping habits are managed and monitored by principals in order 'to attain 100% participation.'[43]

Perhaps the fastest growing trend in school commercialism is the production of sponsored educational materials: unsolicited advertising and promotional material sent directly to schools and teachers, targeted by grades and subject areas. Examples include 'an environmental curriculum video produced by Shell Oil and concentrated heavily on the virtues of the internal-combustion engine while offering students pearls of wisdom like, "You can't get to nature without gasoline or cars."'[44] A lesson plan and video from Exxon titled 'Scientists and the Alaska Oil Spill' 'praises the oil company's role in restoring the ecology of Prince William Sound while avoiding any discussion of what (or who) caused the Alaska oil spill in the first place.'[45] Read-a-Logo is a reading software program that uses corporate logos in place of some common words. Students are required to recognize corporate logos in magazines and newspapers and bring them into class.[46]

Another trend is in-school corporate-funded performances in classrooms and school assemblies. McDonald's has developed in-school presentations that have been brought to several schools throughout Canada as a part of their 'GO ACTIVE!' campaign. Following a dazzling light-and-sound show, several costumed figures with microphones announce that they're from McDonald's and are going to talk about healthy nutrition and healthy lifestyles. They announce, 'We've all gone to teachers college, so we're just like your teachers.'[47] The National Theatre for Children is often solicited by advertisers who want to sponsor plays about their products in schools. It has performed plays about 'nutrition, smoking prevention and energy conservation [that] were sponsored by health care or insurance firms, utilities or government agencies. While the for-profit theater aggressively courts brand-name firms, it will not accept business from companies that want to sell guns, liquor, tobacco or candy.'[48]

In order to more readily gain access to schools, Coca-Cola co-founded the Council for Corporate and School Partnerships, which 'works with educators and businesses to identify, create, recognize and support exemplary business–school relationships that improve the student experience in K–12 schools.'[49] The CEO of Coca-Cola Enterprises confirms its motive: 'The school system is where you build brand loyalty.'[50] Cola contracts have provoked significant conflict, and in addition to obvious health and dietary problems, have also been associated with increasing control over the student body. In some cases students have been discouraged or even prohibited by corporations from engaging in activities to support their school teams. For example, several high school students attempted to raise money for a school trip by selling bottled water to the audience at a sporting event, but were later forced to pay the money back to Coke because a condition of the schools' cola contract stipulated that no one was permitted to sell a comparable product on school grounds. In other cases, students have been punished for opposing cola contracts. At a rally during a 'Coke Day' at one

Georgia school, all students came to school wearing Coke T-shirts in hopes of winning a $500 prize. Several Coke representatives arrived for a photo-op, and one student was suspended for wearing a Pepsi T-shirt.[51] This demonstrates how private corporations gain control over what students can and can't do in public schools, and will even prevent student fundraising projects.

These dynamics are perhaps most apparent in research into the impact of Channel One, a corporation that requires that students watch its closed-circuit programming for ten to twelve minutes per day in exchange for its 'donated' television equipment. Erika Shaker of the Canadian Centre for Policy Alternatives (CCPA) argues that Channel One has an even more profound influence on children than TV at home, because 'the school environment itself reinforces the legitimacy of the messages taught within.'[52] A study done by the CCPA indicated that students who watched Channel One were more likely to agree that 'money is everything, designer labels make a difference, a nice car is more important than school, I want what I see advertised, and wealthy people are happier.'[53] Furthermore, many students were often unable to differentiate between advertisements and news, and others were more likely to remember the advertisements shown than the news content.[54] Even more troubling, one recent study showed that 'students may view commercials that are shown in a school setting as more credible than those that are viewed at home.' The effects of these commercial inroads has been confirmed: perhaps unsurprisingly, 'students tended to remember a greater number of ads than news stories, and students had purchased up to 8 of the 11 advertised items listed on the survey.'[55]

Advertisers are trying to capitalize on every moment in the daily life of students, even while in transit. Like Channel One, a recent start-up called BusRadio offers its equipment and programming for free in exchange for mandatory air time on school buses, including eight minutes of advertising per hour. As Commercial Alert warns, 'In its contract with school districts, BusRadio does not rule out advertising any particular type of products. If Channel One is any guide, we might expect BusRadio to advertise junk food, soda pop, violent and sexualized entertainment, and movies that encourage school children to smoke tobacco.'[56]

Children today are so thoroughly immersed in advertising's world of images and logos that they have no trouble identifying dozens of consumer brands and corporate slogans; they have developed a new kind of literacy. Literacy discourse is characterized by tensions over what 'literacy' means, whom it serves, how it ought to be measured, and how it should be taught and learned. There is much written about emotional literacy, functional literacy, and so on. However, what is increasingly apparent in today's students is what could be called the literacy of consumption. Even at a very early age, many children can more readily identify countless logos and meanings associated with them than they can important historical figures. A provocative display of this dynamic occurs in the documentary *Super Size Me*.[57] Several school children were shown dozens of corporate logos and were more successful at identifying them than when shown pictures of Jesus, Martin Luther King, and Mother Theresa. A 1986 study showed that already over twenty years ago the popularity of Ronald McDonald among students was so high that '96% of them could identify Ronald McDonald, second only to Santa Claus in name recognition.'[58]

Principals who permit corporate partnerships are often motivated by the desire to enhance the reputation of their schools so as to reduce the likelihood of school closing. As desperate schools turn to corporate advertisers for revenue, well-intentioned principals and administrators all too often welcome the benefits and additional income. For example, their arguments concerning fast food in the cafeteria and pop machines in the halls are that 'kids eat junk anyhow' and 'advertising is everywhere.' In fact, several principals, boards, and regional governing bodies have established taxpayer-paid positions to facilitate this process. Missouri has its own director of school–business partnerships, and some districts like East Hartford have permanently established and publicly funded School–Business Partnership offices.[59]

Perhaps most troubling, rather than functioning as sites to research and critically engage school commercialism, some faculties of education help to facilitate the development of partnerships with business. For example, the partnership between the University of Calgary Faculty of Education and Imperial Oil, called Teaching and Learning for a Knowledge Era[60] seeks to advance K–12 school–business partnerships in the province of Alberta. Its general manager, Brenda Gladstone, and education professor Michele Jacobsen argue, 'Educational partnerships are an important strategy for increasing the authenticity and value of school for our future citizens. In addition to the financial benefits that business–school partnerships often bring to schools, there are a variety of teaching and learning benefits of making links with the community at large.'[61] In fact, they go so far as to argue, 'Educational partnerships promote civic responsibility and good citizenship, leadership and volunteer opportunities, and increase social contacts for our students with diverse members of their community.'[62] Their Teachers in Business Summer Program, sponsored by Imperial Oil, 'provides summer positions to classroom teachers' that allow teachers to 'identify specific programs and individuals that would best fit with their own students and curriculum.'[63]

These many examples indicate the extraordinary commercial presence in the school environment, a process in which the state is complicit in handing over students to corporations. Although we have touched on the reasons why corporations are interested in gaining access to schools, this issue is worth closer examination.

Commercial Inroads

There are six main reasons why corporations seek access to public schools:

1. First and most obviously, schools provide a direct opportunity for immediate profit, and corporations are in pursuit of the money spent every day by students. Market researchers estimate that 'there are more than 60 million kids aged 5 to 19 with over $100 billion of their own money to spend.'[64] Nine- to nineteen-year-olds in Canada spent approximately $13.5 billion in 1999.[65]
2. Schools are vast sorting sites that students are obligated to attend, where they are organized by age and grades, which marketers note creates 'very refined and specific targeting and message segmentation.'[66] Marketing firm Youthography notes on its website that schools provide a much more targeted market than that available to TV broadcasters, as schools contain specific age groups and are also organized by income, race, and language, reflecting the local ethnicity and economic status of the surrounding population.[67] Kenway and Bullen ask, 'What better place than an all-girls school, for instance, for gender-targeted marketing such as Johnson and Johnson's "Follow Your Dream" Promotion?' (CC, 94–5). Schools help assemble a target audience, which is then made available to corporations.
3. Advertisers compete to reach a market in an environment of growing 'clutter' or 'noise' from other advertisers. Kenway and Bullen note, 'With "ad glut" or "clutter" a major problem, advertisers are finding it increasingly difficult to make products appear distinc-

tive in a marketplace saturated with ads. As they are relatively commercial-free, schools offer advertisers a largely competitor-free environment' (CC, 96). Students in schools are what marketers call a 'captive audience,' required to 'be there approximately 6½ hours a day, five days a week, nine months a year until the age of 16.'[68] With changes in television watching, such as TiVo (which allows recording without commercials), and the growing popularity of online video games, advertisers are continually trying to develop new ways of gaining a captive audience. Furthermore, schools are places where advertisers can bypass parental 'gatekeepers' who might otherwise control their children's exposure to advertising.

4. Once bypassed, kids in turn can market back to their parents on behalf of advertisers. In-school advertising allows advertisers to bypass parents and speak directly to children – often so that they can regain access to parents. In fact, this is its primary advantage over other forms of advertising: it provides a targeted opportunity to market to kids, through parents and/or to parents, all at once. Children become corporate representatives within the family and exert tremendous sway over their parents' spending habits. One advertising executive notes that 'this generation's influence on the consumer economy is immense. Generation Y's needs and opinions drive many adult purchase decisions, and they, literally, represent the future market for most consumer brands.'[69] Schooling is thereby used to access not only youth but also their parents through what marketers term the 'nag factor' or 'pester power.'[70] Market researchers estimate that in 2003 'children age four to 12 influenced some $565 billion of their parents' purchasing each year.'[71] One marketer observed, 'The *influence market* is five to seven times the size of the primary market.'[72] It could be said that this is a new form of child labour, as children become the 'Trojan Horse'[73] of the home market and thereby do the work of marketers within the family. Sut Jhally, the founder and executive director of the Media Education Foundation, argues that youth marketing is a new form of child labour because children become corporate spokespeople and unknowingly do the work of marketers within the family. Jhally goes so far as to suggest that even as we make efforts to protect our children from bullying and physical molestation, 'we have opened up our doors and allowed people to come into our homes to manipulate our children and draw value out of them.'[74] In addition to creating animosity between children and their families,

many marketing strategies seek to exploit the already fragile emotional landscapes of divorced families. Parents who spend less time with their children because of work or divorce may be more likely to show their love and ease their guilt through spending. Kids may interpret the absence of consumer goods as an absence of affection. It may seem overly suspicious to claim that marketers exploit these societal trends, if it weren't for the fact that *nag factor* and *pester power* were terms created by the marketing industry itself.

5. Corporations seek access to schools because they are sites where cultural values are taught and ideological messages are internalized. Consumerism shapes the subjectivities and world views of students, who have been called 'consumers in training.' They are developing 'brand loyalties' that may last for their entire lifetime, and may include life-long addiction to tobacco, cola, and other substances. As one marketing journal asserts, 'Millions of people, especially young people, identify with certain brands the way they once did only with film stars and sports heroes.'[75] Considering how young they are, and that they have years of consuming to look forward to, they are a much more sought-after demographic than older consumers, because 'they have a lifetime of spending ahead of them.'[76] Marketers measure this in terms of 'customer lifetime value,'[77] which calculates the total amount of money expected to be made from a customer through his or her lifetime.

6. Last, and perhaps most abstractly, corporations capitalize on the social legitimacy accorded to schools because corporate involvement in schools can be construed as benevolent and used to improve their image. A 2006 *New York Times* article cites Molnar to this end: 'One standard goal corporations have in their marketing programs is making the corporation itself seem more desirable and good, and it's hard to find something more desirable and good than public schools.'[78] Erika Shaker of the Canadian Centre for Policy Alternatives argues that 'merely by being associated with the school, the product and the sponsoring corporation appear to have additional legitimacy and the implicit endorsement of the educational system.'[79] Such partnerships are a 'cheap and effective way for corporations to gain goodwill in the community, and in return ... the schools can give them an enormous amount of exposure.'[80] Even as their public image is improved, corporations are also eligible for tax deductions – creating a loss in revenue that could have gone to the schools in the first place. The Canadian

Centre for Policy Alternatives explains the several ways this constitutes a loss to taxpayers: 'Partnerships usually represent a financial
loss to taxpayers. The donation is always tax-deductible, which
means less tax revenue for education ... Taxpayers pay for educational time being diverted to activities to promote the corporation
... As we accept these donations, we can expect an exponential loss
through a reduction in the funds we receive from the Ministry of
Education.'[81]

From Plato through Dewey to contemporary philosophy of education and critical pedagogy, schools have been recognized as sites where
cultural values are taught and ideological messages are internalized.
Through the influence of consumerism and school commercialism,
students internalize consumer values and take on commercial world
views; it is the values of the marketplace and business world that become dominant. Public dispositions are replaced with private commercial ones, blurring the line between schools as public realms and
schools as commercial spheres.

Heather-Jane Robertson identifies a paradoxical and ironic shift: 'Just
when education has adopted "marketese" and "globalspeak" as its vernacular, the privatization alliance has begun to couch its school reform
agenda in the argot of equality and opportunity.'[82] For example, a new
textbook publisher called Textbook Media Press includes ads mixed
with lessons and course material and offers its books for free online.
'Students, or anyone else who fills out a five-minute survey, can down-
load a PDF file of the book, which they can store on their hard drive and
print.'[83] Textbook Media Press argues that this commercialization trend
addresses the issue of increasing textbook costs and will therefore help
improve equity and accessibility. School commercialism is presented as
the solution to the very problem it creates. Kenneth Saltman notes that
'rather than addressing the funding inequalities and the intertwined
dynamics at work in making poor schools, the remedy is commodification.'[84]

Corporate Motives

Peter Cowley of the Canadian pro-business lobby group The Fraser Institute suggests that corporate support simply picks up where government leaves off: 'Many educators and parents welcome such initiatives
because they know taxpayer funding for education is inevitably lim-

ited.' Corporate support is construed as a generous and benign supplement, and welcomed by all. He claims that there are great rewards for everybody and no downside, since 'there is no evidence that displaying the logos of corporate sponsors in schools has any effect on learning.'[85] However, corporate involvement has many effects beyond measurable learning, and each type of involvement varies. To narrow the issue of corporate funding to the direct relationship between logos and learning reduces the issue to the point of absurdity and obscures the larger issue of the public function of schooling.

While corporations might describe their relations with schools as 'partnerships,' and emphasize the advantages that schools reap, they are in fact motivated only by profit. This is not corporate benevolence but is what marketers describe as 'strategic philanthropy.' There are several reasons why it is not benevolence:

1. The cost of school advertising is already factored into the price of the consumer product; it is we as consumers who pay for corporations' involvement with schools when we purchase their products. However, paying for schools with consumer purchases rather than our tax dollars bypasses the democratic process and public responsibility, because decisions are passed over to corporations with dramatically different aims and interests.

2. Corporate involvement in education is undertaken only if corporations expect to make more money than they pay, either directly through sales or indirectly through brand promotion or tax write-offs. In fact, this is the claim of well-known free market advocate Milton Friedman, who famously insisted, 'There is one and only one social responsibility of business – to use its resources and engage in activities designed to increase its profits.'[86] Because corporate funding of school activities is intended to draw attention to their brand and their products, it is easy to forget that the bulk of educational funding comes from public sources. Advertisers and marketers use the most visible and high-profile strategies to project their presence, grabbing the limelight while other services are often left neglected and underfunded. Government involvement – which in fact covers most of the expenses – is easily overlooked because corporations play a small part of education funding, yet gain the most recognition. For example, a school may receive money from Nike to renovate its gymnasium in exchange for the prominent display of the Nike name and logo, while equally important but

less high-profile budgetary needs are neglected. Thus, in our hasty gratitude we forget that we as taxpayers not only pay for the bulk of school expenses but also pay to assemble this audience – or market – in the first place.

3. If schools received sufficient income directly from the public through taxes rather than highly questionable school–business partnerships, it wouldn't be necessary to spend extra money promoting products in the school. Ironically, the same economic organizations pushing for cuts to schools establish partnerships in order to resolve this same financial crisis. Heather-Jane Robertson notes, 'It is absurd of us to ask the same organizations that have clamoured for lower taxes and less public spending to rescue the schools that these politics are damaging.'[87] Deborah Cowen of York University suggests that public obligations become business opportunities because 'we've transformed what used to be an obligation placed on firms [in the form of taxes] into a marketing opportunity that provides tax relief for firms and is entirely voluntary.'[88] As a result, 'school fundraising reinforces the problematic notion of education as a charity, rather than as a basic human and social right.'[89]

4. Corporations will often dictate the conditions of their involvement with schools. Heather-Jane Robertson argues that there is no level playing field when education and commercial interests mix, and that the term *partnership* misrepresents what is really going on in these arrangements. 'When you talk about partners it implies that both parties have an equal say. That's simply not the case here. Corporations have the power and the money, and schools are dependent because they are cash-strapped.' She observes, 'In interpersonal relationships, when one person needs the other in order to survive, we call the relationship dysfunctional. In nature, when one biological organism feeds off another, we call it a parasite. In education, we call this relationship a partnership.'[90] For example, decisions about when, where, and how a playground sponsored by Home Depot is built are no longer made democratically but instead at the whim of corporations. 'Relying on corporate relationships allows the private sector to make decisions previously made by elected officials.'[91] Furthermore, corporations will prevent opposition or criticism of their products or policies within schools, and principals and administrators are required to enforce these conditions or risk losing their funding. Widely documented examples

range from suspending students who criticize their products to preventing teachers from turning off Channel One or the Youth News Network.[92]

Built into most contracts is a non-disclosure or confidentiality clause, which prevents students or teachers from criticizing the corporation with which they have a contract.[93] Although these contracts vary between schools and their corporate partners, some opponents of school commercialism have successfully argued that such contracts are public property under freedom of information laws. Yet when three Toronto area teachers criticized YNN and founded a group called People against Commercial Television in Schools, the company charged them with defamation and sued them for damages of $900,000.[94] 'When the lawsuit came down, all of a sudden, those who had been openly discussing the pros and the cons of YNN didn't feel comfortable talking about it anymore. What began as a debate over the merits of YNN's programming and the ethics of trading class time for technology became a fight over the rights of parents, educators and students to express their opinions about what's taught in their schools, and the role of the school in facilitating that discussion.'[95] Although these charges were eventually dropped, the implications for democracy and debate about school commercialism are far-reaching. 'The silence that the defamation suit has enforced teaches kids, by example, that getting involved, speaking out and expressing dissent will only lead to trouble. That's far more dangerous than making kids watch commercials in class.'[96] This trend blurs the line between educating students and acquiring new consumers, between schools as commercial spheres and educational environments, and demonstrates the extent to which corporations will go to ensure they have access to students.

Soon it may be the case that more money is spent marketing to students than educating them, as students become targeted as present and future consumers rather than future participants in the public world or agents of social change. Statistics confirm the trend in which increases in advertising budgets far exceed the increases to spending on education. Benjamin Barber notes, 'While the United States spent about $16 billion in foreign aid in 2003, the projected American expenditure for advertising for 2005 was $276 billion,' and 'worldwide advertising [is] expected to increase by 5 percent a year' (CN, 11, 13). Mark Evans of the *National Post* writes, 'Global advertising spending will increase at a robust 5.9 percent CAGR during the 2005–2009 period, rising to $477 billion in 2009 from $358 billion in 2004.'[97] A PricewaterhouseCoopers headline claims, 'Entertainment and Media Industry in Strongest Position since 2000, Will Grow 7.3 Percent Annually to $1.8 Trillion in 2009.'[98] Yet in Ontario, $10.5 billion was spent on K–12 education. Not only is the total amount of spending on advertising increasing, but also the total amount of daily or weekly exposure. Benjamin Barber argues, 'Teachers struggle for the attention of their students for at most twenty or thirty hours a week, perhaps thirty weeks a year, in settings they do not fully control and in institutions that are often ridiculed in the popular media [while] the true tutors of late consumer capitalist society as measured by time are those who control the media monopolies … who capture sixty or seventy hours a week, fifty-two weeks a year, of children's time and attention' (CN, 231).

Marketing to Teens: The 'Nag Factor' and 'Pester Power'

Because consumerism is a growing part of socialization, it is worth considering the core assumptions and implications of marketing to school-age children. Advertising and marketing have grown ever more prevalent in our society, creating a culture of consumers, a 'consumer culture,' and increasing parts of our day involve exposure to these signs and images. Marketing is rapidly evolving and taking on new forms. Buzz marketing or stealth marketing pays individuals to promote products to friends and family or just to wear a new product. Furthermore, as if there weren't already enough ads in the 'real' world, advertising is now moving into the virtual world by putting ads and product placements in video games. It is for these reasons that Gary Ruskin, former director of Commercial Alert, says that marketers' 'minds do not work to solve the nation's real problems; they work to create new problems for you.'[99]

As a result, contemporary experiences of childhood and adolescence are increasingly the construct of consumer culture, and what has been referred to as Generation X or Y could in fact be called the Branded Generation.[100] Marketer Ann Sutherland calls them the 'more generation': 'If the boomers were the "me" generation, then Generation Y could be thought of as the "more" generation. As one New Yorker cartoon glibly pointed out, these kids have only known a "bull market." The end result: More spending, more experiencing, more demands for more.'[101] However, while such a long period of sustained economic growth itself promotes more consumerism and growth, it would also seem to imply that only a major economic depression or world war could do anything to alter consumerism. Indeed, just as overspending helped precipitate the economic crisis during the fall of 2008, more consumerism is held up as the solution.

Several scholars explore how the rise of consumerism parallels key shifts in the experience of childhood. For example, in *Consuming Children*, Jane Kenway and Elizabeth Bullen outline the changing conceptions of the child throughout history and argue that the prevalence of consumer culture has dramatically altered schooling. In eroding the demarcations between education, entertainment, and advertising, it has brought schooling into what they call the 'age of desire.' 'The "nature" of being young, the relationships of the young to adults, to the family and to other social institutions such as the school, have changed considerably across time and place.' As a result of this change, 'the demarcations between education, entertainment and advertising collapse and … the lines between the generations both blur and harden' (CC, 2). The struggle to mature, develop, and individuate is often impeded rather than facilitated by consumerism, in what psychologists call the Peter Pan syndrome, when we *want* to remain infantile, carefree, and forever young. Consumerism might seem to be like this syndrome, but instead of protecting childhood, consumerism exploits it; instead of keeping children safe from a world of commerce, it exposes them to it so as to create consumers. It *sells* them the ideal of youth; it does not release the imagination but captures it in a commodity. Benjamin Barber notes the paradox that it is like Never-Neverland, 'except that you have to buy it with grown up dollars' (CN, 19).

Marketers know that teens are more influenced by their peers than by any other demographic. To this end they have attempted to recruit teens as marketers for each other. For example, Procter & Gamble recently established a subsidiary called Tremor, which has 'assembled a stealth sales force of teenagers – 280,000 strong – to push products on friends and family.'[102] Teenagers are invited to join a 'network,' described as a 'way for kids to influence companies and find out about cool new products before their friends do.'[103] While movies and television have long contained 'product placement,' musicians have been approached to include references to McDonald's in their lyrics. 'Eminem and 50 Cent could soon have a new lyrical weapon to add to their arsenal: the Big Mac.'[104] With the growing popularity of video games that lure youth away from the television screen, advertisers have begun placing products within the virtual world of games themselves.[105] This development will be further discussed in the chapter on Baudrillard and the simulation of reality.

Some marketers argue that they are performing a public service by educating children. For example, in *Kidfluence* marketers Ann Sutherland and Betty Thompson argue that marketers are part of a dramatic transformation of the traditional family from an authoritarian parent-centred structure to a 'bi-directional relationship' more democratically centred upon children's real needs and interests.[106] The authors suggest that boomers who grew up in authoritarian households are trying to raise their kids differently by involving them in family discussions in a much more democratic manner. Parents increasingly ask their kids opinions about consuming decisions because they are afraid of buying the wrong product. Business responded by marketing directly to younger people, who are now the educated experts within the family and appreciated for their extensive product knowledge. Sutherland and Thompson explain,

> In the new family model, kids feel like a valuable part of the family unit and grow up believing they have the right to vote on all issues affecting their family, including purchasing decisions. Small questions like 'What should we get Grandma for her birthday?' to weightier queries like 'Where shall we spend our summer vacation?' are within the parameters of normal dialogue for most families. In fact, today's parents go as far as to say it is unfair not to include younger members of the family in buying decisions. Families who do not confer with their children about purchases, either of a daily nature or larger one-time acquisitions, deny their kids an opportunity to develop important life skills. Many families who have adopted these democratic practices like the dignity they give the family. They promote the concept that all family members are equally valued and given consideration regardless of age.[107]

According to these marketers, increasing one's ability to make consumer choices is the same as democratizing the family, and marketers are providing a service to society by spreading democracy. This may put the cart before the horse: while some parents may ask for their kids' opinion, many others are simply overwhelmed by constant berating. Few parents will be grateful to marketers while walking through the candy section of a store or driving past a fast food restaurant. Jonathan Rowe and Gary Ruskin argue that 'corporations are literally alienating children from their parents, shifting children's loyalties more toward the corporations themselves.'[108]

Another teen marketer sympathetically argues that marketing to teens involves listening to and empowering teens. 'They are filled with great ideas, but they don't think anyone listens to them.'[109] Yet through this process, schools, teachers, and parents are portrayed as a negative 'Other' and resented as authority figures, while the icons of consumption and entertainment are elevated as symbols of rebellion to identify with and emulate. In linking popular culture and pedagogy, Henry Giroux and Roger Simon note, 'At first glance, the relationship between popular culture and classroom pedagogy may seem remote. Popular culture is organized around the investments of pleasure and fun, while pedagogy is defined largely in instrumental terms. Popular culture is located in the terrain of the everyday, while pedagogy generally legitimates and transmits the language, codes and values of the dominant culture. Popular culture is appropriated by students and is a major source of knowledge for authorizing their voices and experiences, even as pedagogy authorized the voices of the adult world of teachers and school administrators.'[110]

Children today are so thoroughly immersed in advertising's world of images and jingles that they have no trouble identifying dozens of consumer brands and corporate slogans. While Socrates called upon us to know ourselves, and Freud showed that we are largely unknown to ourselves, marketers demonstrate that they often know more than we do about ourselves and our desires. They can readily gain access to our minds, as the name of marketing firm Mindshare indicates. Their website proudly proclaims, 'Gaining a greater share of customers' minds for our clients calls for smart ideas. But they are worth little without rapid decision-making, committed action and faultless execution. In other words, we know the importance of getting things done – and doing them well.'[111] A new trend in marketing called 'neuromarketing' uses magnetic resonance imaging to map brain patterns and reveal how consumers respond to a particular advertisement or product. Researchers at the Brighthouse Institute for Thought Sciences measure the discrepancy between a participant's stated preference and the pleasure centres of his or her brain that the product activated. The results show that brands and images often have a greater impact than physical sensations. Researchers can thereby determine the effectiveness of marketing campaigns and branding strategies, and plan new and more effective ones. Advocates say they're doing consumers a favour by helping determine what we like and want. A *Forbes* article states that the intention is to 'find a buy button inside the skull.'[112]

Soon the search for this 'buy button' will replace the unreliability of surveys and focus groups as it turns from a 'soft' social science to a 'hard' neurological science in which our preferences become understood at the molecular level. Mapping the shopper's mind in this way allows unlimited reach into the most private dimensions of human thought and desire. The company is secretive about whom they sell this knowledge of our minds to. Researcher Adam Kovol contends that their work is benign because 'they only observe and learn,' and even benevolent because they are helping address the school funding problem by offering money to willing participants.[113]

Many theorists argue that the language of advertising has become the most important influence in socialization – in Baudrillard's terms, 'a form of socialization' (SO, 23). For Henry Giroux, 'growing up corporate has become a way of life for American youth ... it is apparent in the accelerated commercialism in all aspects of everyday life, including the commercialization of public schools.'[114] After observing a Toronto high school classroom, cultural critic Hal Niedzviecki suggests that students' 'minds have clearly been invaded, filled with information they are too young to process or need.'[115] It is not only schools themselves that have been invaded, but the very minds of students.

Scholars who have researched employment trends argue that those children who worked outside the home in other historical periods either did not go to school or turned their earnings over to the household. Melissa K. Lickteig asserts that 'historically, children who worked did so largely to help supplement their family's household income; their wages contributed to the collective needs of family maintenance.'[116] She argues that in contrast, teenagers today in many cases work to buy consumer products for themselves. Unfortunately this may diminish school spirit as students may be more inclined to work rather than participate in school activities or volunteer for school programs.[117] Companies like Nike, Coke, MTV, and countless others would be much less successful were it not for the growth in discretionary spending money among this demographic cohort.

These examples may explain why, according to the Millward Brown Global Market Research Agency, 'nowhere else in the world [but America] are 8–12 year olds more materialistic or likely to believe that their clothes and brands describe who they are and define their social status.'[118] Critic of consumerism Juliet Schor writes, 'The United States is the most consumer-oriented society in the world [and] the architects of this culture ... have now set their sights on children ... Kids and teens are now the epicenter of American consumer culture. They command the attention, creativity, and dollars of advertisers. Their tastes drive market trends. Their opinions shape brand strategies.'[119]

It is ironic that, even as education is expected to be 'value neutral' and teachers are not to 'impose their values' on students,[120] advertising does just the opposite: it teaches values based on consumption. However, unlike education and educators, advertisers do not work towards a better future for society. Henry Giroux states that corporations 'substitute corporate propaganda for real learning, upset the requisite balance between the public and the private, and in doing so treat schools like any other business.'[121] This reinforces students' roles as consumers, spectators, and passive citizens. Consumerism thereby erodes democratic life by reducing education to the reproduction of private accumulation, and advances political apathy in place of social change, ultimately transforming human relations into commercial transactions of calculated exchange. Deron Boyles argues that consumerism 'reduce[es] searching, being, and thinking to objectified and reductionistic particulars. For schooling it means that students see their roles as "getting" right answers to questions instead of searching for meaning and understanding by contesting standardized curriculum.'[122] Critical pedagogue Svi Shapiro notes that 'TV, movies, popular music, and fashions, for example, powerfully disseminate the culture of consumption; against school's emphasis on deferral is the insistence on immediate gratification; in place of the concern with future investment and career planning is the demand for present satisfaction and "letting things happen"; and instead of discipline or restraint is a demand for spontaneity or "letting go."'[123] Consumerism may lead students to devalue their own curiosity and learning and its potential contribution to a richer democratic society, and instead focus entirely on stimulation and extrinsic material rewards.

While it is the goal of education to ensure the well-rounded development of our youth, the goal of advertising is unapologetically and narrowly focused on encouraging consumption and brand loyalty. Critical perspectives on advertising are encouraged insofar as children are able to differentiate between the different brands of choice for sale, and choice is encouraged insofar as choice is a product rather than a genuine political or pedagogical alternative. As an example of the discourse of 'choice' in education, the newsletter *EdInvest News* published by the World Bank Group examines the Canadian Education Freedom Index developed by the business-oriented Canadian think tank The Fraser Institute.[124] The index measures 'educational freedom' based exclusively on 'choice,' and seeks to reduce the role that 'governments play in creating or obstructing educational freedom.'[125]

In the next section, a growing trend in school commercialism will be discussed, perhaps the most direct attempt to commercialize education: the rise of the educational management organization.

Trends in School Commercialism: Edison and Allegiance

In *School Commercialism*, Alex Molnar distinguishes between marketing *to* schools, *in* schools, and *of* schools.[126] In fact, they would seem to follow logically: rather than trying to get into schools, why not just run them? Running schools makes it even easier to directly profit from advertising and marketing within schools. It is the prospect of running schools that is the focus of Kenneth Saltman's *The Edison Schools*. His book is unique among works that consider school commercialism in its focus on one particular manifestation of corporate influence. I will briefly comment on this book as an example of a specific form of school commercialism that is a logical outcome of the emergence of the discourse of the student as 'client' or 'consumer' of education.

In *The Edison Schools*, Saltman chronicles the dramatic rise and fall of America's first educational management organization (EMO), the largest and most ambitious attempt to launch a publicly traded, nationwide, for-profit manager of public schools. Whereas private schools collect tuition directly from parents, the EMO's aim is to use tax money to run public schools, and capture profits from money that would otherwise go to pay for smaller class sizes, more books and other supplies, and higher teacher salaries.

Saltman opens the book with an evocative description of Edison schools, as an example of the transformation of national reverence into corporate adulation and replacement of citizens with educational 'consumers': students line up in front of the American flag before classes start, but rather than pledging allegiance to the flag they pledge themselves to the Edison Corporation.[127] In the same way that beer ads use nationalism to sell beer, Edison uses nationalism to 'sell' Edison.

Saltman's chronicle is made even more compelling by his focus on the central figure behind Edison, the founder of both Channel One and

Whittle Communications, Chris Whittle. This grand 'edupreneur' is an ambitious 'advertising ideaman'[128] whose self-proclaimed mission is the spread of advertisements and whose demonstrated expertise lies in the transformation of public institutions and resources into privately owned for-profit endeavours. A frequent outspoken critic of public schooling, Whittle has done little to improve their condition but instead positions himself to profit from their beleaguered condition. His early career of commercializing public space began with forays into health care, such as advertising in doctors' waiting rooms. Saltman shows that the frequent failures of Whittle's controversial business ventures designed to profit from schooling did little to discourage him, but instead led him to launch Edison schools in 1995.

At present Edison has 136 schools in twenty states, with a total of 132,000 students. Saltman chose Edison by not only because it is the largest and most influential EMO in America but because it is considered the bellwether of the EMO movement. Edison is closely followed by the media, academics, parents, and educators to determine the possible success or failure of the EMO movement as a whole. This book then stands as an essential document of the trials and tribulations, failures and successes, of this test case. Saltman notes, 'The most pressing issues about the Edison schools involve the role of public schooling in a democracy, and more broadly the meaning of the privatization of the public sector in a democracy. The success or failure of Edison is not so much about the alleged skills or alleged corruption of a group of business people as it is about the fundamental issues of school funding, the purpose of public schools, the role of teachers and administrators, the society's commitment to educating youth to become not merely consumers or disciplined workers but active participants in forging the future with the hope that they will make a better, more just, equal and fair nation and world.'[129]

Saltman's chronicle depicts the role of countless illustrious movers and shakers of American politics, business, and education that Whittle's powerful connections brought on board for Edison. These range from former secretary of education Lamar Alexander and Yale president Benno C. Schmidt Jr, to both Bush brothers. Corporate donors range from publishing (Time-Warner, Inc.) to clothing (The Gap) to several high-tech corporations (IBM and Apple), all seeking access to public schools and their students so as to better create – or 'brand' – future consumers. Thus, corporations that target youth no longer need to do so only through advertising, because as investors they can gain direct access to school administrators; they may not have to pay to get their products and ideas placed before young people because the education industry will do it for them. For example, Saltman describes how high-tech corporations on the Edison board push for mandatory computer-based assignments and activities.

In privatizing our public schools it is the values of the marketplace and business world that take over: efficiency and measurement, cost and competition come all too often at the expense of quality, inclusion, and equity. For example, the market model is said to empower parents because it allows for more 'choice,' but it often empowers certain schools more than others because some schools can choose the students they would like to admit. Saltman describes problematic Edison practices such as charges of racism and cases of excluding students who may negatively alter test results. Philosopher of education Ruth Jonathan suggests that the problematic implications of this aspect of school commercialism arise because often democratic principles are undermined by the larger political and pedagogical implications of consumer choice. 'When each exercises consumer rights individually, the aggregate outcomes of citizens' choices are removed from any deliberative process, which democratic control – whether central or local – of the conduct of education and of its distribution sought (however imperfectly) to realize. Whilst seeking to restrain the tentacular reach of the state, we shall see that the shift to control by market forces licenses a "war of all against all" such as even the most "minimal state" is designed to avoid.' This gives rise to what she calls the 'destructive power of consumer sovereignty on a society's educational provision.'[130]

However, even as a business, the Edison schools have been less than successful. Saltman notes that 'the company did not file tax returns in many states that require them. Whittle faced more than $10 million in unpaid taxes and penalties.'[131] The remedy has been numerous government bailouts, and even offers of Edison shares to teachers, including the Florida and California Public Teachers Pension Plan – which would ironically make the retirements of public school teachers dependent on the success of private schools.[132] Fortunately, intensive lobbying prevented such a conflation of public schools with private profit.

Through the Edison schools, Saltman presents the problematic implications of the prevalence of the free market model. When education becomes a business venture, it also becomes a high stakes gamble, subject to all the risks inherent to economic fluctuations, global economic instabilities, and a highly volatile stock market. Recent events reveal that 'what's good for General Motors' often means laying off thousands or turning back to the state for bailouts after years of profits. We too should be warned of what equating the corporate good with national good might mean for schools and our children. Yet with education the stakes may be even higher. Saltman asks, 'What happens to school kids when the company running their school goes under?'[133] This question raises even greater concerns in light of economic events of the fall of 2008. Children are placed in the hands of unpredictable, impersonal, and essentially unaccountable economic interests, exposed to the perils of the marketplace. Freedom and choice are often said to benefit all, but as Ruth Jonathan points out, spreading choice may harm more than it helps: 'To extend similar choices to all *is not to correct an injustice, but to foist on everyone implicit acceptance of a conception of justice which many do not share.*'[134] The paradox is that we are to celebrate economic freedom, yet embrace increasing corporate control.

Reproducing Consumerism: The World Education Market

Our reverence for the free market and faith that it adheres to laws both natural and universal implies that we must simply obey its logic – and public schooling is shown to be no exception. Gordon Bigelow argues that there is often a near-religious attitude towards economics and the market as 'the cosmology and the theodicy of our contemporary culture. More than religion itself, more than literature, more than cable television, it is economics that offers the dominant creation narrative of our society, depicting the relation of each of us to the universe we inhabit, the relation of human beings to God ... this understanding of markets – not as artifacts of human civilization but as phenomena of nature – now serves as the unquestioned foundation of nearly all social and political debate.'[135] However, rather than permitting schooling to succumb to this trend, Ruth Jonathan argues that 'in any open society the social practice we call education must represent the limiting case of the free market.'[136]

Alex Molnar agrees, arguing that school commercialism compromises the democratic function of education:

Today, across the nation and around the world, the ideal of the public school as a pillar of democracy is being transformed by a wave of commercialism. Commercialism is an expression of advanced capitalist culture and a profound threat to democratic civic institutions. Its impact on schools is, at its most basic, to transform the guiding ideal of public schools as centers of learning serving the public good to centers of profit benefiting private interests. Once held to be a public good that could be measured by their contribution to the community's well-being, schools have come to be seen as markets for vendors, venues for advertising and marketing and commodities to be bought and sold ... Their mission has been transformed conceptually into a 'service' that can be delivered by private businesses responding to the profit motive. (SC, 16)

Molnar is the director of the U.S.-based Commercialism in Education Research Unit (CERU), which releases annual reports on school commercialism, for-profit education management organizations, and market-oriented school reforms, going back over a decade.[137] Molnar describes eight categories used to indicate changes in schoolhouse commercialism: sponsorship of programs and activities; agreements giving corporations exclusive rights to sell in school; incentive programs, such as free pizza for meeting reading goals; appropriation of space, such as advertising in hallways, cafeterias, and classrooms; sponsored educational materials, corporate-sponsored curriculum such as the McDonald's nutritional curriculum; electronic marketing such as Channel One (explored in detail by Saltman); privatization and educational management organizations; and fund-raising practices, such as when corporations 'encourage parents and neighbors to purchase the companies' products so that the labels can be redeemed for rewards' (SC, 26). His research confirms that all of these key indicators point towards dramatic increases in school commercialism.

Molnar sets commercialism within the global context of neo-liberalism and privatization and the governing bodies and legal documents that influence it, arguing that 'the stage is being set to expand the commercialization of education around the world' (SC, 130). Thus we see that North American trends are in fact part of a larger worldwide shift towards school commercialism. Molnar describes the 'world education market,' which 'assumes learning and the educative process to be simply one more bundle of commodities, ripe for globalization and profit maximizers' (SC, 131). This trend is led by such educational corporations as Eduventures, whose website announces that it is 'the leading information services company for the education market, provides research and analysis that enables organizations to develop strategy, increase sales, and improve operational performance. Our offerings include targeted research programs, advisory services, and conferences. As a worldwide authority on the education market, we serve a blue-chip client base of executives and senior managers at hundreds of leading educational organizations and technology companies,' and 'Eduventures helps organizations serving education make sound investments in strategy, marketing, and product development. Our consulting draws on research and best practices developed through our Learning Collaborative programs to provide fact-based assessments and recommendations. We track and report on trends as they emerge and leverage that knowledge to bring unique, actionable insights to clients.'[138] Schooling is construed as a business like any other, one worth $2 trillion annually, 5 per cent of global GDP.[139] The world education market has profound implications for Canadian schooling, to which I will now turn.

Canadian Case: Cultural Invasion?

Those same trends so prevalent in the United States are also increasingly apparent in Canada, as the porous border between the two countries allows for a tremendous influence of American commercial forces on the Canadian educational system.

The Canadian Teachers Federation and the Canadian Centre for Policy Alternatives (CCPA) recently focused on the commercialization of Canadian schools at their annual meeting, and a detailed recent national survey exploring key empirical indicators of school commercialism affirms that the same trends are at work in Canada. The aim of the report was to 'examine the nature and extent of commercial activity in Canadian schools, and to determine the degree to which public funding is being replaced by alternative funding sources.'[140] This report shows that there is considerable opposition to this trend in Canada, that 70 per cent of Canadians agreed that advertising has 'no place in schools.'[141] However, Quebec has been a national leader in the regulation of school commercialism and has developed a Consumer Protection Act that limits advertising to children, and *Guidelines for Schools on Advertising and Financial Contributions*. The CCPA notes, 'While our survey results clearly indicate that Quebec schools are not commercial-free, it appears this may be the only province where an attempt has been made to limit the effects and influence of advertising on the most vulnerable segment of its population – children.'[142]

Canadian educational commentator Heather-Jane Robertson explores the implications of the influence of consumerism on Canadian schooling in her book *No More Teachers, No More Books: The Commercialization of Canada's Schools.* In most cases it is either specific American corporations or American neo-liberal educational values that are affecting Canada; for American marketers, 'the road [to schools] doesn't detour when it hits our border.'[143]

This is not to suggest that schools in Canada would otherwise be untouched by school commercialism, or that Canada would otherwise be an uncommercialized island in a global sea of consumerism. It is possible that even if no foreign corporations or commercial trends in education were allowed into the country, Canadian schools would succumb to commercial forces nevertheless. Instead, school commercialism in Canada reveals that the commercialization of education takes place within a global context governed by internationally negotiated free trade agreements and a highly competitive environment in which corporations seek to outdo and take over smaller corporations. The 'world education market' displays the neo-liberal imperative to permit the free movement of capital, even at the expense of national sovereignty and democratic processes in the formation of school policy. Regardless whether what's good for General Motors is good for America, it is rarely good for Canada.

Consumerism can be linked to Freire's account of cultural invasion, through which 'the invaders penetrate the cultural context of another group.'[144] Inroads made by advertisers into the educational environment constitute a form of cultural invasion by commercial interests when the cultural context of the school environment is 'penetrated' by the symbols and values of consumerism in such a way that schools become the location of ever-greater domination. 'In their passion to dominate, to mold others to their patterns and their way of life, the invaders desire to know how those they have invaded apprehend reality – but only so they can dominate them more effectively.'[145] Market research of schools and students is done by advertisers only so they can better sell a product.

Consequences of School Commercialism: Erosion of the Public

Schools become colonized and colonizing spaces where a foreign power gains extraordinary access over our young, evidenced by their remarkable familiarity with the latest developments in Hollywood rather than in Canada. Yet some educational administrators not only see nothing wrong with school commercialism, they argue that we should complacently accept consumerism as inevitable.

Some argue that since consumerism is so prevalent in society it should also be equally present in schools. For example, Wade Marshall, chairman of the Halifax Regional School Board, claims that 'Canadians have sort of embraced that everything we do has an aspect of advertising to it.'[146] The CCPA observes, 'The issue of a growing commercial presence in the classroom is often minimized by the claim that since kids are marketed to on a regular basis, why is it worse to target them in the school?'[147] Nevertheless, many things like guns and drugs are prevalent in society, yet we seek to keep them out of schools. More relevant for my argument, schools have an essential public function as sites for democratic renewal. This sentiment is echoed by Canadian teacher Larry Kuehn: 'The public schools are an integral part of the institutions of democracy. Democracy requires public space, places where debate and discussion inform decision making. And it requires education that prepares people to participate as critical citizens in that public space. If we are to achieve the democratic ideal of equity, there must be a commons, and it must be accessible for all to participate effectively. Public education is an important part of that commons.'[148]

Through the influence of consumerism, student empowerment becomes equated with the strengthening of purchasing power, and the development of self-esteem is reduced to the development of consumer confidence. Yet the prevalence of consumerism and the inroads made into the educational environment not only influence spending habits but alter the entire educational experience. First, the student body itself becomes represented as 'consumable,' sold as a commodity to advertisers. Second, the student is increasingly described as a 'consumer' of educational services, as the discourse of school choice and students-as-clients becomes ever more prevalent. Third, teachers become construed as curriculum delivery machines, as instruments for transmission of data, and also as 'edutainers' in competition with that other Great Educator, television.

In *Teaching after the Market*, Allan Luke laments how teaching has 'increasingly been appropriated both by curriculum and instructional commodities and the extent to which teachers have moved towards consumer-like behavior,' and argues that 'the effect is to turn teaching into a neoclassical form of commodity fetishism.'[149] Knowledge becomes construed as a 'consumable' purchased in a financial transaction in which the classroom becomes a site of commercial exchange and learning itself an act of consumption. Under such circumstances, immeasurable and intangible public aspects of education are easily neglected.

Several contemporary theorists suggest that there is a profound tension between the commercial objectives and the political functions of education. Political philosopher Michael Sandel writes, 'The commercialization of the classroom highlights the tension between unbounded markets and civic ideals. The purpose of public education is not to provide basic training for a consumer society, but to cultivate citizens capable of thinking critically about the consumer society they inhabit. Infusing the classroom with consumerism is at odds with this civic purpose.'[150] Alex Molnar concurs, arguing that the pedagogy of advertising reduces freedom to the 'execution of impulses' rather than the 'freedom of the intellect' (SC, 82) and promotes 'pseudo-communities based on consumerism or the uncritical acceptance of a particular policy or point of view' (SC, 83). Henry Giroux emphasizes the distinction between the commercial and civic aims of education: 'Schools are being transformed into commercial rather than public spheres as students become subject to the whims and practices of marketers whose agenda has nothing to do with critical learning and a great deal to do with restructuring civic life in the image of market culture. Civic courage – upholding the most basic non-commercial principles of democracy – as a defining principle of society is devalued as corporate power transforms school knowledge.'[151]

Considering that the young will determine the character of our future, the commercialization of school space and curricula has significant long-term social implications. Henry Giroux states that 'when public education becomes a venue for making a profit, delivering a product, or constructing consuming subjects, education reneges on its responsibilities for creating a democracy of citizens by shifting its focus to producing a democracy of consumers.'[152] He later adds that corporations 'substitute corporate propaganda for real learning, upset the requisite balance between the public and the private, and in doing so treat schools like any other business.'[153] This reinforces students' roles as consumers, spectators, and passive citizens.

As school commercialism becomes more widespread and integrated into school practices, it also becomes increasingly difficult to reverse; opening school doors to marketers now will invariably result in compromises down the road. As relations with private sources of funding become normalized and incorporated into school planning, schools become dependent on business for funding essential school activities, giving further legitimacy to government cuts. One journalist asks if 'each time private money fills the gaps left by public financing, does it enable legislators and taxpayers to shrug off responsibility for supporting education?'[154] The CCPA report noted, 'In fall 2004 the Ontario government implemented an accounting change requiring school boards to include school fundraising in their general revenue, along with governmental grants. This move raised significant concerns that private money was being entrenched in the public system, making it easier for the government to argue that public funding for education could be reduced where it appeared private funding was available.'[155]

Allowing high-profile school activities to be funded by corporations will make it even more difficult to critically examine them. For example, if Nike is sponsoring a school athletic team, there will be tremendous opposition to the loss of income if the contract is questioned.

It is for these and other reasons that there is growing opposition to these trends. In their campaign to address school commercialism, Commercial Alert discouraged companies from engaging in school–business partnerships, noting, 'According to a 2004 Harris poll of youth advertising and marketing professionals, only 45% "feel that today's young people can handle advertising in schools." Not surprisingly, 47% believe that "schools should be a protected area" and that "there should not be advertising to students on school grounds."'[156] Gary Marx, associate executive director of the American Association of School Administrators, argues that 'the classroom should be a marketplace of ideas, not products.'[157] Yet it is noteworthy that while his opposition to the commercialization of the classroom is important, he succumbs to the use of commercial language even in this critique when he construes the classroom as a 'marketplace.'

It is worth noting that recent limits on corporate influence have often come through interventions from parent groups, religious organizations, or the medical profession. Witness the recent regulation of candy and soft drink vendors in several jurisdictions,[158] and many interventions by the religious right to prevent pharmaceutical companies that produce contraceptives and publishers of textbooks with controversial content such as homosexuality from establishing school–business partnerships.[159] Stephen Petrina describes recent developments in British Columbia: 'Complaints were made about a multimedia history textbook because of its pro-labour bias and its realistic depictions of "male-to-male intimacy" in the American west and "illegal" abortion. Similarly, the Surrey School District in British Columbia, the lower mainland's largest district, banned children's books with pro-gay and lesbian content.'[160] The religious right is not unified against the commercialization of education as such but does engage the issue when Christian values are directly and adversely affected.

Some educational theorists are critical of teachers' inadequate response to these trends. Allan Luke laments 'the ways in which teaching has increasingly been appropriated both by curriculum and instructional commodities and the extent to which teachers have moved towards consumer-like behaviour.'[161] Alex Molnar suggests that, 'with notable exceptions, educators' reactions range from tacit acceptance to outright embrace of [advertisers'] actions' (SC, 121). Perhaps this is because teachers are all too often either explicitly prohibited from addressing school commercialism, or simply overwhelmed by the task of meeting the demands of daily teaching. In the final chapter I provide a more detailed investigation of how school commercialism can be addressed at the policy level in a limited and preliminary sense, and in the classroom in a more substantial and effective manner.

For philosopher of education Kerry Burch, 'most schools are not producing critically reflective democratic citizens; they are far more engaged in the *mass production of idiocy*. I use this phrase with precision: the ancient Greek etymology of *idios* refers to a "purely private person," one who could participate in the *polis* as a citizen, but did not.'[162] This distinction between an *idios* and the participant in the *polis* also parallels the distinction between *idios* and *puberty*, emphasized by educational theorist Walter Parker: 'When aimed at democratic ends and supported by democratic means, schools can help children enter the public consciousness needed for citizenship, or what the ancient Greeks called *puberty*. This includes the habits of reasoning and caring necessary for public life: the cosmopolitan respect, the insistence on fair play, and the knack for forging public policy with others whether one likes them or not. The opposite is what the Greeks called *idiocy* – absorption in one's private affairs. Public schools are good places to help young people grow from idiocy to puberty.'[163]

This discussion of *idios* and the private realm presages the discussion of Hannah Arendt in the next chapter, which will demonstrate how education should renew the public realm rather than facilitate its erosion.

Conclusion

We have looked at key ways in which the rise of consumerism affects schooling: the inroads made by commercial forces into public schools and the resulting displacement of pedagogical values with consumer values. It is noteworthy that this is the first generation of students who notice nothing unusual or problematic about the trends described above. For today's students, school commercialism is so normalized that it is like the water in which they swim. However, perhaps it is more accurate to say that they are like lobsters who don't notice the gradually increasing temperature in the water.

My concern is twofold: not only is consumerism compromising the public and democratic function of education, but schools also facilitate the spread of consumerism by 'reproducing' consumer society. If schools are caught up in consumerism, they become institutions that facilitate the emergence of a society increasingly centred upon consumerism. Instead, I would argue that schools are sites where consumerism can be resisted rather than facilitate the emergence of a consumer society.

Because consumerism can be best understood through the lens of the public/private distinction and the semiotic character of commodities, we will consider it in relation to Arendt's account of the public followed by Baudrillard's account of signs. Arendt's examination of the public realm and its eclipse allows us to more fully explain the political and pedagogical implications of the rise of consumerism.

3 Hannah Arendt:
Consuming the Polis

We are by nature political animals [*zoon politikon*] ... Whoever lives outside the polis is either a beast or a god.

– Aristotle[1]

Only the loss of a polity itself expels [one] from humanity.

– Hannah Arendt[2]

What is most noteworthy in the work of Hannah Arendt is how she extends the meaning of both politics and the public realm so as to equate them with reality and the world itself. Yet Arendt acknowledges the difficulty of taking seriously the idea of a 'public realm,' observing that 'misunderstanding and equating the political and social realms ... has become even more confusing in modern usage and modern understanding of society,' and speaks of 'the extraordinary difficulty with which we ... understand the decisive division between the public and private realms' (HC, 28). This sentiment is echoed by American philosopher of education Maxine Greene, who laments that increasingly 'there is a general withdrawal from what ought to be public concerns,' and that 'Americans generally do not perceive the "darkness" Arendt described, nor do they perceive the significance of a public space that might throw light.'[3] Greene shares much with Arendt's account of publicity. She emphatically asserts that freedom grounded in a common world is not simply the power to choose but rather the power to act and the opening of spaces of possibilities. Greene is deeply critical of freedom – understood as merely unrestrained entitlement – as 'a lassitude, a disinterest, an absence of care,' and laments the 'rootless subjectivities' that result when 'there is a general withdrawal from what ought to be public concerns.'[4] Instead we are 'all too likely to remain immersed in the taken-for-granted and the everyday. For many, this means unreflective consumerism; for others, it means a preoccupation with *having* more than *being* more.'[5] For both Arendt and Greene, publicity is not pre-existent but rather a collective endeavour and ongoing achievement that is compromised by consumerism.

There are several reasons why it is increasingly difficult to talk about or take seriously the idea of a 'public realm.' First, the public realm seems to be a highly intangible and ethereal concept, because it does not necessarily refer to a specific physical place. Consumerism seems to affect other more tangible and physical things in a more immediate and dramatic way: the health costs of consumption are tangible and obvious (diabetes, obesity, and diseases), as are the environmental costs (pollution and global warming). In contrast, Arendt emphasizes the changes to society and culture that increasingly structure our experience of the world, ourselves, and each other. Arendt shows that a fundamental propensity of the human being is to long for a place in the world and to seek to create one through political action. The public is not an abstract category but a very fundamental component of human life. She shows that consumerism offers only a false promise of a place in the world, delivering alienation and what Aristotle calls the 'loss of a polity,' leaving us 'either a beast or a god' (1253a1-29). However, this concern about 'beast or god' is not intended to evoke a high/low culture distinction. Arendt does not suggest we aspire to become 'godly' by transcending the public, or that those unable to transcend the public are mere beasts, but that we are fully human and realize our fullest humanity only through public life. Simply because the public seems intangible doesn't mean we don't suffer from the effects of its demise.

A second challenge to taking the public realm seriously is that we no longer experience the public because it is already so thoroughly undermined by consumption. It is increasingly difficult to know or conceive of what is not already affected by consumerism, because we live in a world already so deeply shaped by it.

Third, there is often a tendency to think that the public is simply any gathering of people; a TV show audience and a shopping mall would create a public simply because they gather people together. However, Arendt shows that these gatherings are commodified and transformed into a market such that the public realm becomes vacuous. Benjamin Barber notes that 'more than anything else, what has been lost in the clash of Jihad and McWorld has been the idea of the *public* as something more than a random collection of consumers or an aggregation of special interests or a product of identity politics' (JM, 286).

Last, it is very easy to complacently accept consumerism, because the images it presents are so persuasive and seductive and they encourage comfortable and complacent acceptance of the status quo. The consumer would seem to be increasingly independent and self-sufficient, and we are able to live considerably more comfortable lives in the private realm than ever before. As a result, consumerism conceals its destructive character and problematic implications, and makes the public realm or political change seem unimportant and unnecessary. Joe Heath and Andrew Potter confirm this dynamic by asking, 'If we all hate consumerism, how come we can't stop shopping?' and argue that people are 'getting what they want when they act in a consumerist fashion.'[6]

In fact, public space itself is often used to advance consumerism when viewed by marketers as a resource to be exploited. Not only is the public lost, but it is replaced with things that advance consumerism: monstrous billboards hanging down apartment buildings, political leaders like Bush calling upon people to shop, and the widespread use of the media to advance consumerism. It is easy to continue to assume that the public realm exists as long as there are 'public' places – even as consumer messages spread to park benches, postal boxes, public washrooms, and library cards.

A concrete and tangible example of how public space is used by marketers to promote consumerism may help demonstrate this trend. Recently in the city of Toronto several buildings on a downtown corner were demolished to make way for a new public square. According to the municipal government, the function of this square is to 'promote economic development activities.' The surrounding buildings display dozens of billboards and huge TV screens, and the job description for the recently advertised new position of manager for Dundas Square reveals how public space is now conceived: 'The successful applicant will be an innovative, dynamic entrepreneur with demonstrated ability to successfully lead a business unit of similar scope ... and will support the preparation of business plans and develop and implement both marketing plans to attract commercial events and activities, and new ideas and initiatives for revenue generation.'[7] As this description makes apparent, the public square is construed as an opportunity for revenue generation and the promotion of consumerism, best managed by marketers and operated according to the same principles of profit and return on investment as a private corporation. Dave Meslin of the Toronto Public Space Committee asks, 'Instead of the Yonge-Dundas Square why don't they just name it the Yonge-Dundas Business Unit?'[8]

While the practice of producing, promoting, and profiting from the public realm becomes increasingly lucrative, Arendt's account of the public reveals this conception of a public square as anemic. All sides of the public square are lined with screens and advertising; people are entirely surrounded by symbols of consumerism. This dearth of a meaningful public realm gives power to those who can fill such a void by *seeming* to speak of something larger and more substantial than private consumption. Arendt argues that although we live in a time that privileges the private and neglects the public, we as human beings remain inherently political. These examples indicate that we are unaccustomed to meaningful engagement in the political realm and are left vulnerable to corrupt evocations of the public.

Some scholars argue that modern changes to the relationship between public and private are not new and have previously brought about significant political decline. Richard Sennett argues that the decline of the Roman Empire was closely tied to a widespread retreat from the *res publica* as public involvement was increasingly construed as an obligation or duty. One increasingly 'sought in private a new focus for emotional energies, a new principle of commitment and belief. This private commitment was concerned with escaping the world at large and the formalities of the *res publica* as part of that world.'[9] Sennett also points to the etymologic of public: while the Latin *publis* refers to public, *res publica* implies 'matters of the public' from which we derive 'republic.' Considering the fate of the Roman Empire read in light of the examples above, Sennett's analysis raises concerns about contemporary trends concerning the private and public spheres.

As consumerism becomes more prevalent, questions about the public realm and its relation to education grow at once both more imperative and increasingly complex. Considering that schooling is a project undertaken for the preservation and renewal of a public realm, it is imperative that such questions be addressed. Democracy, as more than a set of institutions and procedures, rests on a public that is actively engaged beyond private concerns, on the human capacity to alter the political world we experience as a central part of our lives. A genuinely democratic society is composed of citizens who are not merely preoccupied with the private realm, but active public participants. Motivated by public commitments, the citizen transcends self-preoccupation and engages with the public. Arendt critiques the elevation of the private individual construed as the locus of rational self-interest used to determine the most effective means towards its realization. This liberal discourse obscures the possibility that politics and pedagogy might be concerned with more than self-interest, that humans might be driven to be a part of something larger than private subjectivity and seek to participate in what lies beyond the self, that we are political animals interested in not merely living privately but also public life. Yet because consumerism has become so pervasive, we remain limited in our ability to discern the forces that erode the possibility of establishing such a relationship with public life.

Arendt remains relevant today because of the centrality of the public realm to human life, and because she makes apparent what is otherwise taken for granted and unnoticed. Perhaps the public becomes most apparent when at risk; we become aware of the profound importance of the public only as it disappears, even as its disappearance obscures our awareness of it.

Introduction: Life and Influence

Biographical background on Arendt will help situate her historically and describe the development of her political ideas. Life experiences affect intellectual development, ground thought in the personal character of philosophical reflection, and convey the drama of ideas as they unfold through a lifetime. This is particularly true of Arendt, as her approach is both theoretical and experiential. Such biographical considerations can help ensure the relevance of philosophy to the wider political world by demonstrating the interconnection between philosophy and politics, and how lives and thought are in turn influenced by that same world.

Hannah Arendt is widely considered to be among the most original and provocative philosophers since the Second World War – yet ironically she never viewed herself as a philosopher in the traditional sense: 'I neither feel like a philosopher, not do I believe that I have been accepted in the circle of philosophers.'[10] Arendt was foremost a theorist of the public sphere who drew from the history of Western philosophy in order to cast light on our age, an era she termed 'dark times.'[11] Her work continually returns to political themes, and her lifetime spanned some of the most important events and disturbing convulsions of the twentieth century. Yet she had the good fortune to study with some of the most influential philosophers of the early twentieth century: Martin Heidegger, Edmund Husserl, and Karl Jaspers. Born in 1906, Arendt studied philosophy and theology at the University of Marburg and completed her doctorate at the University of Freiberg at the age of twenty-three. Her most influential teacher, Martin Heidegger, had begun writing his magnum opus, *Being and Time*, shortly before they met.

As the Nazis rose to power, Arendt fled to Paris, where she remained for a decade during and after the Second World War. Following the war and a brief period of internment at a concentration camp, she settled in New York City, where she spent much of the remainder of her life. Arendt remained bound by no academic institution and held visiting fellowships and professorial positions at a variety of American universities. In 1975 she died with the first page of the final volume of *The Life of the Mind* in her typewriter, yet by then her work was already becoming noted, and today she is remembered as one of the most illuminating and provocative intellectuals of our time.

Arendt is a challenging thinker to approach: she produced no systematic or summative work of philosophy. Her work instead ranges widely from theological issues in her doctoral thesis on St Augustine, to her study of the 'banality of evil' as embodied in Adolf Eichmann, to her work on Kant's political philosophy. Most important for the present topic of consumerism, her work also includes an account of the decline of the public realm and political action in one of the most influential works of twentieth-century thought, *The Human Condition*.

Arendt is a theorist of ruptures, reversals, and distinctions: ruptures within the history of the West, reversals of human activities and their location, and the distinctions necessary for their conceptual illumination. Nowhere is this more apparent than in *The Human Condition*, where she outlines the three central human activities of labour, work, and action, which are each in turn grounded in corresponding given 'conditions' of human existence: life, worldliness, and plurality. This account of ruptures in the history of Western philosophy illuminates the retreat of human freedom and potentialities through the reduction of action and plurality to the private activities of consumption. Her aim was not to protect the private sphere of free, rights-bearing, rational autonomous agents who engage in politics only so as to preserve their privacy. This tendency is prevalent among many liberal readers of Arendt seeking to align her with such thinkers as the contemporary American political philosopher John Rawls and his procedural liberalism and emphasis on juridical and administrative concerns, or to locate her within the neo-Kantian tradition emphasizing autonomous subjectivity.[12] Rather, her aim is to critique the modern reversal of the relative importance of activities that correspond to the private realm and those of the public. This is not to say that she either abandoned the private subject or the importance of individual liberty, or engaged in an unreflective celebration of community, but rather feared such contemporary trends as the emergence of consumerism.

Arendt wrote only briefly on education, in her essay 'The Crisis in Education,' where she asserts that 'education is the point at which we decide whether we love the world enough to assume responsibility for it and by the same token save it from that ruin which, except for renewal, except for the coming of the new and young, would be inevitable.'[13] Her critique of modernity and account of political action and the public realm is profoundly relevant for educators and educational theorists who seek to locate their activity within the context of the eclipse of public life by consumerism. Arendt's work points towards how we can fall short in our responsibility for renewing the world, and how education can become complicit in the erosion of a vibrant and robust public realm.

Hellenic Nostalgia?

Because Arendt drew widely from the history of Western thought in order to cast light on our own age, her work is a powerful reminder of our own place in history and the significant political transformations we witness. However, her occasional use of Greek terms and favourable description of the Athenian polis has led some contemporary scholars to accuse her of nostalgia for pre-modern political thought and practice. Because her account of threats to the public realm rests on her exploration of the emergence of dangerous developments in modernity, some critics have suggested that her method was to resurrect lost texts and forgotten political experiments. For example, Noel O'Sullivan states, 'It need hardly be said that admiration for the ancient world has waned somewhat since the days of Machiavelli and Renaissance political thought. What principally distinguishes Arendt from other contemporary political philosophers is the fact that her enthusiasm for that world goes considerably beyond even Machiavelli's.'[14]

In the introduction to *The Human Condition*, Margaret Canovan acknowledges that because 'the book is laced with criticism of modern society, it is tempting to suppose that she intended to present a utopia of political action, a kind of New Athens.'[15] However, Canovan goes on to argue that Arendt's account of the public and private realms is not 'an exercise in nostalgia for the Greek *polis*.'[16] Arendt would agree, as her work is tempered with wariness towards the city that put Socrates, that rare exemplar of action, to death. In her own words, 'All efforts to escape from the grimness of the present into nostalgia for a still intact past, or into the anticipated oblivion of a better future, are vain.'[17]

There are several more reasons her work is not simply nostalgic. Arendt is much more concerned with newness and natality than with nostalgia; in her work she repeatedly celebrates the human capacity to bring new and unprecedented things into the world. Second, she suggests that solutions to political crises are available to us at any time and place, including modernity, through the fundamental capabilities that characterize the human condition. She asserts that 'action and speech create a space between the participants which can find its proper location almost any time and anywhere' (HC, 198). In *On Revolution*, she describes several exemplary political developments within the twentieth century that confirm this point, including the American Revolution, the Paris Commune, and the Hungarian uprising of 1956. That Arendt speaks so highly of these modern political phenomena suggests that she is not being merely 'nostalgic' for an irretrievably lost golden age. Kimberly Curtis summarizes this defence of Arendt: 'If, however, we pay attention to the structure of Arendt's argument, it looks less romantic in tone and orientation.'[18] Benjamin Barber notes that 'when Hannah Arendt defined politics as the active life (*vita activa*) in her book *The Human Condition*, what was curious was not the definition itself but the degree to which her colleagues received it as a radical antiquarian critique of modern liberal democracy, as if action had nothing to do with politics.'[19]

Activities and Conditions

As mentioned earlier, Arendt's theoretical method consists of exposing ruptures, reversals, and distinctions: ruptures within the history of the West, reversals of publicity and privacy, and of the categorical distinctions between human activities necessary for their conceptual illumination. Nowhere is this more apparent than in *The Human Condition*. This account of ruptures in the history of Western philosophy points towards the retreat of the public realm and the human potential for political action through the reduction of difference and plurality into the sameness and conformity of 'the social.' Perhaps what is most notable and unique about her approach to political thought is the firmness with which she insists on certain categorical distinctions, and her intention to clarify these distinctions and restore a sense of conceptual clarification. Arendt is concerned that the growing incapacity to make distinctions results in 'a generalization in which the words themselves lose all meaning ... this kind of confusion – where everything distinct disappears and everything that is new and shocking is (not explained but) explained away either through drawing some analogies or reducing it to a previously known chain of causes and influences – seems ... to be the hallmark of the modern historical and political sciences.'[20]

The basis for Arendt's distinctions frequently lies in her appeal to the ancient meanings of certain terms that she evokes in order to reawaken us to the dangers inherent in the erosion of the capacity for language to convey meaning. This is not to imply a true, pure, or unchanging meaning of such terms but rather to indicate a way of understanding that strikes our ears as strange; that words might also mean something quite different from their common and contemporary usage. In her search for etymological explanations, she presents distinctions that she argues are fundamental to understanding the challenges consumerism presents to a healthy and active political life.

For example, she begins her chapter on labour in *The Human Condition* by insisting that although the distinction between the terms *labour* and *work* might appear unusual in modern English, there is striking 'phenomenal evidence in its favor ... that every European language, ancient and modern, contains two etymologically unrelated words for what we have come to think of as the same activity, and retains them in the face of their persistent synonymous usage.'[21] In the preface to *Between Past and Future*, Arendt states that her concern is 'to discover the real origins of traditional concepts in order to distill from them anew their original spirit which has so sadly evaporated from the very key words of political language ... leaving behind empty shells with which to settle almost all accounts, regardless of their underlying phenomenal reality.'[22] Her work chronicles the blurring and loss of distinctions, resulting in a fundamental political problem: the 'extraordinary difficulty with which we ... understand the decisive division between the public and private realms' (HC, 28). She argues that only when these distinctions are acknowledged and affirmed can political life be protected from the erosion of our sense of reality.

At the apex of Arendt's hierarchy of distinctions are the two central 'ways of life,' the *vita activa* (the life of action) and the *vita contemplativa* (the life of contemplation). The *vita activa* refers to 'a life devoted to public-political matters' (HC, 28) and involves the activities of labour, work, and action. In contrast, the *vita contemplativa* refers to Plato and the 'life of the philosopher devoted to inquiry into, and contemplation of, things eternal' (HC, 13). Contemplation is the 'conscious cessation of activities,' a state of stillness or 'passive speechlessness' that is 'untranslatable into words' (HC, 302). Philosophic *apolitia* expresses disdain towards the 'unquiet' polis life because contemplation demands 'freedom and surcease from political activity' (HC, 14) rather than political engagement. Perhaps one of the reasons she hesitated to consider herself a philosopher was because she felt that philosophers had historically depreciated political life, even rendering political life subservient to the *bios theoretikos* of the philosopher. This is consistent with the distinction she develops between the life of political action, the *vita activa*, and the life of contemplation looking beyond the world, or *vita contemplativa*. Jacques Taminaux describes Arendt's critique: 'The mode of appearing of the objects in *theoria* is infinitely superior, so the philosophers claimed, to the mode of appearing of human affairs.'[23] Arendt asserts that the entire project of Plato's political philosophy 'is not only directed by the superior insight of the philosopher but has no aim other than to make possible the philosopher's way of life' (HC, 402) and that his philosophy influenced 'the later Christian claim to be free from entanglement in worldly affairs' (HC, 14). It was her aim to dismantle the elevation of Being over Appearing, so long dominating Western metaphysics, by emphasizing the importance of political appearance in the public realm.

It is primarily with respect to this distinction that Arendt can be contrasted with her former teacher Martin Heidegger. For Arendt, Heidegger was largely hostile towards public life, and her elevation of the public can be seen as a response against his emphasis on authenticity and resoluteness towards death. Heidegger's *bios theoretikos* was construed as a largely private or apolitical endeavour pursued in solitude and silence in which the public is characterized by the rule of the They (*das Man*). 'Thus we find the old hostility of the philosopher toward the *polis* in Heidegger's analysis of average everyday life in terms of *das Man* in which the public realm has the function of hiding reality.'[24] It is for this reason that Kimberly Curtis argues that Heidegger was a 'worldless thinker,' that while Heidegger's phenomenology was apolitical or even anti-political, Arendt sought to develop a phenomenology of the public realm as a 'space of appearance.'[25]

In contrast to the *bios theoretikos* and *vita contemplativa*, the *vita activa* is based on three human conditions: the life process, worldliness, and plurality. Three activities correspond to each of these conditions: labour, work, and action. What is perhaps unique and most illuminating about Arendt's account of the public/private distinction is that she connects the notion of 'realm' or 'sphere' to these three conditions and to their corresponding activities by locating conditions and activities in a particular 'place.'[26] This approach stands in stark contrast to that advanced in the Rutledge overview of the public realm in *On the Public*, which claims that 'there is no characteristic activity or set of activities that sets you off as an instance of the public.'[27]

These conditions and activities constitute the central theme of *The Human Condition* and provide the conceptual structure Arendt uses to explain the rise of our consumers' society. These conditions refer to how we experience ourselves and others, and relate to the world around us. She terms these the 'basic conditions under which life on earth has been given.'[28]

These conditions and activities provide a theoretical framework to explain how the public realm has been eroded by the private forces of production and consumption, and the threat that consumerism presents the *vita activa*. For Arendt, activities like labour and work are important human undertakings, but she insists that profound problems follow if they come to hold a dominant position in politics. Arendt's public/private distinction applies to her interpretation of key historical thinkers and her analysis of contemporary society. Her distinctions among these three activities are not based on a priori structures nor universal and transcendent categories but distinctive self-understandings and ways of being in the world.

Labour

Labour, the first of the three activities, is grounded in 'the human condition of life,' the biological life process to which we are bound by virtue of being human, compelled to submit to and preoccupy ourselves with self-preservation and species-preservation. Labour is the private activity that provides for the biological continuation of life, in which the human body 'concentrates on nothing but its own being alive' (HC, 115). Labour as 'the source of all property' is the endless taking from nature and returning to it through consumption. Because none of the products of human labour are lasting or durable, labour is described as 'futile.' It is the activity in which we are irrevocably bound to the unending cycle of production and consumption, the 'two stages through which the ever-recurrent cycle of biological life must pass' (HC, 131). This cyclical character of labour makes private life uniform and the private realm, or *oikos*, a location of conformity and sameness.

There are several 'labour theorists' whose writings have contributed to advancing the importance of this activity. Arendt identifies John Locke, Adam Smith, and Karl Marx as theorists who considered acquisition, property, exchange, and labour to be located among the highest human activities. Despite political differences, the common element of these thinkers is their unprecedented elevation of the labour activity itself, now 'considered to be the supreme world-building capacity of man' (HC, 101). Arendt continues, 'The sudden, spectacular rise of labor from the lowest, most despised position to the highest rank, as the most esteemed of all human activities, began when Locke discovered that labor is the source of all property. It followed its course when Adam Smith asserted that labor was the source of all wealth and found its climax in Marx's "system of labor," where labor became the source of all productivity and the expression of the very humanity of man' (HC, 101). Kimberly Curtis notes that these theorists considered labour our 'highest purpose': 'The dynamic devouring social life process becomes, for all three, the highest purpose of collective life.'[29]

Privacy here implies 'privative,' to be deprived of something essential. Although Arendt describes this realm as 'privative,' we have misunderstood her if we accuse her of simply condemning labour or the private realm; labour is considered an essential human activity, and the *oikos* respected as a place where we can feel 'sheltered against the world,' a place where consumption 'should be hidden' (HC, 59, 72). The importance of privacy can be determined only to the extent that it contributes to those activities within the *vita activa* that it must serve if human existence is to be considered worldly and free. Yet as long as we are bound within this process and restricted to our own privacy, our efforts are futile and we remain isolated within ourselves, unable to engage in the realm of human affairs and effectively disclose ourselves and our experiences through speech. *Animal laborans*, as labour personified, is bound to necessity and therefore does not appear to others, unable to communicate experience and subjectivity: 'It is as though he did not exist' (HC, 58). We are pulled into the cyclical process of consumption and exist in a 'mere togetherness' within the private realm where we are neither seen nor heard in our full humanness.

Action

Continuing with Arendt's account of the rise of consumerism, labour is contrasted with action both in its location in the world and its importance within the *vita activa*. Action is the highest activity in which humans can engage. It expresses our highest potentialities and possibilities through which we are known by others, disclose our uniqueness, and participate in something larger than ourselves. A life without action 'is literally dead to the world; it has ceased to be a human life because it is no longer lived among men' [*sic*] (HC, 76). Whereas labour was grounded in the 'human condition of life,' action is grounded in the human condition of plurality. It is the articulation of difference, of *alteritas*, where we distinguish ourselves from others. She contends that both the meaning of the action and the identity of the actor can be established only in the context of human plurality, in the presence of others who are able to understand and recognize the uniqueness of our acts. Because action is the 'only activity that goes on directly between [us] without the intermediary of things or matter' (HC, 7), by acting we experience ourselves and each other without mediating these relations with objects or commodities.

It is through action that our identity and our uniqueness can be disclosed and made known to others, through which we 'insert ourselves into the human world.'[30] This human world Arendt calls the 'space of appearance,' the public realm, or the polis: 'Before men began to act, a definite space had to be secured and a structure built where all subsequent actions could take place, the space being the public realm of the *polis*' (HC, 195). The polis 'assures the mortal actor that his passing existence and fleeting greatness will never lack the reality that comes from being seen, being heard, and, generally, appearing before an audience of fellow men' (HC, 198). Thus, action is not lost to decay or the maintenance of life, but rather constitutes the process by which we present ourselves and appear to others.

By characterizing action as performance and drama, Arendt underlines its improvisational nature and inherent unpredictability, which ensures its status as an end in itself. Action's unpredictability is identified with the newness and beginning found in the introduction of each unique person into the world. Thus 'action has the closest connection with the human condition of natality,' the miracle of birth in which 'the faculty of action is ontologically rooted' (HC, 279).

For Arendt, although we may be 'political animals,' the public realm does not exist 'by nature.' Only through our own efforts does an always fragile public realm emerge, in need of continual renewal through political action and the movement from private concerns to public engagement. Thus the polis and action are mutually interdependent, because while action is needed to preserve the polis, so too is the polis needed to preserve action; while the polis is the location for action, so too is it the place where action is preserved through speech. The polis is where we not only differentiate ourselves from others but also differentiate between production and consumption as 'activities related to a common world and those related to the maintenance of life' (HC, 28). The polis provides the location for both self-disclosure and its preservation by providing a remedy for the futility of action and speech by preventing it from fading into obscurity. Through self-disclosure Arendt closely links action with speech, stating that 'speechless action would no longer be action' (HC, 178), for, along with 'deeds,' it is through speech that actors both disclose themselves and preserve or 'memorialize' action. Kimberly Curtis comments that 'the political actor needs liberation from nature's compulsion for a life in the world of human affairs in which speech and action are at stake.'[31] Although labour and the *oikos* may include 'speech' of a sort, she insists that 'no other human performance requires speech to the same extent as action' (HC, 179). With action we not only bring new things into the world, but we bring ourselves into the world.

It may seem that Michel Foucault was the first to express concern about a growing influence of the life process in his 1976 account of 'biopolitics' in *The History of Sexuality*.[32] However, as Georgio Agamben observes, Arendt's earlier account of the entrance of the life process into the public arena is the central focus of *The Human Condition*: 'Almost twenty years before *The History of Sexuality*, Hannah Arendt had already analyzed the process that brings *Homo laborans* – and, with it, biological life as such – gradually to occupy the very center of the political scene of modernity. In *The Human Condition*, Arendt attributes the transformation and decadence of the political realm in modern societies to this very primacy of natural life over political action.'[33] Agamben goes on to echo Arendt's emphasis on the importance of language and political life, noting that language helps to move one from private *zoe* to political *bios*:

Politics therefore appears as the truly fundamental structure of Western metaphysics insofar as it occupies the threshold on which the relation between the living being and the *logos* is realized. In the 'politicization' of bare life – the metaphysical task *par excellence* – the humanity of living man is decided. In assuming this task, modernity does nothing other than declare its own faithfulness to the essential structure of the metaphysical tradition. The fundamental categorical pair of Western politics is not that of friend/enemy but that of bare life/political existence, *zoe/bios* ... There is politics because man is the living being who, in language, separates and opposes himself to his own bare life and, at the same time, maintains himself in relation to that bare life in an inclusive exclusion.[34]

Many liberals have incorrectly construed Arendt as a champion of individual rights, disregarding her critique of *Animal laborans* and the private sphere. Liberal wariness towards the public and attempt to strictly delimit the 'domain of the political' led Carl Schmitt to claim that 'there is absolutely no liberal politics, only a liberal critique of politics.'[35] However, Arendt's endeavour was not to describe the public as something intrusive from which the private sphere of free and rights-bearing agents must be protected, but instead to point out the dangers of its erosion. The transition from private life to political life was based on the distinction between mere life (*zoe*) and an 'authentically human way of life' (*bios*) (HC, 36).

The thinker with which Arendt is perhaps most often compared is her contemporary Jurgen Habermas, the well-known German social theorist who has also written about the public sphere. Some theorists suggest that he was the first to develop the concept of 'the public,' even though *The Human Condition* was written years earlier.[36] In *The Structural Transformation of the Public Sphere: An Inquiry into a Category of Bourgeois Society*, Habermas links the public sphere to the formation of public opinion through the 'public use of reason' in rational discourse and debate 'oriented toward the achievement of public consensus.'[37] Like many communitarians, Habermas appreciates Arendt's elevation of the public sphere as a locus of commitment, communication, and publicity. In his essay on her work, he portrays her account of political action as a consensus-driven undertaking of 'unimpaired intersubjective dialogue' tied to reasoned deliberation and 'nondistorted communication' by rational agents.[38]

Perhaps what is most problematic in his analysis is that he suggests that the public realm emerged alongside capitalism and the Enlightenment, that it 'arose for the first time only in the eighteenth century.'[39] This notion is echoed in *On the Public*, which claims that 'the ideal of a public sphere, a sphere of open and free discussion, arose in the eighteenth century.'[40] In contrast, Arendt argues that the Enlightenment was the very same era in which the public was in fact most profoundly threatened; Habermas's account of the emergence of the public in fact parallels the rise of consumerism. Habermas even goes so far as to include 'consumers' within the public: 'In seventeenth-century France *le public* meant the lectures, *spectateurs*, and *auditeurs* as the addresses and consumers, and the critics of art and literature.'[41]

It has often been said that Arendt developed a political phenomenology or phenomenology of politics insofar as she brought Heidegger's ontological categories of Being and revealing (*aletheia*) to bear on political questions. Politics for Arendt is the activity by which we publicly present ourselves before others to be seen and known and heard. The move from the 'darkness' of the private to the light of public appearance is not equivalent to the emergence from the Platonic cave of *doxa* and ignorance into the full light of the Good, as outlined in Book 7 of *The Republic*. Arendt's account is not the journey of the philosopher, but of the political actor for whom the public constitutes a realm for self-disclosure and appearance before others. She insists that 'without the space of appearance … neither the reality of one's self nor the reality of the surrounding world can be established' (HC, 208). We only *are* when we *appear*, and that appearance is contingent on a public. However, our entry into the human world 'is not forced upon us by necessity, like labor, and it is not prompted by utility, like work' (HC, 177). Appearance is not driven by a rational-purposive concern oriented toward instrumental ends but is the condition under which freedom appears only after such concerns are set aside. This appearance is contingent on difference and plurality, which emerge from contrasting perspectives: 'the reality of the public realm relies on the simultaneous presence of innumerable perspectives and aspects … Being seen and heard by others derive their significance from the fact that everyone sees and hears from a different position. This is the meaning of public life … Only where things can be seen by many in a variety of aspects … can worldly reality truly and reliably appear' (HC, 59).

Aristotelian Influence

The epigraph from Aristotle that opens this chapter is not intended to suggest that his account of politics or political life is to be held up as an exemplar to be idealized and emulated. Rather, it is intended to make his emphasis on the public realm apparent by suggesting that contemporary dangers to political life are not unanticipated, nor are contemporary theories about the public realm historically unprecedented.

Aristotle opens *The Politics* by differentiating between the polis and the *oikos*, arguing that they are not different in degree but different in kind; the polis is not simply a large household functioning according to the same principles but is categorically different. While the *oikos* exists for 'the sake of daily life,' the city 'exists not just for the sake of living but living well' (1252a6). For this reason Aristotle expresses deep gratitude for whoever has first brought about this possibility of 'living well': 'The one who first constituted the city is responsible for the greatest of goods' (1253a30), because to be without a city is to be 'without clan, without law, without hearth' (1253a5). In contrast, Aristotle recognizes the political dangers of unleashing what he called *pleonexia*, disordered and misdirected desire driven by those possessive parts within us that grow inflamed and insatiable and concerned with wanting more of and more than.[42] Maintenance of the *oikos*, 'household management,' requires what he calls 'business expertise' and 'expertise in acquiring possessions' (1253b13, 1253b22) directed towards satisfying *pleonexia*.

Pleonexia has been translated and described as 'disordered and misdirected desire' that is driven by those overreaching and possessive parts within the human soul. These parts are endlessly insatiable and concerned with wanting more of, and more than. He argues that the 'unjust person' and 'unjust acts' are motivated by *pleonexia* because 'we are stirred up against one another by profit and by honor – not in order to acquire them for themselves ... but because they see others aggrandizing themselves' (1320a37–b1). Here, *pleonexia* has been translated as 'aggrandizing' and is said to lead invariably to factions and conflict. As an antidote to *pleonexia*, Aristotle recommends *sophrosyne*, or soundmindedness, the virtue that controls the desires, in combination with *phronesis*, prudence or good sense.

What these statements emphasize, appearing in the early pages of one of the first texts on politics, is the political dangers that any elevation of 'household management' might entail. While Arendt shares this emphasis on the importance of political life, of *zoon politikon*, she saw political community as not existent by nature but arising and continuing through human efforts. Arendt's account of 'the social' makes evident the nature and implications of consumerism.

Consumer Society and the Rise of 'the Social':
From *Vita Activa* to *Vita Accumulativa*

For Arendt, the public and private realms and their corresponding activities are not historically static in their relation to each other; that is, they may change in relative importance throughout history – a trend that has become even more pronounced today: 'Although misunderstanding and equating the political and social realms is as old as the translation of Greek terms into Latin and their adaptation to Roman-Christian thought, it has become even more confusing in modern usage and modern understanding of society' (HC, 28). In fact, 'the social' affects both private and public realms, 'changing almost beyond recognition the meaning of [private and public] and their significance for the life of the individual and the citizen' (HC, 351). Arendt argues that, beginning with the rise of the 'labour theorists' (John Locke through Adam Smith to Karl Marx), action and the *bios politikos* (political life) have been marginalized as the private concerns of the *oikos* (consumption and production) were elevated to a place of political dominance. Arendt defines this reversal of public and private spheres as 'the rise of the social realm,' 'a relatively new phenomenon whose origin coincided with the emergence of the modern age' (HC, 28).

With the loss of action and the public sphere, freedom becomes reduced to routinized 'behaviour,' difference and plurality to conformism and uniformity, and speech and self-disclosure to production and consumption. Instead of 'appearing' through action and speech in the public realm, humans are reduced to mere adjuncts to the cycle of production and consumption, while the polis is required to enable this cycle's smooth functioning and progressive acceleration. The social realm is a community centred on the cyclical process of production and consumption, in which human self-understanding becomes based on 'possessive individualism' and speech subjugated to commercial discourse. It is the end of action and speech.

Between action and labour Arendt situates work, the activity that corresponds with the human capacity to build and maintain those physical things essential for political life. While always a fundamental activity, work became increasingly significant during the Enlightenment and the rise of modern science. Work can be differentiated from labour on at least two levels: its relationship with nature, and the duration of its products.

Whereas *Animal laborans* is 'bound to the recurring cycles of nature,'

Homo faber 'works upon' and values nature for its 'use' and sees it as the 'almost "worthless material" upon which to work' (HC, 98, 155). *Homo faber* reduces nature to a mere means, shaping and transforming it according to human needs and desires, thoroughly 'instrumentalizing' it. While working, we are engaged in the endless process of resisting the persistent threat of being overwhelmed by the cyclical growth and decay of nature, of sustaining existence in the face of nature. It is the process by which we transform nature into the lasting and enduring human artifice that constitutes the location for political life. Quoting John Locke, Arendt argues that 'Nature seen through the eyes of the *Animal laborans* is the great provider of all "good things," which belong equally to all her children, who "take them out of her hands" and "mix with" them in labor and consumption. The same nature seen through the eyes of *Homo faber*, the builder of the world, "furnishes only the almost worthless materials as in themselves," whose whole value lies in the work performed upon them' (HC, 135).

Whereas *Animal laborans* 'leaves nothing lasting' (HC, 87), because its products are immediately consumed, work creates an enduring 'human artifice.' Rather than disappearing through consumption, the human artifice provides a 'home' through the 'stability and solidity' of the world made by human hands. Work corresponds to worldliness, because it is a world-building activity, and *Homo faber* creates the public world both physically and institutionally by constructing such things as buildings and laws. It is within the realm of these durable artifacts that we 'dwell.' Arendt finds this activity exemplified in the physical objects of a table and chair, which indicates that while the products of labour are to be immediately consumed, work differs in duration: tables and chairs last long enough to provide the stability required for political life to emerge. Furthermore, this example points towards the way in which the human artifice draws humans together at the same time that it separates them, allowing for distinctness and plurality to become manifested. This example also demonstrates that Arendt doesn't condemn it outright, but is concerned about the implications when other dimensions of human existence are altered.

Arendt is concerned about the conflation of work and action, and argues that the emphasis on making and fabrication as the central activities of *Homo faber* applies the 'process' character of action to all human undertakings. However, Arendt argues that Being is contingent on political appearance, and that what she calls the concept of Process is to be held within the *oikos*: 'In the place of the concept of Being we now find the concept of Process. And whereas it is in the nature of Being to appear and thus disclose itself, it is in the nature of Process to remain invisible' (HC, 296–7). Once *Homo faber* enters the political realm and transforms politics into 'work,' an expectation that human undertakings be subject to the same standards of predictability and control as work will be created. The result of the victory of *Homo faber* is what Arendt calls 'earthly alienation.' We come to live surrounded by objects and their signs, which for Arendt do not comprise a political world but a world of consumption. As a result, something fundamental to our humanity and political existence is lost.

However, Arendt is quick to point out that *Homo faber*'s rise soon became dominated by *Animal laborans* and the human condition of life, because 'we have changed work into laboring' (HC, 126). 'What needs explanation is not the modern esteem of *Homo faber* but the fact that this esteem was so quickly followed by the elevation of laboring to the highest position in the hierarchical order of the *vita activa*' (HC, 306). It is important to note that the modern decline did not stop with the establishment of the rule of *Homo faber* and the threat of modern science, but continued to the final victory of 'the social,' completing the decline from action, through work, to labour. Whereas work resulted in what Arendt called earthly alienation, the primacy of *Animal laborans* results in worldly alienation – an experience that arises when humans are left without a world in which to dwell. We instead dwell in a world of what we produce and consume. Arendt describes the character of this worldlessness: 'One of the obvious danger signs that we may be on our way to bringing into existence the ideal of the *Animal laborans* is the extent to which our whole economy has become a waste economy, in which things must be almost as quickly devoured and discarded as they have appeared in the world, if the process itself is not to come to a sudden catastrophic end. But if the ideal were already in existence and we were truly nothing but members of a consumers' society, we would no longer live in a world at all but simply be driven by a process in whose ever-recurrent cycles things appear and disappear, manifest themselves and vanish, never to last long enough to surround the life process in their midst' (HC, 234). The danger is that we become surrounded by artificial things and therefore suspicious and even resentful towards what we did not make or cannot reduce to consumption. In becoming surrounded by commodities, we grow hostile to anything that is not a commodity and anything that is not of our making. Arendt speaks of 'modern man's deep rooted-suspicion of everything he did not make himself': because we resent what we did not make, we seek to 'exchange it for something [we have] made' and thereby 'rebel against the world as it has been given' (HC, 3). Something fundamentally important about ourselves is compromised as a result.

Arendt states that 'this earthly home becomes a world in the proper sense of the word only when the totality of fabricated things is so organized that it can resist the consuming life process of the people dwelling in it, and thus outlast them' (HC, 210). Instead, in a consumer society, the products of work are increasingly 'consumed' and drawn into the cyclical movement of production and consumption. They no longer provide a lasting and stable human artifice for political community, because 'a consumers' society cannot possibly know how to take care of a world and the things which belong exclusively to the space of worldly appearances, because its central attitude toward all objects, the attitude of consumption, spells ruin to everything it touches.'[43] Arendt states that, in consumer society, 'the rate of use is so tremendously accelerated that the objective difference between use and consumption, between the relative durability of use objects and the swift coming and going of consumer goods, dwindles to insignificance' (HC, 125). Consumerism is therefore not so much like the tendency to view the world as objects to *use*, but rather to *use up*. Arendt describes the consequences of the unleashed devouring life process of consumerism as follows:

> Painless and effortless consumption would not change but would only increase the devouring character of biological life until a mankind altogether 'liberated' from the shackles of pain and effort would be free to 'consume' the whole world and to reproduce daily all things it wished to consume. How many things would appear and disappear daily and hourly in the life process of such a society would at best be immaterial for the world, if the world and its thing-character could withstand the reckless dynamism of a wholly motorized life process at all. The danger of future automation is less the much deplored mechanization and artificialization of natural life than that, its artificiality notwithstanding, all human productivity would be sucked into an enormously intensified life process and would follow automatically, without pain or effort, its ever-recurrent natural cycle. (HC, 132)

Worldly alienation arises when our physical structures, built to provide the lasting and durable environment for political life, are caught up in the accelerating process of decay and lost to the endless stream of consumption and production. The activities of labour and work are anti-political and destructive of politics and culture, because they result in the 'leveling of all human activities to the common denominator of securing the necessities of life and providing for their abundance' (HC, 126).

While Arendt emphasizes the importance of a public realm, she does not celebrate any or all forms of human community. A group or assembly of people is not necessarily a public but may be simply a collection of private persons, what David Reisman calls *The Lonely Crowd*.[44] Regarding the title of Liz Cohen's book *The Consumers Republic*,[45] Benjamin Barber points out that the term *consumer republic* is in fact a contradiction in terms: 'Champions of the idea that consumers are democratic citizens have tried to have their civic cake and consume it too by talking about consumer sovereignty and a "consumers republic." Yet a republic is defined by its public-ness (*res publica* meaning "things of the public"), and what is public cannot be determined by consulting or aggregating private desires. The consumers' republic is quite simply an oxymoron. Consumers cannot be sovereign, only citizens can' (CN, 126). In Arendtian terms, a 'republic' of consumers is a community of private persons all behaving in a normalized and predetermined fashion without any experience of plurality or sense of their political character. Arid, impersonal, and inhospitable, it is a collection of grasping persons united only by their self-preoccupation, unable to leave behind the self-absorbed self.

Such a community arises from the activity of work: the agora, the exchange market. However, unlike the polis, this community is motivated by 'the desire for products, not people,' where humans express themselves 'not [as] persons but producers of products' (HC, 209). Like tables and chairs, the products of work enable a context for action and speech, not merely exchange. It is noteworthy that the agora is physically held within the polis, not vice versa. However, the fundamental danger in a consumer society is the reversal, when the agora eclipses – even consumes – the polis.

This dynamic is well summarized in a classic sales book that describes the importance of creating 'the buying mood,' worth quoting at length:

The president of a large chain organization recently revealed the methods that he uses in selecting the locations for his stores. His conclusions suggest an important aspect of selling. He said:

The big thing is to be where people pass who are in the buying mood. It does not matter how many people are going along the sidewalk if they are thinking of something other than buying. If they are intent on getting to their work or on getting to lunch or on getting home – if they have some other purpose in mind – then their number means little to us. That is why we like to be near other stores. You might think that we would want to get away from competitors. Nothing of the sort. They bring business. We want to be where there are lots of people and most of them are in the buying mood.

This successful merchant expresses a truth that many salesmen never discover – that the sale is possible only when the customer drops all other interests and activities and passes into that mental state which we call the buying attitude ... The central question is 'How to arouse this mood!!'[46]

This 'buying mood' is highly destructive of political life and transforms the polis into the site of a frenzied exchange. We could add that the central question is not only how to arouse this mood, but how can this mood be made as socially pervasive and permanent as possible such that it eclipses all other concerns. The aim is to gather people together, provoke the 'buying mood,' and then sell this 'public' for profit – even if the public is schoolchildren.

The construction of 'the buying mood' is the primary function of the shopping mall. What was referred to in the last chapter as the 'malling of America' is said by Ashish Kumar Sen to have begun in 1956 with the opening of the first shopping mall in Minneapolis, Minnesota.[47] Sen notes, 'The shopping center space has increased by a factor of 12 in the last 40 years ... By 2000, there were more than 45,000 shopping malls in the United States, with 5.47 billion square feet of gross leasable space.'[48] It is easy to mistakenly believe that malls are an example of public space. Although free to enter, they have highly controlled physical environments, impose restrictions on freedom of speech, prohibit any activities not intended to promote consumerism, and perhaps most important, are owned and operated for profit by private companies.

For Arendt, 'the social' in fact 'excludes the possibility of action' and substitutes the uniqueness of each actor for the predictability and conformity of 'the social': the 'phenomenon of conformism is character-istic of the last stage of this modern development' (HC, 40). In place of action, we find only 'a certain kind of behavior, imposing innumer-able and various rules, all of which tend to "normalize" its members, to make them behave, to exclude spontaneous action or outstanding achievement ... [Behavior is] by no means a harmless scientific ideal; it is the no longer secret political ideal of a society' (HC, 43). 'The social' is an elevation of economic and private concerns pertaining to the preservation and 'maintenance of life,' combined with related characteristics of uniformity, sameness, and behaviour.

In the final pages of *The Human Condition*, Arendt provides a frightening description of this state: 'The last stage of the laboring society, the society of jobholders, demands of its members a sheer automatic functioning, as though individual life had actually been submerged in the over-all life process of the species and the only active decision still required of the individual were to let go, so to speak, to abandon his individuality, the still individually sensed pain and trouble of living, and acquiesce in a dazed, "tranquilized," functional type of behaviour ... [I]t is quite possible that the modern age – which began with such an unprecedented and promising outburst of human activity – may end in the deadliest, most sterile passivity history has ever known' (HC, 322).

We can now see the danger of 'the social': it is endowed with the remarkable capacity to 'grow' and 'devour,' not only regarding activities of the *vita activa* but even their worldly locations: 'Since the rise of the social, since the admission of household and housekeeping activities to the public realm, an irresistible tendency to grow, to devour the older realms of the political and privacy as well as the more recently established sphere of intimacy, has been one of the outstanding characteristics of the new realm' (HC, 45).

Many of the characteristics of 'the social' result from its correspondence to one single human condition: 'life itself.' The life process reflects the very devouring character of life itself. As a consequence, consumerism threatens the highest activity within the *vita activa*, and the highest 'condition under which life on earth has been given' (HC, 7): the human condition of plurality. In place of the human condition of plurality we find only sameness: 'The end of the common world has come when it is seen only under one aspect and is permitted to present itself in only one perspective' (HC, 58). Moreover, 'the monolithic character of every type of society, its conformism which allows for only one interest and one opinion, is ultimately rooted in the one-ness of man-kind' (HC, 46). Because human existence is conditioned existence, consumerism threatens to eradicate the very ground of human existence itself, to eradicate the condition of the highest human activity. Resentment against the human condition and 'rebellion against human existence as it has been given' (HC, 2) reaches its most dramatic proportions.

Contemporary social theorist Zygmunt Bauman agrees with Arendt's concern about public/private conflation, lamenting that 'the passages between private and public have been thrown wide open,' and that one consequence of this conflation and loss of the public is the 'individualization of political problems.'[49] He describes several examples of the problematic implications of allowing privacy into the public realm. The individualizing and privatizing of political problems through 'confessional television' obscure their more pressing political character: 'Around the institution of the chat show, a community is created; it is, however, an oxymoronic community, a community of individuals united only by their self-enclosure and self-containment.'[50] This undermines the possible development of a political language or ability to deal with political problems by reinforcing isolated subjective and private experience. Concurring with Arendt's account of the potentialities of action, he argues that politics is the project of transforming subjective experiences into collective political action, private malaise into public engagement. Instead, as the private becomes explicit, the political becomes obscured, and what is strengthened is a language for expressing private and subjective experience without an equivalent or comparable political language. 'Politics is many things, but it would hardly be any of them were it not the art of translating individual problems into public issues, and common interests into individual rights and duties.'[51] Private issues are permitted into the public realm, yet political problems such as consumerism are left to private 'choice.' The individualizing and privatizing of political problems obscures the extent to which private problems may in fact have political solutions.

What emerged in the place of the public realm is a community centred on consumption, in which human self-understanding becomes based on possession, action reduced to acquisition, and self-disclosure reduced to consumption. Instead of experiencing action in the public realm, humans become reduced to mere adjuncts of the cycle of consumption. 'Through society it is the life process itself which in one form or another has been channeled into the public realm ... society constitutes the public organization of the life process ... the form in which the fact of mutual dependence for the sake of life and nothing else assumes public significance and where the activities connected with sheer survival are permitted to appear in public' (HC, 45–6). Within Arendt's framework there is a hollowness to this transitory character of life as objects rapidly become irrelevant and 'unfashionable,' passing through use into decay. In a consumer society the pursuit of possession means that products no longer provide the lasting and durable physical world within which humans can engage in meaningful politics and self-disclosure, but are themselves consumed. In her essay 'The Crisis in Culture,' Arendt carries this argument further, arguing that mass society 'does not mean that culture spreads to the masses, but that culture is being destroyed in order to yield entertainment,' that the consumer 'wants not culture but entertainment, and the wares offered by the entertainment industry are indeed consumed by society just like any other consumer goods.'[52] It is the forces of commodification and 'functionalization' that erode culture: 'Culture is being threatened when all worldly objects and things, produced by the present or the past, are treated as mere functions for the life process of society, as though they are there only to fulfill some need, and for this functionalization it is almost irrelevant whether the needs in question are of a high or a low order.'[53]

Consumption becomes a self-perpetuating dynamic: just as the rise of consumption erodes the public realm, consumerism is strengthened when we are denied meaningful political life. We are no longer Aristotle's *zoon politikon*, political animals, but live as if merely *zoon*: according to our possessive proclivities. The human being becomes narrowed down to working and consuming as the mall becomes an archetypal institution. Work and labour are mistakenly thought to transcend the imperatives of biological preservation, and political life is replaced by the accumulation of goods rather than political action. As we make and remake the world to suit our needs and reduce all things to human use as objects for human consumption, we come to live surrounded by objects and their signs. For Arendt, this is not a political world but a world of consumption in which we are thrown back upon our own privacy. It is for these reasons that Arendt observes, 'It is frequently said that we live in a consumer society' (HC, 126).

In the most advanced form of a consumer society, even the public sphere itself becomes a commodity, an economic resource to be exploited like another other, demonstrated in the opening example of the 'Yonge-Dundas Business Unit.' Ironically, even as the public becomes increasingly hard to define or experience, it is evoked for purposes that are destructive of the public; publics are created only so that they can be sold.

As will be elaborated in the next chapter on Baudrillard, the new mantra of marketing is to not produce advertising but to commercialize public reality itself; the aim is not to sponsor culture but to *be* the culture, not to advertise within public spheres but to *be* the public sphere. Baudrillard shows that the public is not only a commodity to be sold but is itself turned into a brand. As a result, something fundamental to our humanity and political existence is lost. Kimberly Curtis notes, 'We need a vigorous and diverse public and democratic life not for the sake of individual glory, or of winning immortality and defeating a nauseating futility, or for the sake of "making the world beautiful," so as to redeem appearances, or of acting in concert, or of sheer survival. Rather, we need such a public realm to sustain and intensify our awareness of reality.'[54]

Action as Redemption

Arendt writes that 'we have almost succeeded in leveling all human activities to the common denominator of securing the necessities of life and providing for their abundance' (HC, 126). Yet she also insists that this can be reversed by certain qualities of 'another and possibly higher faculty' (HC, 236) that may 'redeem' those activities beneath them.

I take my cue from Arendt's statement that 'the *Animal laborans* could be redeemed' through *Homo faber*, who 'erects a world of durability,' and that *Homo faber*, in turn, could be redeemed through 'action and speech' (HC, 236). In the case of *Animal laborans*, this refers not only to the tools and instruments that *Homo faber* develops to ease the toil of labour but rather to the fabrication of a lasting world that reverses the subjection of *Animal laborans* to the privative preoccupation with the life process: '*Homo faber*, the toolmaker, invented tools and implements in order to erect a world, not – at least, not primarily – to help the human life process' (HC, 151). The worldlessness of *Animal laborans* is redeemed by the worldliness of *Homo faber*. Arendt alludes to this redemption in the final pages of her chapter on labour, where she states that in order for *Animal laborans* to survive he must see nature as the 'great provider of all "good things"' (HC, 134). Moreover, she asserts that 'without being at home in the midst of things whose durability makes them fit for use and for erecting a world whose very permanence stands in direct contrast to life, this life would never be human' (HC, 135). In short, the danger of modern life is that we may lose our awareness of our own preoccupation with the life process: 'the danger that such a society [of consumers], dazzled by the abundance of its growing fertility and caught in the smooth functioning of a never-ending process, would no longer be able to recognize its own futility' (HC, 135).

Although the worldliness of *Homo faber* may redeem *Animal laborans*, work stands in need of redemption from its 'predicament of meaninglessness' (HC, 236). The predicament of *Homo faber* is caused by his tendency to 'instrumentalize' nature, to view a tree as merely wood, as material to be worked upon and drawn into the human artifice. Once all things have been reduced to mere objects, they become subjected to the instrumental character of utilitarian calculation. However, Arendt asserts, 'the perplexity of utilitarianism is that it gets caught in the unending chain of means and ends without ever arriving at some principle which could justify the category of means and end, that is, of utility itself' (HC, 154). The utilitarianism and instrumentality of *Homo faber* inevitably leads to the 'loss of all standards' and the 'limitless devaluation of everything given' (HC, 157).

In addition to the predicament of meaninglessness resulting from utilitarianism and instrumentality, *Homo faber* stands in need of redemption from work itself. Although *Homo faber* is able to establish an exchange market for his goods, *Homo faber* encounters others as those who 'did not meet as persons but as owners of commodities and exchange values' (HC, 162). Further, work entails a risk that the appeal of its 'greater reliability' (HC, 195) may result in the attempt to apply this activity to the realm of politics itself, to conceive of politics in terms of 'making.' Applying the model of the relationship that holds between a craftsman and material to the political realm is profoundly dangerous because it inevitably results in attempts to 'make' politics.

Furthermore, Arendt continues, modernity is characterized by a growing tendency to conflate work and labour such that 'work is now performed in the mode of laboring' (HC, 230), culminating in *Homo faber*'s predicament of 'earthly alienation.' According to Arendt, such a state can be redeemed 'only through the interrelated faculties of action and speech' (HC, 236) through which a political actor's self-disclosure can establish a space of appearance that assures a sense of reality and meaning in what otherwise would be a meaningless cosmos. In *The Human Condition*, Arendt often makes note of the importance of speech. For example, she warns us in the prologue that while 'speech is what makes man a political being,' we are threatened by 'a way of life in which speech is no longer meaningful,' and because we increasingly 'move in a world where speech has lost its power' (HC, 4). Arendt likens speech to action, considering them to be 'of the same rank and the same kind,' because 'finding the right word at the right moment ... is action' (HC, 26). Speech and narratives correspond to the uniqueness and distinctness of each human and are how the actor discloses self-identity and is inserted into the realm of human affairs.

This impulse to speak and insert oneself into the human world has its origin in natality, for 'its impulse springs from the beginning which came into the world when we were born and to which we respond by beginning something new on our own initiative' (HC, 177). Moreover, action itself depends on speech, as 'speechless action would no longer be action because there would no longer be an actor' (HC, 178). Although *Animal laborans* and *Homo faber* each possess the capacity to speak, their speech is merely a 'means of communicating information' (HC, 179) and does not reveal unique personal identities nor entail the 'disclosure of who.' However, 'action without a name, a "who" attached to it, is meaningless' (HC, 180). The importance of speech also lies in its performative dimension: words and self-disclosure contain a theatricality that confirms the interrelatedness of humans as 'actors.' The re-enacting of stories on a stage entails a revealing through the mimesis of acting. Indeed, for Arendt, 'the theater is *the* political art par excellence' (HC, 188). It is the importance of speech and its relation to our sense of the real that we are primarily concerned with in the next chapter.

Conclusion

Arendt attempts to release us from the narrow constraints of modern political discourse by extending the meaning of politics, with the aim to advance consumerism. She shows that a gathering of consumers is not a public, because something fundamental about the human condition is compromised when the public becomes a commodity to be sold for profit. In Arendt's view, what is widely held to be politics is in fact not politics at all but a preoccupation with the anti-political habits of consumption. The 'political speech' of George Bush following 9/11 exemplifies Arendt's assertion that in modernity 'the dividing line is entirely blurred between the public and private' (HC, 28). Arendt acknowledges the difficulties we face today in attempting to discern what is public: 'What concerns us in this context is the extraordinary difficulty with which we, because of this development, understand the decisive division between the public and private realms, between the sphere of the polis and the sphere of household and family, and, finally, between activities related to a common world and those related to the maintenance of life, a division upon which all ancient political thought rested as self-evident and axiomatic' (HC, 28).

Yet we remain limited in our ability to discern the forces that transform all things in the world into commodities. Arendt's account of politics emphasizes a human togetherness in which we have a place in the world that is not determined by consumption. A key implication is also the loss of what Arendt scholar Kimberly Curtis calls 'our sense of the real,' lamenting that 'the greatest casualty of the world Arendt describes is our sense of reality.'[55]

4 Jean Baudrillard: Consuming Signs

A revolutionary age is an age of action; ours is the age of advertisement and publicity. Nothing ever happens but there is immediate publicity everywhere.

– Søren Kierkegaard[1]

In order to become an object of consumption, the object must become a sign.

– Jean Baudrillard[2]

Connecting Arendt's analysis with the postmodern philosopher Jean Baudrillard provides a deeper understanding of the semiotic character of consumerism. Although connections between these two thinkers have not been explored by scholars, there are significant areas of overlap that can help us better understand the issue at hand: both observe that human relations have been altered and increasingly mediated by consumerism, and both explain the process by which what is private becomes public. Both thinkers reveal the extent to which we are immersed in consumerism and highlight for us the urgency of the question of politics today. Baudrillard helps illuminate the important developments in the fifty years since Arendt wrote, as the dramatically new postmodern character of consumerism requires equally dramatic new modes of critique. What Baudrillard offers is not only an unusual and original semiotic account of consumerism but also an engagement with the 'hyper' character of modernity.

Like Arendt, Baudrillard is also a theorist of ruptures: between premodernity, modernity, and postmodernity; indeed, Baudrillard himself went through several remarkable ruptures and reversals in his own career. Baudrillard connects the changing character of consumerism with the shift from modernity to postmodernity in terms of the role of signs and symbols. Just as Arendt's account of the ascent of the *oikos* and agora to a place of political dominance entailed the eclipse of the public realm and the loss of action, the rise of consumerism entails what Baudrillard calls 'the proliferation of signs' and the loss of reality. However, while he accepts many of her categories and concepts, he carries them forward to their logical extreme.

Commercial Literacy: The Branded Alphabet

Children today are so thoroughly immersed in advertising's world of signs and logos that they have no trouble identifying dozens of consumer brands and corporate slogans. They have developed a new kind of literacy, what could be called a 'commercial literacy.' While literacy discourse is characterized by tensions over what *literacy* means, whom it serves, and how it should be taught and learned, and while there is much written about various types of literacy such as emotional literacy, functional literacy, etc., what is increasingly apparent in today's students is what could be called the literacy of consumption. Aristotle describes us as political animals, yet we are also what educational theorist Bradley Levinson calls 'symbolic animals,' a species that uses symbols to communicate meaning. In *Schooling the Symbolic Animal*, Levinson links schooling with symbols by exploring the cultural function of learning about symbols and their meaning. He argues, 'We are perhaps the only species to regularly use symbols to understand and act upon the world, and we are probably the only species to systematically transmit the rules of symbol use to succeeding generations ... That is indeed the heart of education' because 'education involves the continual remaking of culture as human beings transmit and acquire the symbolic meanings that infuse social life.'[3]

Consumerism is radically transforming how symbolic meaning is engaged and understood by students. From a very early age, many children can more readily identify countless logos and the meanings associated with them than important historical and political figures, provocatively demonstrated in the documentary *Super Size Me*. In this documentary several school children are shown dozens of corporate logos and are more successful at identifying them than when shown pictures of such important historical and religious figures as Jesus, Martin

Luther King, and Mother Theresa. An example more directly related to the classroom is demonstrated by the work of the American media theorist and high school teacher Carrie Maclean. Maclean describes an in-class activity she undertook that demonstrates the extent to which schoolchildren increasingly possess greater knowledge and awareness of the signs and logos of consumerism than of the natural world around them: 'On the first day of class, I ask students to try and identify several plants and trees common in our Brooklyn neighborhood. They generally fail to name one. Then I show a slide of the alphabet comprised entirely from brand logos, and they name almost all of them.'[4] This activity demonstrates the extent to which their commercial literacy is increasingly eclipsing their literacy of the natural world around them.

I have had the opportunity to present this alphabet in several contexts, from K–12 schools to undergraduate and graduate classrooms to academic conferences, and can discern a significant pattern: while older academics can identify about six to eight logos, university students usually just over a dozen, younger children can generally name all of them – and usually with great enthusiasm. This demonstrates a significant demographic and generational shift in commercial literacy. It is noteworthy that while cultural conservatives like E.D. Hirsch lament the decline of a common knowledge and call upon education to promote 'cultural literacy,'[5] youth today in fact already speak a common language: 'what every American needs to know' is about brands and their meanings.

Life in consumer society for this new generation of students requires commercial literacy much more than knowledge of the natural world around them, because knowledge of commodities and their symbolic function is more important than environmental knowledge. Yet commercial literacy is based on an artificial language manufactured for billions of dollars (paid for by us as consumers), and constitutes what Baudrillard calls a 'simulation' of speech or a 'code' that has profoundly problematic implications. Furthermore, commercial literacy not only obscures the natural world but is produced to advance consumerism with the result of profound damage done to that same natural world it obscures; not only do students know so little about nature but the harm done to it by consumerism is obscured by consumerism itself. Furthermore, commercial literacy is designed to prevent the possibility of communicating alternative messages of resistance; it is manufactured in order to promote consumerism, not communicate resistance.

It is worth exploring these and other problems that emerge as a consequence of such a highly developed and widely 'spoken' commercial literacy. The hegemonic literacy derived from such advertising obscures non-commercial speech and is a mere simulation of learning, a degradation of traditional literacy. While today's students may possess this kind of commercial literacy, they are limited in their ability to use it to communicate dissent or alter symbolic meaning. In an interview about her work as a culture jammer, Carly Stasko argues, 'There's no dialogue when mass media is so focused on selling us stuff.'[6] However, Baudrillard reveals that these consumer brands and logos are not symbols in the conventional manner Levinson describes, but are empty signs without referents. Baudrillard's analysis reveals the symbols of such advertising to be degraded signs, empty of signification.

Baudrillard and Postmodernism

First a few words about Baudrillard. A long-time leading figure in French intellectual circles, Baudrillard is a confounding and playful thinker who connects sociology, cultural studies, media theory, political economy, and semiotics to an analysis of our consumer society. In drawing from these disciplines, Baudrillard provides a remarkably original and insightful analysis of the most central characteristics of consumerism and postmodernism. Although rooted in contemporary Western thought, Baudrillard often dispenses with argument and traditional scholarly methods and instead celebrates contradictions and conflations while playing with language and perspective. For this reason his work is difficult to understand, rather than because his work is characterized by complex linguistic amalgams and original neologisms, as found in Heidegger or Arendt. At times both frightening and humorous, he delights in pushing ideas to their logical extreme – an extreme more often absurd and ironic than logical.

Baudrillard participated in the project to provide a new theoretical framework that would challenge many of the structuralist and modernist tenets of classical Marxist political economy and social theory, perhaps the most important philosophical movement of the twentieth century that came to be known as postmodernism. With roots in Nietzsche and Heidegger and grounded in the deconstruction of metaphysics and the 'linguistic turn' towards the influence of language, postmodernism has radically and permanently altered the landscape of Western philosophy. Although postmodernism is not one monolithic or unitary world view, it does have common characteristics and discernible features. While modernity sought to preserve such foundational metaphysical categories to Western philosophy as essence, linearity, and unity, postmodernism radically alters these notions by advancing alterity, undecidability, and incommensurability. By emphasizing fragmentation, aporia, and multiplicity, postmodernism emerged in part as a critical response to modernity and Marxism, from what Michael Peters describes as 'the desire to bring to an end traditional Marxist intellectual culture ... and to develop an alternative left culture.'[7] It does so by advancing the Nietzschean critique of such pillars of modernity as reason, subjectivity, progress – and even critique itself. While modernity seeks to preserve the idea of historical progress, postmodernism radically calls into question the very conceivability of such a notion. Instead, because history consists of dramatic and unexpected ruptures that can be neither anticipated nor understood, a stance of 'incredulity towards metanarratives'[8] is encouraged.

Born in 1929 in the northern French city of Reims, Baudrillard taught during several tumultuous decades at Nanterre, beginning shortly before the student uprising of May 1968. That same year saw the publication of his dissertation, *The System of Objects*, a study of the meaning derived from consumption as the process by which human social relations become mediated by objects. Consumerism constituted a very central place for Baudrillard from the very beginning of his career – in fact his first book was titled *The Consumers Society*. Certainly among the most important intellectuals of the latter decades of the twentieth century, Baudrillard diagnoses and describes – even evokes – the nihilistic character of consumer society. Just as Nietzsche's Zarathustra announced the death of God, Baudrillard announces the death of the real – or perhaps he is more akin to the feverish Nietzschean madman: desperate and panicky yet fully lucid and far-sighted.[9] Baudrillard's work abounds in confounding paradoxes, contradictions, ironies, and playful ambiguities and absurdities. These cannot be simply dismissed as indications of Baudrillard's own intellectual development and shifts in thought but hermeneutic strategies for unveiling his philosophical project and the semiotic character of consumerism. Baudrillard's preoccupation with simulation and his radical questioning led him to such provocative statements as 'the gulf war did not take place'[10] and 'the collapse of the towers of the World Trade Center is unimaginable, but that is not enough to make it a real event.'[11]

For Baudrillard, the subject is not the unified, rational, and autonomous figure described by Enlightenment thinkers, but always already deeply immersed in the signs of consumerism. Thus Baudrillard scholar Douglas Kellner argues that 'his work was one of the first to appropriate semiology to analyze how objects are encoded with a system of signs and meanings that constitute contemporary media and consumer societies. Combining semiological studies, Marxian political economy, and sociology of the consumer society, Baudrillard began his life-long task of exploring the system of objects and signs which forms our everyday life.'[12] Motivated by the belief that Marxism 'does not adequately illuminate premodern societies that were organized around symbolic exchange and not production' (SO, 58), Baudrillard supplemented Marx's analysis with a semiotics of objects and their cultural power, reflecting an important shift from the influence of economic structures to the importance of culture and signs. He shows how consumerism populates the world with objects that have become divinized and animated and endowed with foreign properties, creating a world of signs in which we have come to dwell.

'Baudrillard's Death Did Not Take Place'

As his career progressed, Baudrillard seemed to implode under the weight of his own concepts as he shifted from sociology and structuralism to semiotics and post-structuralism, from a study of objects to signs and finally to simulation. Baudrillard scholar Charles Levin remarked that Baudrillard's social world grew steadily darker as his career progressed,[13] while Douglas Kellner comments that 'Baudrillard is perhaps more useful as a provocateur who challenges and puts in question the tradition of classical social theory and philosophy, and standard academic disciplines and procedures.'[14] Initially influential primarily in France, by the mid-1980s his work in translation began reaching a wide audience. Yet Keller points out that, even as his work became more popular, his new writings became increasingly obscure and indecipherable, leading to caricatures and dismissal of his work. Robert Fulford in the *National Post* declared, 'As much as any thinker of his time, Jean Baudrillard was willing to drive an idea off the cliff of reason and fall with it into the river below – and all just to prove he could do it.'[15] Baudrillard would likely take this accusation as a compliment.

In countless intellectual eulogies and cultural obituaries, Baudrillard pronounced the death of so many of our own sacred idols: the real, the subject, even history itself. Yet he has now himself died, even as this book was written. In a *Guardian* obituary, Richard Poole insisted that 'Baudrillard's death did not take place'[16] because his ideas and influence will continue. Yet because Baudrillard's work is still new and his death quite recent, there is no way for us to yet be certain how it will be taken up and understood by the larger interpretive community.

Baudrillard argued that the death of certain people 'makes the world more enigmatic, more difficult to understand than it was when they were alive – which is the true task of thought,' and observed that some 'outlive themselves into a world which is no longer theirs.'[17] Until the end, he continued to live in a world he anticipated and articulated so well. In an obituary, the editor of the *International Journal of Baudrillard Studies*, Gerry Coulter, observed that 'Baudrillard's work stands as an exemplar of our times – he spoke to us of what is to come and we know it and that is why he frightens so many.'[18]

From Arendt to Baudrillard: The Sign of the Artifice

Arendt shares many of these fears. She opens *The Human Condition* by asserting that the launch of Sputnik exemplifies all that is dangerous about modernity. The passengers on this 'earth-born object made by man' (HC, 1) would be the first to fully inhabit a realm entirely of human making, in which humans are released from the confines of earthly existence to fully enter the realm of the human artifice. For Arendt, this 'rebellion against human existence as it has been given' (HC, 2) reveals the extent of our alienation. This rebellion means the loss of the polis and erosion of speech such that we 'adopt a way of life in which speech is no longer meaningful' and 'move in a world where speech has lost its power' (HC, 4). Baudrillard points towards the similar implications of more recent events: he argues that the proliferation of signs combined with the separation of the sign from the object leaves humans inhabiting a semiotic realm entirely of their own making, eclipsing 'the real.' Baudrillard demonstrates that it is no longer necessary to leave the earth in order to experience alienation or live in the realm of the human artifice; we don't need to go into outer space to no longer live in the world. Instead we can surround ourselves with the signs and symbols of consumerism to such an extent that we live entirely in the realm of the human artifice. Baudrillard's semiotics provides an insightful and original analysis of consumer society and can help explain how sign systems can preserve consumer society long after speech has been drained of its power and meaning.

Arendt, who is primarily a political philosopher, employs the public/ private distinction and activities of labour, work, and action to explain the rise of consumer society. In contrast, Baudrillard's analysis of consumer society draws from the disciplines of semiotics and the political economy of the production of signs. In drawing from these fields Baudrillard provides a unique and original analysis of the new character of consumption, which extends Arendt's analysis into the contemporary situation. It is best to begin with a discussion of his theory of signification and then examine the implications of the separation of the sign from the commodity. It will then be possible to observe the implications of this development for both the loss of reality and the making public of what was previously private.

We can recall that speech was of great importance to Arendt, particularly its link with action and the polis. While Arendt insisted that speech is associated with action and absent from the isolated private life of consumption and production, Baudrillard outlines the spread of speech through the signs and symbols of commercial discourse. He echoes Arendt's description of the rise of the social and its communicative implications: 'There is no longer any difference between the economic and the political because the same language reigns in both' (SS, 88, 90). Like Arendt, he finds the type of discourse and communication that dominates consumer society to be neither speech nor language: 'The object cum advertising system constitutes less a language, whose living syntax it lacks, than a set of significations. Impoverished yet efficient, it is basically a code' (SO, 193). Elsewhere he asserts that 'there can be no more impoverished language than this one, laden with referents yet empty of meaning. It is a language of mere signals' (SO, 191–2). Advertising and marketing become the signs, language, and entire communicative structure within our society and come to dominate all other forms of discourse and signification.

Today what we are experiencing is the absorption of all virtual modes of expression into that of advertising. All current forms of activity tend toward advertising and most exhaust themselves therein. Not necessarily advertising itself, the kind that is produced as such, but the form of advertising, that of a simplified operational mode, vaguely seductive, vaguely consensual (all the modalities are confused therein, but in an attenuated, agitated mode). More generally, the form of advertising is one in which all particular contents are annulled at the very moment when they can be transcribed into each other, whereas what is inherent to weighty enunciations, to articulated forms of meaning (or of style) is that they cannot be translated into each other, any more than the rules of a game can be. (SS, 87)

While Arendt asserts that labour and work are speechless and emphasizes the link between action and speech, Baudrillard emphasizes the importance of communication systems within the consumer society. Baudrillard writes several decades after Arendt when consumerism has accelerated and moved into a new 'hyper' form, when the discourse of consumption has become even more dominant and increasingly based on a new type of communication. 'Hyper' society can be characterized as an acceleration of Arendt's 'social realm' when dominated by the proliferation of signs. Baudrillard writes in *Simulacra and Simulation*, 'The hypermarket [French word for shopping mall] is already, beyond the factory and traditional institutions of capital, the model of all future forms of controlled socialization ... The "form" hypermarket can thus help us understand what is meant by the end of modernity ... These new objects are the poles of simulation around which is elaborated, in contrast to old train stations, factories, or traditional transportation networks, something other than a "modernity": a hyperreality, a simultaneity of all the functions, without a past, without a future, an operationality on every level. And doubtless also crises, or even new catastrophes' (SS, 76–8). This dynamic demonstrates a fundamental paradox of consumerism. Many twentieth-century thinkers have attempted to describe the instrumentalizing process by which everything that humans encounter in the world is transformed into a lifeless and inanimate thing, ready at hand for human use. Similarly, Arendt describes the instrumentalizing gaze of *Animal laborans* and *Homo faber* for whom 'everything is judged in terms of suitability and usefulness for the desired end, and nothing else [such that] usefulness and utility are established as the ultimate standards for life' (HC, 157). Baudrillard describes a more advanced stage in this process by which the object in turn is 'animated' and endowed with simulated meaning, in a shift from the tendency to reify to the tendency to deify, from the tendency to disenchant the world to the attempt to re-enchant the world through animating objects and turning them into signs.

These signs in turn enter into a series and constitute a language, commercial speech, interpreted with commercial literacy. Kellner suggests that, for Baudrillard, modernity was concerned primarily with the production of objects, while postmodernism is concerned with simulation and the production of signs: 'Modernity thus centered on the production of things – commodities and products – while postmodernity is characterized by radical semiurgy, by a proliferation of signs.'[19] This shift becomes part of Baudrillard's passage through Marx into the conceptual framework of linguistics.

Commercial Discourse: A Language of Signals

The deeper political effect of branding can easily be obscured if understood primarily from the perspective of a distinct commodity or a particular branding campaign. Instead, by examining consumerism from a broader perspective, it becomes apparent that as a totalizing system it comes to constitute a 'code.' Examining Baudrillard's theory of signification in light of the emergence of a new visual consumer culture reveals several implications of the separation of the sign from the commodity.

It is important to note that there is nothing inherently wrong with the human tendency to symbolize. Semiotic representation is how we participate in the world around us and experience ourselves as a part of that world. As political philosopher Eric Voegelin argues, 'The self-illumination of society through symbols is an integral part of social reality, and one may even say its essential part, for through such symbolization the members of a society experience it as more than an accident or a convenience; they experience it as of their human essence.'[20] Baudrillard points out that this process is readily taken up and used in such as way to as to promote consumerism; it is how the consumer is produced.

While Arendt insisted that speech is associated with action and absent from the isolated private life of consumption and production, Baudrillard describes the spread of a kind of 'speech' through the signs and symbols of commercial discourse. Baudrillard agrees with Arendt that the type of discourse and communication that dominates consumer society is not 'speech' or language: 'The object/advertising system constitutes a system of signification, but not language, for it lacks an active syntax: it has the simplicity and effectiveness of a code' (SO, 22). While this syntax of consumption is certainly not 'speech' as understood by Arendt, the mode of communication within consumer society effectively drowns out any political speech. It is so pervasive that we don't even notice it anymore; we become blind to this new visuality.

Through the transformation of the commodity into a sign, the sign is able to enter into a 'series' in which it becomes immersed within the endless stream of other signs. The pitch of this discourse relentlessly increases as each sign seeks to drown out the 'noise' generated by other signs.[21] The result becomes deafening; but to mix metaphors, it dominates our vision, blinding us and blurring into an endless stream of flashing images. For Baudrillard, as a result of this separation 'we disappear behind our images.'[22] In a consumer society, the personal modes of communication used to produce a sense of intimacy between advertisers and consumers, and between consumers and commodities, is so prevalent that human relationships themselves becomes simulated. For example, 'buzz' or 'stealth' marketing pays individuals to promote products to friends and family.

Ironically, while we all complain about paying taxes, we are in fact paying even more to have products endowed with symbolic meaning so they can be sold to us in the first place. It is notable that often advertising is a larger component of the price of a commodity than taxes, what Dave Meslin of the Toronto Public Space Committee calls 'advertising sales tax' (AST). As mentioned in chapter 2, it is troubling that in the last decade the increase in spending on advertising and marketing in North America outpaces increases to spending on education.

Remarkably, because the signs of consumption constitute a language, many marketers and advertisers claim their work should be protected as a right to freedom of speech. For example, marketer Steven Shugan laments that 'market folks continue to face extremely vocal, relentless, and powerful antagonists who want to silence them.' Because 'marketing folks' are burdened with the responsibility of preserving the market, they should be awarded an equal right to freedom of speech: 'There is no free lunch. Someone must pay the price of maintaining the market, and often it is the marketing folks.'[23] In contrast, University of Alberta law professor Roger Shiner argues that, because corporations cannot possess an original autonomous right to free expression, and the free communication of commercial information is not a public good equally beneficial to all, the regulation of commercial speech is neither paternalistic nor anti-democratic. He claims that 'this doctrine is the thesis that so-called commercial expression (commercial advertising, for example) deserves the same, or sufficiently similar, constitutional protection as any other form of constitutionally protected expression or speech, because it serves essentially the same purposes in essentially the same way.'[24]

For Baudrillard, advertising is a meaningless code of signals, because it constructs a false world of signifiers that don't refer to the signified. Consumers must be able to 'read' the system of consumption in order to know what to consume, because commodities are no longer defined by their use, but rather what they signify. Yet as we become educated in this language of consumption, we are lost within our own linguistic simulations. Because one can't consume a signifier, the latent promise of the signifier is perpetually unconsummated. Since these signs are systematically ordered to command consumption, they conceal the same experience of incompletion they create.

The Commodity as Sign: The Symbolic Function of Consumption

Like many of his colleagues and contemporaries within the French postmodern scene, Baudrillard critically engaged Marxist social theory and political economy. Douglas Kellner argues that Baudrillard's critique of Marx was that, in his emphasis on exchange value and use value, he overlooked the political and cultural importance of 'sign value' and the code of consumption: 'His polemics against Marxism were fuelled by the belief that sign value and the code were more fundamental than such traditional elements of political economy as exchange value, use value, production and so on in constituting contemporary society.'[25]

Perhaps the most central issue in Baudrillard's engagement with Marx concerns the shift from the production of objects to the production of signs, from the means of production to the means of consumption, or 'the simultaneous production of the commodity as sign and the sign as commodity.'[26] This shift is evident in the new kind of 'heroes' that characterize a consumer society in contrast to those of the earlier era of production: 'The impassioned biographies of heroes of production are everywhere giving way today to biographies of heroes of consumption. The great exemplary lives of self-made men and founder, pioneers, explorers and colonizers, which succeeded those of saints and historical figures, have today given way to the lives of movie stars, sporting or gambling heroes, of a handful of gilded princes or globe-trotting barons – in a word, the lives of great wastrels ... it is always the excessiveness of their lives, the potential for outrageous expenditure that is exalted' (CS, 45–6).

As a result of this shift, the Marxist categories of consciousness, power, subordination, and authority are to be found in the mode of signification more so than production. Peter McLaren and Zeus Leonardo describe this dynamic: 'Domination no longer resides primarily in the control of the means of production. Rather, domination can be attributed more to control of the means of consumption. Moreover, this is accomplished at the level of the mode of signification (previously mode of production) in everyday life.'[27] The sign proves to have much more impact than the physical commodity itself because sign value exceeds use value. Because consumerism is a socially regulated system of signs, it is no longer based on economic rationalism or a production-oriented political economy. This spells the end of the era diagnosed by Marx and characterized by the centrality of labour and production as described through political economy; for Baudrillard, these have all come to their end: 'The end of labor. The end of production. The end of political economy.'[28]

Baudrillard connects simulation with many other central features of modern society such as waste and excess, scarcity and abundance. In his work *The Consumer Society*, he discusses the tribal practice of potlatch, in which precious goods were destroyed or given up in ceremonies intended to deepen group cohesion, establish rank, demonstrate bounty, and appease divine forces. Rites would include the burning of precious herbs and tobacco, tossing valuable metals into lakes and rivers, leaving food on mountaintops, spilling blood on objects and the earth, and so on. For Baudrillard, these gestures were symbolic because they disregarded notions of utility, calculation, and necessity. Baudrillard calls these practices 'productive waste' and argues that in contemporary consumer society the economic predilection for disposability and excess contributes to a mentality of wastefulness. However, rather than thinking of waste in ritual terms as an occasional meaningful sacrifice, we think only of convenience without regard for ceremony, reverence, or the social and environmental consequences of perpetual waste. Contemporary culture's waste is instead a hedonistic simulation of tribal societies' practices of accumulation and disposal as a living spiritual practice. This analysis links back to the earlier discussion of the etymological character of consumerism, supplemented with Baudrillard's analysis of waste and destruction: '*Does not affluence ultimately only have meaning in wastage* ... wastage which defies scarcity and, contradictorily, signifies abundance ... The consumer society needs objects in order to be. More precisely, it needs to *destroy* them ... destruction remains the fundamental alternative to production: consumption is merely an intermediate term between the two' (CS, 44–5, 47).

In his next work, *The System of Objects*, Baudrillard explores another kind of simulation in his examination of not only the central properties of objects but their character and function as a *system* in modern consumer society. For Baudrillard scholar Mark Gottdiner, Baudrillard concerns himself in *The System of Objects* with how 'home furnishings and interior decoration have passed from an ersatz, subjective, and personalized activity to one that is highly regulated by a code of design and appearance.'[29] Baudrillard explores how commodities such as home furnishing and interior decoration are taken up in ways that are highly regulated and codified. Through a detailed description of particular objects such as household goods and appliances, he presents a larger account of the hegemonic and ideological character of consumerism, arguing that modern objects in the household point towards 'the desire for technology under the sign of progress.'[30]

Objects are in fact not what they seem; they are allegorical and metaphorical. Advertising endows objects with meaning such that we do not simply consume the object but rather the *system* to which all objects belong as signs. In his own words, 'We shall not be concerning ourselves with objects as defined by their functions or by the categories into which they might be subdivided for analytic purposes, but instead with the processes whereby people relate to them and with the systems of human behaviour and relationships that result therefrom' (SO, 2). It is through our participation in this system of objects that we come to know ourselves: 'This modern home-dweller does not "consume" his objects. Instead of consuming objects, he dominates, controls and orders them. He discovers himself in the manipulation and tactical equilibration of a system' (SO, 25). The consequences of this type of participation are quite frightening: 'The fact is that this formal achievement papers over an essential lack; our technological civilization tries to use the universal transitivity of form as a means of compensating for the disappearance of the symbolic relationship associated with the traditional gestural system of work, as a way of making up for the unreality, the symbolic void, of our power' (SO, 56–7).

Through this lack it is we ourselves who become an 'abstraction': 'There is no reason to assume that the unceasing forward march of *techne* will not eventually achieve a mimesis which replaces a natural world with an artificial one. If the simulacrum is so well designed that it becomes an effective organizer of reality, then surely it is man, not the simulacrum, who is turned into abstraction ... in the face of the functional object the human being becomes dysfunctional, irrational and subjective' (SO, 60). One is reminded again of Arendt's concern about the emergence of the human artifice. This profit-driven attempt to attach meaning that does not inhere in the object, an object often incapable of providing the experience of meaning promised by advertisers, is another form of simulation. This results in a disenchantment with the traditional world through the intrusion of systems of signification, such that the reality of the natural world disappears as the sign is naturalized and normalized into a system. This dynamic results in a troubling paradox of consumerism: even as the natural world is transformed into a lifeless and inanimate thing, ready at hand for human use, it is the object in turn that is 'animated' and endowed with simulated meaning.

While humans have always and will always endow objects with attributes of our own making through signification, in consumer society this activity is appropriated by commercial forces such that instead of seeing the world around us we see only the signs of consumption. While Max Weber described modernity as 'disenchanted,' because the prevalence of instrumental reason drained the world of meaning, Baudrillard suggests that consumerism responds by attempting to 're-enchant' the world through animating the commodity. However, this attempt to 'humanize' objects by endowing them with symbolic meanings and characteristics of human personalities furthers the dehumanization of the world by making it a place of artificial and simulated meanings.

This dynamic is a fundamental feature of what sociologist George Ritzer calls 'McDonaldization,' which 'tends to bring with it disenchantment, or a loss of magic and mystery. However, disenchanted structures are unlikely to attract consumers. In response to this problem, the new means of consumption have, at least to some degree, been re-enchanted, incorporating ever more spectacular features to draw in consumers seeking euphoria in a world lacking in emotion.'[31] This sentiment is echoed by media theorist and critic of consumerism Sut Jhally, who argues that consumerism succeeds because it begins by 'emptying [commodities] of meaning, of hiding the real social relations objectified in them through human labor, to make it possible for the imaginary/symbolic social relations to be injected into the construction of meaning at a secondary level. Production empties. Advertising fills. The real is hidden by the imaginary ... The hollow husk of the commodity-form needs to be filled by some kind of meaning, however superficial. This is why advertising is so powerful.'[32]

Consumer society is not driven by the needs and demands of consumers, but rather by excessive productive capacity because of a contradiction between higher levels of productivity and the need to dispose of the product: 'It becomes vital for the system at this stage to control not only the mechanism of production, but also consumer demand' (CS, 41). Baudrillard describes the overwhelming deluge of objects that swamp society, transforming human relationships: 'With the advent of consumer society, we are seemingly faced for the first time in history by an irreversible organized attempt to swamp society with objects and integrate it into an indispensable system designed to replace all open interaction between natural forces, needs and techniques' (SO, 132). The system at this stage must control not only production but also consumer demand as part of planned socialization by the code:

> In the planned cycle of consumer demand, the new strategic forces, the new structural elements – needs, knowledge, culture, information, sexuality – have all their explosive force defused. In opposition to the competitive system, the monopolistic system institutes *consumption* as control, as the abolition of the contingency of demand, as planned socialization by the code (of which advertising, style, etc. are only glaring examples) ... Thus consumption ... signifies the passage ... to a mode of strategic control, of predictive anticipation, of the absorption of the dialectic, and of the general homeopathy of the system ... Needs lose all their autonomy; they are coded. Consumption no longer has a value of enjoyment per se; it is placed under the constraint of the absolute finality which is that of production. Production, on the contrary, is no longer assigned any finality other than itself. This total reduction of the process to a single one of its terms ... designates more than an evolution of the capitalist mode: it is a mutation.[33]

We have passed through capitalism into hyper-capitalism. Baudrillard's account of simulation and consumption helps differentiate between modernity and postmodernity: while modernity was concerned primarily with the production of objects, postmodernism is concerned with simulation and the production of signs. In Baudrillard's words,

> Traditional symbolic goods (tools, furniture, the house itself) were the mediators of a real relationship or a directly experienced situation, and their subject and form bore the clear imprint of the conscious or unconscious dynamic of that relationship. They thus were *not arbitrary* ... From time immemorial people have bought, possessed, enjoyed and spent, but this does not mean that they were 'consuming' ... It is ... the organization of all these things into a signifying fabric: consumption is *the virtual totality of all objects and messages ready-constituted as a more or less coherent discourse ...*

To become an object of consumption an object must become a sign. That is to say: it must become external, in a sense, to a relationship that it now merely signifies ... This conversion of the object to the systematic status of a sign implies the simultaneous transformation of the human relationship into a relationship of consumption ... all desires, projects, and demands, all passions and relationships, are now abstracted (or materialized) as signs and as objects to be bought and consumed. (SO, 2001).

The shift in emphasis from production to consumption parallels the tendency within postmodern linguistics to separate the signifier from the signified; within Baudrillard's semiotic analysis of consumer society, this takes on the character of a separation between the commodity and its sign. To consume the commodity is to consume the sign and its meaning, as 'it is in this way that it becomes "personalized," and enters into a series, etc.: it is never consumed in its materiality, but in its difference' (SO, 25). Advertisements have become more powerful and persuasive as a result of this separation.

Previously, goods were presented on the basis of their material qualities and function. Now, advertisers focus more on selling their brand and brand meaning. This gradual transition results in an association of the sign with a lifestyle and its integration into the social life of people. Through the transformation of the commodity into a sign, it is able to enter into a 'series' in which it becomes immersed within the never-ending stream of signs. In *The Consumer Society*, Baudrillard outlines how consumers buy into the 'code' of signs more so than the meaning of the object itself. His analysis of the process by which the sign ceases pointing towards an object behind it but rather to other signs that together constitute a cohesive yet chaotic 'code' culminates in the 'murder of reality.' The rupture is so complete, and the code so 'totalitarian' that Baudrillard speaks of the 'violence of the image.' Any liberating activity becomes complicit in the reproduction of its opposite, because 'the code is totalitarian; no one escapes it: our individual flights do not negate the fact that each day we participate in its collective elaboration.'[34] Baudrillard describes how consumers buy into the 'code' of signs more so than the meaning of the object itself such that as we 'consume the "code," we "reproduce" the system.'[35]

Although humans have always been meaning-makers by engaging in symbolic production and expression, the language of advertising has become increasingly prevalent as 'a form of socialization' (SO, 23), a dominant discourse that characterizes consumer society. His account of the 'implosion of meaning' entailed by the proliferation of signs and the reduction of the sign to the status of commodity points toward the simultaneous experience of the loss of reality and the encounter with hyperreality.

Politics, religion, education – every human undertaking is swept up and absorbed by this process. Media theorist Sut Jhally notes that this trend directly affects the electoral system such that 'politics is largely conducted on a symbolic realm.'[36] Marshall McLuhan claimed that 'politics will eventually be replaced by imagery. The politician will be only too happy to abdicate in favor of his image, because the image will be much more powerful than he could ever be.'[37]

Baudrillard argues that the dominance of the code, the proliferation of signs, and the violence of the image entail the eclipse – even death – of the real. 'The image ... is violent because what happens there is the murder of the Real, the vanishing point of reality' (CS, 1). An example of this eclipse might help clarify: in the novel *Everyone in Silico*,[38] Toronto writer Jim Munroe describes a dystopian future in which we are unaware that the sky is blue or that the moon and stars come out at night, because the sky has become entirely filled with continuously projected billboards and commercials. Humans live fully surrounded by the signs and symbols of commercial discourse, and legends are passed down of what lies behind the ads. This violent erasure of even the sky itself points towards the overwhelming power of the sign to obscure. This dynamic is self-perpetuating, because signs must proliferate indefinitely 'in order continuously to fulfill the absence of reality' (SO, 28). However, Baudrillard argues that this proliferation and erasure invariably induces indifference towards the real: 'The more exponential the marketing of images is growing the more fantastically grows the indifference towards the real world. Finally, the real world has become a useless function.'[39]

Because of consumerism we live in the first period in the history of life itself when one species has brought about the systematic destruction of other species, the first time since life began to diversify that one of its species undermined that process of diversification. Yet ironically, even as we destroy the natural world around us, we evoke those same remnants of nature so as to even better destroy nature: cellphone commercials show exotic and endangered frogs and lizards; insurance ads show brightly coloured fish; Coke commercials show polar bears. In perhaps the most ironic feature of consumerism, ads become an archive of what the very advancement of consumerism is destroying. Perhaps we can save nature only by capturing it as a sign used to promote its own destruction. Perhaps one day such images of nature will become a mere simulation of what has become lost.

Hannah Arendt would share this concern, observing that we 'did not gain this world when [we] lost the other world' (HC, 320). Arendt describes the loss of reality and loss of the world through the ascent of the *oikos* and agora to a place of political dominance. Just as reality is lost, so too is the polis, the realm of human affairs, the only place in which we experienced each other 'without the intermediary of things of matter' (HC, 7). For Baudrillard, 'men of wealth are no longer surrounded by other human beings, as they have been in the past, but by *objects*. Their daily exchange is no longer with their fellows, but rather, statistically as a function of some ascending curve, with the acquisition and manipulation of goods and message' (CS, 32).

Baudrillard sought to provide an understanding of the new 'hyper' form of advanced capitalism that emerged through the virtual and simulated character of contemporary experience. This steady stream of private banality has done little to preserve publicity or 'the real,' but is only a public display of our own private preoccupations, creating a community in which we are united only by our self-enclosure and self-preoccupation. This parallels Arendt's description of the historical process by which the private realm rose to a place of political dominance. Just as Arendt outlined the ascent of labour and work, the *oikos* and the agora, Baudrillard asserts that 'we [are] becoming functional. We are living the period of the objects: that is, we live by their rhythm, according to their incessant cycles. Today, it is we who are observing their birth, fulfillment, and death; whereas in all previous civilizations, it was the object, instrument, and perennial monument that survived the generations of men' (CS, 32).

The making explicit of the inner workings of privacy implies an analysis of the psychodynamics of consumerism, which Baudrillard explores throughout many of his key works. Recalling that Max Weber associated capitalism with puritanism, Baudrillard asserts that consumer society 'replaces a puritan morality with a hedonistic morality' (SO, 16). Consumerism does not correspond to the notion of need, desire, or pleasure – a confusion that occurs because the sign and object have been separated and the sign has become a commodity to be consumed. For Baudrillard, 'material goods are not the objects of consumption: they are merely the objects of need and satisfaction' (SO, 24). Consumerism does not satisfy needs because there are no limits to consumption; we want to consume more and more. Baudrillard speaks of the compulsion to consume: 'There are no limits to consumption ... people simply want to consume more and more. This compulsion is attributable neither to some psychological condition ("once a drunk always a drunk," and so forth), nor to the pressure of some simple desire for prestige. That consumption seems irrepressible is due, rather to the fact that it is indeed a total idealist practice ... Its dynamism derives from the ever-disappointed project now implicit in objects' (SO, 204–5). Consumerism does not delay gratification, it makes it impossible.

Furthermore, consumption does not satisfy desire: 'The discourse of advertising only arouses desire in order to generalize it in the most vague terms' (SO, 21). It is this confusion that occludes the more insidious dynamics concerning consumption, that consumption is more deeply associated with the experience of lack: 'It is ultimately because consumption is founded on a lack that it is irrepressible' (SO, 28). The signs of consumption impose a profound lack as a longing for something that is not there and can never be completed: 'there can be no final, physical satiation' (SO, 69). There is nothing behind the sign, only an endlessly accelerating noise and blur. Consumption cannot be consummated because it is the 'frustrated desire for totality' (SO, 28). As we become 'educated' in this language of consumption we become silent to ourselves and to political life, disappearing behind our own linguistic simulations.

Transparency and Disappearance: The Private as Obscene

Consumerism entails the loss of reality in part because it brings what was previously private into the public realm. In *The Violence of the Image*, Baudrillard outlines how the violence of the image makes what was once private become explicit. In much more dramatic and apocalyptic language than Arendt, Baudrillard warns of the murder of the real through the 'violence of transparency' and the 'total elimination of secrecy.'[40] Ironically, even as the reality of the public world recedes, the private realm is exploited for material that is then displayed in public, for profit. This can be seen in the countless reality shows and confessional television, the use of hand-held digital cameras with grainy images, the popularity of documentaries, all intended to suggest greater intimacy with and proximity to reality. Even as the task of politics is construed as the protection of the private realm, privacy is 'mined' for an insatiable viewing appetite.

Baudrillard argues that when everything is explicit, everything be-comes public, yet when everything becomes public, nothing is public. Echoing Bauman's discussion of confessional television, philosopher of education Kenneth Wain observes that this situation arises because 'the media show us everything instantaneously and without any scruple or hesitation, rendering it for this reason "obscene."'[41] In Baudrillard's words, 'The era of interiority, subjectivity, meaning, privacy and the in-ner life is over; a new era of obscenity, fascination, vertigo, instantane-ity, transparency and overexposure begins' (SS, 56). Baudrillard carries the logic of Arendt's public/private distinction to the nihilistic conse-quences of overexposure, explicitness, and 'delirious exhibitionism':

> There are two ways of disappearing, of being nothing. Either to be hidden, and to insist on the right not-to-be-seen (the actual defense of the private life). Or one shifts to a delirious exhibitionism of his own platitude and insignificance – ultimate protection against the servitude of being, and of being himself. Hence the absolute obligation to be seen, to make oneself visible at any price ... Then we are in the double bind – not to be seen, and to be continuously visible ...This means that people are decipherable at every moment. Overexposed to the light of information and addicted to their own image. Driven to express themselves at any time – self-ex-pression as the ultimate form of confession, as Foucault said. To become an image, one has to give a visual object of his whole everyday life, of his possibilities, of his feelings and desires. He has to keep no secrets and to interact permanently.[42]

Baudrillard suggests that even as our meaning-making propensities are drawn ever more quickly into a symbolic order centred on con-sumption, it is through consumption that we participate in our own disappearance. 'This is transparency to force all the real in the orbit of the visual. And this is obscene. Obscene is all what is unnecessarily visible, without desire and without effect. All that usurps the so rare and so precious space of appearances.'[43] The effect of the hyperreal is to obliterate distinctions, such as between private and public, in an implosion of meaning and a blinding proliferation of visuality when taken to the obscene extreme of transparency. This transparency and disappearance is driven by the simulated character of contemporary consumerism, as described by Benjamin Barber: 'The branding game targets consumers, but it also helps erase the boundaries between con-sumer and what is consumed. In thinking he has conquered the world

of things, the consumer is in fact consumed by them. In trying to en-
large himself, he vanishes' (CN, 35). Each signifier signifies only itself
as signification becomes self-referential, implying a presence, but con-
cealing an absence. We become extras in a spectacle of our own making.

Disneyland and the Hyper-Polis: The City of the Sign

Baudrillard describes the new 'hyper' form of consumerism by outlin-
ing several orders of simulation. The first order is the original as an
accurate reflection of reality based on an antecedent model. Second is
the counterfeit or emulation, notable for its falsity but still based on
forms of nature or an antecedent model. Third is the mechanical copy,
reproduced for equivalence and exchange in which commodities gain
importance not as objects but as signifiers whose value is measured
only in relation to other exchangeable commodities. Fourth and most
important is his notion of the hyperreal, a simulation without referent,
a copy of a copy. Unlike previous orders of simulation, the hyperreal
breaks the bonds with any pre-existent referent because it is 'without
origin or reality' (SS, 1). Simulation is exemplified by virtual reality,
information technology, and electronic media. A complete rupture between signifier and signified occurs such that each signifier signifies
only itself and other signifiers, and reality loops around itself in an
'implosion of meaning.' The simulacrum displays colonizing tendencies as it eventually replaces and obliterates the real. Recalling Arendt,
just as 'the social' devours the polis, so too does simulation devour the
real.

His critique of 'the real' is frequently thought to imply a denial of
physical reality. Towards the end of his career Baudrillard offered this
important clarification: 'Let us be clear about this: when we say reality has disappeared, the point is not that it has disappeared physically
but that it has disappeared metaphysically. Reality continues to exist;
it is its principle that is dead.'[44] Baudrillard doesn't aim to promote the
simulacrum any more than Marx sought to promote industrial capitalism. His aim was to diagnose and describe the operation of Western semiotic systems and the forms of social control that produce and
govern us today. To criticize Baudrillard for his sometimes frightening
characterization of consumerism would be like the mob in an episode
of *The Simpsons* that reacts to a meteorite bearing down on the town by
calling for the burning of the observatory. Baudrillard anticipated this
tendency: 'The reality-fundamentalists equip themselves with a form

of magical thinking that confuses message and messenger: if you speak of the simulacrum, then you are a simulator; if you speak of the virtuality of war, then you are in league with it and have no regard for the hundreds of thousands of dead.'[45]

Baudrillard opens *Simulacra and Simulation* by describing a society whose cartographers create a map so detailed that it covers the very things it was designed to represent. Eventually the map fades into the landscape and neither the representation nor the real remains – just the hyperreal. He argues that 'simulation is no longer that of a territory, a referential being, or a substance. It is the generation by models of a real without origin or reality: a hyperreal. The territory no longer precedes the map, nor does it survive it. It is nevertheless the map that precedes the territory – *Precession of simulacra* – that engenders the territory … today it is the territory whose shreds slowly rot across the extent of the map' (SS, 1). As a result of the shift from hiding something to hiding that there is nothing, we come to experience the simulated effects of the real world's absence. A 'new and improved' reality is manufactured for 'public' consumption. Yet this simulation is even more dangerous in its falseness; it is more real than real.

This fourth order is described as 'hyperreality,' 'the simulation of something which never really existed' (SS, 46). Simulation entails the move from hiding something to hiding that there is nothing, the 'transition from signs that dissimulate something to signs that dissimulate that there is nothing' (SS, 6). Because simulation entails hiding an absence, it is far more radical than imitation: 'To dissimulate is to pretend not to have what one has. To simulate is to feign to have what one doesn't have. One implies a presence, the other an absence. But it is more complicated than that because simulating is not pretending: "Whoever simulates an illness produces in himself some of the symptoms." Therefore, pretending, or dissimulating, leaves the principle of reality intact … whereas simulation threatens the difference between the "true" and the "false," the "real" and the "imaginary"' (SS, 3).

An example will help clarify this point. Baudrillard argues that since Disneyland is so explicitly a simulation it hides the fact that the rest of American culture is itself also a simulation, a culture of signs without referents. The imaginary world of Disneyland is intended to suggest, by juxtaposition, that the rest of America is real. Baudrillard argues instead that mainstream American culture is itself a simulation, that Disneyland conceals that all of 'real' America is as simulated as Disneyland: 'Americans had to invent Disneyland to convince themselves that America is real' (SS, 12). Baudrillard's description of this dynamic is worth quoting at length.

> Disneyland exists in order to hide that it is the 'real' country, all of the 'real' America that *is* Disneyland (a bit like prisons are there to hide that it is the social in its entirety, in its banal omnipresence, that is carceral). Disneyland is presented as imaginary in order to make us believe that the rest is real, whereas all of Los Angeles and the America that surrounds it are no longer real, but belong to the hyperreal order and to the order of simulation. It is no longer a question of a false representation of reality but of concealing the fact that the real is no longer real. The imaginary of Disneyland is neither true nor false, it is a deterrence machine set up in order to rejuvenate the fiction of the real in the opposite camp. Whence the debility of this imaginary, its infantile degeneration ... Disneyland: a space of the regeneration of the imaginary as waste-treatment plants are elsewhere. Everywhere today one must recycle waste, and the dreams, the phantasms, the historical, fairylike legendary imaginary of children and adults is a waste product, the first great toxic excrement of a hyperreal civilization. (SS, 12–13)

It is noteworthy that just as Bush called upon the American people to go shopping in the weeks after 9/11, he also encouraged Americans to take trips to Disney World: 'Get down to Disney World in Florida. Take your families and enjoy life, the way we want it to be enjoyed.'[46] Yet Baudrillard asserts that the production of 'unreality' in Disneyland hides that all of America is itself already like Disneyland; Disneyland conceals the fact that the real is no longer real. The aim is to 'capture' reality and transform it into a spectacle or reality show, to make the real a spectacle: 'Disney, the precursor, the grand initiator of the imaginary as virtual reality, is now in the process of capturing all the real world to integrate it into its synthetic universe, in the form of a vast "reality show" where reality itself becomes a spectacle [*vient se donner en spectacle*], where the real becomes a theme park.'[47] The production of simulation in a specific location conveys the impression that the simulation is not already present in, even determinant of, the rest of society. By extension, it could be said that the reason we have shopping malls is to convince ourselves that the rest of the world is not itself becoming a shopping mall. To connect this account to education and extend Baudrillard's analysis, it could be said that the function of the numerous shopping malls on university campuses is to convey the impression that the rest of the campus – and perhaps even education itself – is not itself already a mall, that students do not already move through education as if in a mall.

In the postmodern environment Baudrillard describes, brands no longer come to us but it is we who go to the brands and become fully immersed in them. Perhaps the most extreme example of this dynamic is Celebration, Florida, a town developed entirely by the Walt Disney Company and directly connected to the theme park. Naomi Klein describes Celebration: 'It's not about just going there on your vacation or extending a fantasy from a film just a little bit longer. You can live your whole life inside the brand full-time. They send their kids to the Disney school, and they elect representatives to the Disney council. It's a fully privatized life.'[48] Klein also points out that ironically there is in fact no advertising in the town of celebration: 'What's interesting about the world's first branded town is that there are no brands there ... Disney says that this is because they built Celebration as a monument to the ideal of public space. That may be true but when you have finally reached your absolute brand nirvana where you actually have people living there full-time, the first thing you want to do is slam the door behind you and make sure that there aren't any competing messages that are interrupting this perfect synergized, cross-promoted marketing moment.'[49] We witness the end of privatization within a fully privatized world, the end of branding within the fully branded world, the end of signs within the city of the sign. 'Celebration is not even a sales vehicle for Mickey Mouse licensed products; it is an almost Disney-free town – no doubt the only one left in America. In other words, when Disney finally reached its fully enclosed, synergized, self-sufficient space, it chose to create a pre-Disneyfied world – its calm, understated aesthetic are the antithesis of the cartoon world for sale down the freeway at Disney World.'[50] What characterizes Celebration is its protection and promotion of public space. 'What is most striking about Celebration, however, particularly when compared with most North American suburban communities, is the amount of public space it offers – parks, communal buildings and village squares. In a way, Disney's branding breakthrough is a celebration of brandlessness, of the very public spaces the company has always been so adept at getting its brands on in the rest of its endeavors.'[51] Yet Celebration itself is an ad for Disney, and the ultimate aim of branding is not to market a product but to create a fully self-enclosed branded world that we inhabit. The new mantra of marketing is no longer to simply produce advertising but to commercialize reality itself, not to sponsor culture, but to *be* the culture. This totally branded world is no longer what Arendt would call a dwelling place, because the whole town is itself private. We have moved into the city of the sign.

A response to Disney emerges, an anti-Disney movement. The tourism board for the Canadian province of Newfoundland and Labrador proclaims that a vacation there is 'about as far from Disneyland as you can possibly get.'[52] Such ad campaigns reveal a desperate desire to experience the physical tangibility of what is hidden or obscured in our sign-saturated society. Such increasingly frantic attempts arise to regain something before and beyond the sign demonstrate the growing desperation with which we seek to find an alternative to simulated life. But for Baudrillard these attempts are ineffective; resistance proves impossible because the subject as a consuming spectacle itself is thoroughly caught up and penetrated by the signs of consumption that any liberating activity becomes complicit in the reproduction of its opposite.

Baudrillard extends his account of the hyperreal and simulation beyond Disneyland to the 'real' city of Las Vegas – one of the fastest growing cities and most popular tourist destinations in America. The atmosphere of a Las Vegas casino is intended to promote a sense of fantasy and unreality in which everything is a simulation. It is very much in the interest of the casino owners to create an environment of fantasy and simulation in the hopes that it will evoke a sense of unreality, which more readily inclines people to give up their very real money. Yet in the casino-as-polis, it is very real money that is lost.[53] When completely surrounded by signs, we lose 'sight' of what is not a sign – yet we are invariably affected by loss. It could be argued that the function of the casino is to convey the impression that the rest of society – and the economy – is itself not already a casino.

The Meta-Brand of Capital: Legitimizing Capitalist Meta-Narratives

We have moved from a society of the commodity to a hyperreal society of the simulacrum. In the hyper-polis, the public, a nation, the corporation, and even capitalism itself become signs.

The description of Dundas Square in the last chapter revealed the imperative to turn the public into a commodity required to generate income. Baudrillard describes an even more advanced stage when the public becomes a sign. But the semiotic imperative of consumerism doesn't stop there: a new British company called Placebrand performs this branding service, claiming it will ensure effective branding so as to encourage maximum 'on-brand behaviour' because otherwise people 'will quickly become confused about what the place brand stands for.'[54] A new field of marketing has emerged called 'nation branding' that specializes in developing marketable brand images for countries, turning a nation into a sign.[55]

Even the stock market itself becomes a sign as they compete with each other's signs. Witness the 'sign wars' between the two New York–based stock markets as each competed to better represent the global market for capital: The 'NYSE and NASDAQ waged a brand sign war against each other ... each competing to link itself to the imagery of technology and global markets. Each sought to represent itself as an animated spirit (Geist) that forms the center of global capitalism ... NASDAQ not only branded itself as the core of a global capitalist economy, but as capital itself.'[56]

Eventually capitalism itself becomes a sign, a 'meta-brand' whose aim is to represent itself. While the aim of specific advertisements is to distinguish products from each other, important legitimizing functions of branding become apparent when advertising is viewed as a whole. Goldman and Papson argue in their brilliant article 'Capital's Brandscapes' that 'in the overall branding landscape, the semiotics of branding bleeds into fuzzy capitalist metanarratives ... Taken as a whole, corporate brands construct grand narratives that ascribe a teleological direction to globalization and high technology.'[57] This meta-narrative of the meta-brand permits capital to represent itself, to legitimate and promote capitalist narratives of progress into overarching meta-narratives of commercial utopianism: 'The sum of all corporate branding campaigns yields a metabrand that stands for capital formations associated with globalization, innovative technologies and flexible accumulation ... A metanarrative of capital emerges out of the interplay of hundreds, or thousands, of branding campaigns. Though most branding actively seeks to differentiate one firm from its competition, the cumulative "brand" of capital displays a remarkable consistency of visual signifiers, narrative formulae, and ideological themes.'[58]

In its last moments, even the subject itself becomes a consuming spectacle, displayed as a sign of consumption. The consuming subject is caught up in this global meta-brand, in the great act of self-branding as 'Me, Inc.' A Fast Company article titled 'The Brand Called You' announces, 'It's time for me – and you – to take a lesson from the big brands, a lesson that's true for anyone who's interested in what it takes to stand out and prosper in the new world of work … our most important job is to be head marketer for the brand called You.'[59] The 'possessive individual' of C.B. Macpherson has arrived.

Advertising Consumerism and Raiding Referent Systems

Marketer and president of 'Youthography' Max Valiquette claims, 'Advertising pays for most of the culture we consume.'[60] This claim confuses the forces at work because it implies that advertising is a form of public service without which we would have no culture. Yet culture has certainly been around much longer than advertising! Perhaps it could instead be said that what advertising pays for is a particular kind of culture: consumer culture. Or perhaps that advertising consumes pre- or non-consumer cultures.

Marshall McLuhan once said that 'all advertising advertises advertising.'[61] But it may be closer to the truth to say that what advertising advertises is not a specific product but rather the values of a life centred upon consumption. Advertising advertises consumerism.

Cultural theorists Goldman and Papson go even further by arguing that advertising also consumes cultural meaning, because it 'raids referent systems.'[62] They describe how marketing and advertising appropriate – even steal – cultural values and symbols and then 'capitalize' on them for commercial purposes such that the original cultural meaning is commercialized and consumed. They argue that the 'continuous raiding of cultural meanings for the purpose of generating commodity sign values [and] carving up systems of meaning to fit the semiotic requirements of branding'[63] results in a hollowing out of meaning. There are significant cultural 'costs' incurred when symbols of cultural meaning are appropriated and altered for commercial purposes. 'What most brand practitioners and brand managers seem to ignore is that their acts of cultural appropriation entail costs, that the act of borrowing "brand equity" from cultural formations does have consequences.'[64] These costs are profound: the erosion of value and meaning, the emergence of what Baudrillard calls a 'fractal' stage of value: 'The frenzied pursuit of all things branded contributes to a "fractal" stage of value where nothing has value because every surface has been loaded with value claims.'[65] Barber argues in *Jihad vs McWorld* that this 'fractal stage' of consumerism brings about radical backlashes: 'The same conditions of semiotic weightlessness breed fundamentalist political backlashes as people once again search for the security and moral certitude of fixed meaning that will see them through an epoch of bewildering changes' (JM, 351).

The Code Is Totalitarian: The Impossibility of Resistance

Marketers help deepen our attachment to commodities, reinforce the notion that happiness and a positive self-image come from acquisition, and ensure that we associate products only with the symbolic meaning that marketers create. In doing so, they create a culture of consumers at the same time that the possibilities of any alternatives are made invisible, in addition to questioning what is represented in advertising we must ask where the non-commercial narratives have gone.

The central question Baudrillard leaves us with is what kind of world and subjectivity consumerism produces. Baudrillard reveals that our habits of consumption are not merely 'preference communication' but in fact contribute to our own subjugation. A fundamental feature of consumerism is the inseparability of advances in technologies of domination, because the development of consumer subjectivity entails the subjugation of that same subject. 'For this is the price of making objects appear: the disappearance of the subject.'[66] What is perhaps most disturbing is his description of the capacity for consumer society to incorporate and negate any form of political resistance. This is because technologies of social repression become ever more sophisticated and effective as new forms of resistance arise. Thus emerges the totalizing image of compliance through consumption, a society without opposition. Just as nature is subdued and material progress advances, consumerism functions as a technology of control. Michel Foucault's emphasis on productive power has been supplanted by the seductive power of signs and 'voluntary servitude.' While panoptic institutions train people in regimented and monotonous behaviour, consumerism seduces through the fascinating movements of dazzling images. As philosopher of education Kenneth Wain observes, 'Foucault's disciplined subject is Baudrillard's mediatized terminal.'[67]

For Baudrillard, not only are we never satiated and always frustrated, there is little possibility of resistance, for 'the collective function of advertising is to convert us all to the code ... The code is totalitarian; no one escapes it: our individual flights do not negate the fact that each day we participate in its collective elaboration.'[68] The code comes to dominate us by 'imposing a coherent and collective vision, like an almost inseparable totality. Like a chain that connects not ordinary objects but *signifieds*, each object can signify the other in a more complex super-object, and lead the consumer to a series of more complex choices' (CS, 34). Consumers essentially 'buy' into the code of consumption so completely that they lose the capacity for critical reflection. Rather than allowing dissent, they in fact maintain order because the code, 'simultaneously arbitrary and coherent, is the best vehicle for social order, equally arbitrary and coherent, to materialize itself effectively under the sign of affluence' (SO, 20). In Baudrillard's words, our contribution to the elaboration of the code is a form of 'organized regression':

> One could argue that nothing more is involved than an infantile disorder of the technological society, and attribute such growing pains entirely to the dysfunctionality of our present social structures – i.e. to the capitalist order of production. The long-term prospect of a transcendence of the whole system would thus remain open. On the other hand, if something more is involved than the anarchic ends of a productive system determined by social exploitation, if deeper conflicts in fact play a part – highly individual conflicts, but extended onto the collective plane – then any prospect of ultimate transcendence must be abandoned forever. Are we contemplating the developmental problems of a society ultimately destined to become the best of all possible worlds, or, alternately, an organized regression in the face of insoluble problems? … What, in short has made a civilization go wrong in this way? The question is still open. (SO, 133)

Baudrillard shows that even as the sign becomes animated and humanized, the subject becomes dehumanized and rendered impotent. Because personal identity is now in flux and decreasingly bound by rigid traditions and permanent constellations of meaning, consumption might seem to provide the opportunity for the cultivation of personal identity and a coherent sense of self. But Baudrillard also argues that such attempts at cultivation invariably contribute to ever-greater 'integration': 'Choosing one car over another may perhaps personalize your choice, but the most important thing about the fact of choosing is that it assigns you a place in the overall economic order … "personalization" … is actually a basic ideological concept of a society which "personalizes" objects and beliefs solely in order to integrate persons more effectively … Personalization and integration go strictly hand in hand. *That is the miracle of the system*' (SO, 141, 144).

Through consumption we attempt to differentiate ourselves from others and assert our identity, to mark ourselves as different and insert ourselves into the world of human relations, and thereby experience ourselves as part of a larger political whole. Arendt and Baudrillard reveal how both aims are illusory. Consumerism promotes the tendency to endow objects with cultural features to such an extent that we are surrounded by the signs of consumption. Yet Arendt and Baudrillard reveal that when politics is dominated by the images and signs of consumption, our public realm and reality are eclipsed. This is precisely why questions of agency and resistance are so problematic after Baudrillard. Indeed, these questions link with many larger questions Baudrillard poses for the consumption of virtuality, artificialization, and the post-human. But perhaps through this process we will find what it is to be human. In his inimitable style Baudrillard puts it this way: 'Perhaps we may see this as a kind of adventure, a heroic test: to take the artificialization of living beings as far as possible in order to see, finally, what part of human nature survives the greatest ordeal. If we discover that not everything can be cloned, simulated, programmed, genetically and neurologically managed, then whatever survives could be truly called "human": some inalienable and indestructible human quality could finally be identified. Of course, there is always the risk, in this experimental adventure, that nothing will pass the test – that the human will be permanently eradicated.'[69] The road that led Baudrillard to this insight, one not so far from Arendt's more fearful moments, began with the analysis of consumer society.

Unconsummated History: Deferring the End

Baudrillard's semiotic analysis of consumerism is only part of his social analysis. It is his starting point and eventually leads him to larger reflections on meaning and history towards the end of his career. Baudrillard argues that, contrary to many predictions, we have not reached the end of history. Hegel once advanced this notion in his account of history as a series of dialectical resolutions of subject and object, thesis and antithesis. Marx applied this 'idealist dialectic' to the material conditions of political economy and class consciousness, asserting that a revolution would resolve class contradictions and establish a final regime. More recently and quite differently, Francis Fukuyama celebrated liberal democracy and capitalism as the final regime at the 'end of history.'[70]

While some detractors criticized this argument for suggesting historical closure, Baudrillard suggests instead that the experience of speed and acceleration has thrown us free of conventional categories of reality and historical meaning such that 'we have passed that limit where, by dint of the sophistication of events and information, history ceases to exist as such.'[71] Kenneth Wain explores Baudrillard's account of 'hypertelia,' a fantastic situation in which things go beyond themselves and destroy their own objective and identity: '"Hypertelia" is Baudrillard's metaphor for a postmodern society that has advanced the modernist project to the stage *beyond* the completion of its own internal logic of a technologized universe into a transpolitical, destructured, and dehistoricized universe emptied of event and rendered transparent and obscene by a glut of information.'[72] The experience of this 'beyond' leads us to witness not the end of history but its total denial and erasure: the disappearance of history into the immediacy of all happenings. Careening out of control in cyclical self-replication, consumer society implodes under the weight of its own intensification and acceleration. We cannot even speak of an 'end of history' because of its erasure and short circuit into an instant: 'No end is conceivable, not even the end of history.'[73] Acceleration becomes so overwhelming that it enables the realization of an 'escape velocity' sufficient to escape history, the 'vanishing point' of 'man' in which fulfillment becomes disappearance rather than completion. The hyper-polis has made incoherent and short-circuited metanarratives into a single instant, for if we have left reality, we have left history behind too: 'We are leaving history to move into the realm of simulation.'[74]

But this is not the end of Baudrillard's argument: history has not only disappeared but turned back on itself and become infinite, leaving no place for eschatology or apocalypticism. The moment of historical consummation never arrives; its completion is always deferred. Much as it is for the modern consumer, satiation and salvation are always anticipated. Consumption is always unconsummated and we mourn what is incomplete yet cannot come to pass, and we are left in the interminable condition of melancholia: 'We have to get used to the idea that *there will no longer be any end*, that history itself has become interminable.'[75] In contrast to Habermas's notion of an 'unfinished project of modernity,'[76] Baudrillard suggests that modernity has in fact surpassed itself, has 'turned inwards, imploded onto itself.' We are no longer 'a protagonist of history.'[77]

Voluntary Servitude: Abandoning the Subject

Baudrillard shows that our pathological preoccupation with the commodity and the release of our extractive powers and appropriative endeavours entails the erosion of the public realm and eclipse of the real. Just as Arendt's account of the ascent of the *oikos* and agora to a place of political dominance entailed the loss of reality and worldly alienation, so too in Baudrillard does the proliferation of signs and the transformation of the sign into a commodity entail the loss of reality. However, in contrast to Baudrillard's account of the all-encompassing character of consumer society, able to absorb any form of resistance, Arendt reveals the possibilities that action and speech can provide. In spite of the political dominance of the *oikos* and agora, she holds that action remains within our grasp: 'Needless to say, this does not mean that modern man has lost his capacities or is on the point of losing them ... the capacity for action ... is still with us' (HC, 323).

Furthermore, Arendt links action with natality, arguing that the 'new beginning inherent in birth can make itself felt in the world only because the newcomer possesses the capacity for beginning something anew, that is, of acting' (HC, 9). It is through action and speech that we bring newness into the world and express the human capacity to begin. Arendt's account of natality points towards the resilience of the constant source of the new through which the world is preserved from decay and decline. If this unending wellspring of beginnings is eroded and absorbed into the endless cycle of production and consumption through the signs of consumption, it is our polis – even reality itself – that we stand to lose. There are many points of intersection between Arendt and Baudrillard on the question of consumer society, but it is here on the matter of agency they diverge and where Baudrillard offers his most significant challenge to Arendt.

For Baudrillard, this is precisely what has changed since Arendt wrote *The Human Condition* in 1958. While he has been much criticized for his stance, Baudrillard radically challenges concepts such as agency and subjectivity, arguing that even as modernity opens new possibilities for the subject, there are ever greater pressures towards commodification and simulation. In his book on Baudrillard, Paul Hegarty notes that concepts such as *hyper simulation* and *illusion* are much more important to Baudrillard than *agency*, because the paradoxical side of Baudrillard's *agency* would provide a way out of simulation, which Baudrillard sees as all-encompassing. Baudrillard's position is that theory, which can exist only as a challenge to the real, cannot provide us with a firm critical position, but instead 'illusions, seductions, and paradoxes, even what we might call evil'[78] can do so. Baudrillard's problem with much theory is that it allows us to deceive ourselves with a sense of agency that consumer society does not permit. For Baudrillard, it is not a question of being for or against 'agency' but a need to address a deeper problem of how little space is left for enacting such a concept. Baudrillard's focus on symbolic exchange leads him to positions anathema to traditional critical theory, such as his understanding that the silence of the masses is an effective fatal strategy of resistance.[79]

Remarkably, Baudrillard encourages us to abandon the subject and side with the object, a 'fatal strategy' of surrendering to the object and submitting to the power of seduction, necessary because critique and resistance invariably tend to reproduce and bolster its opposition: a fatal strategy is to duplicate the 'profound duplicity' of the object; a 'voluntary servitude,' to 'bend willingly' to its purposes,' a 'siding with the object.'[80] The signs of consumption become endowed with agency and consumptive capacities, even as we lose our own, so only through complete immersion and 'strategic indifference'[81] can the sign be stopped. The aim is 'to bring about an excess of reality, and have the system collapse beneath that excess.'[82]

What Baudrillard shows is that signs of some type have always existed, that there is no experience that is unmediated by signs, and that we never exist before or beyond the sign. We are constituted by them even as we (de)sign them.

Baudrillard and the Pedagogical Turn: Schooling before the Sign

Baudrillard's radical questioning of signs, symbols, and simulation at the vanishing of history points towards the necessity to reconsider the role of contemporary educational practices as sites of resistance to the code. Is education invariably complicit in the 'murder of the real'? Earlier chapters highlighted how schools have begun to acquiesce to – rather than resist – these phenomena. Let us, then, directly consider schooling in relation to Baudrillard.

Baudrillard's discussion of such concepts as simulation, the hyperreal, and the proliferation of signs could be linked with a wide range of commercial activities in schools. The separation of the commodity from its sign could be described as a 'pedagogical turn' in advertising, which increasingly 'teaches' important lessons about the cultural and symbolic meanings of products. In a consumer society, the primary site for 'learning' is advertising, and the most valuable knowledge concerns signs and their meaning. As mentioned in chapter 2, the increases to spending on advertising are outpacing the increases in spending on schooling, as students demonstrate increasingly extraordinary commercial literacy.

Following Baudrillard, I argue that the colonization of education by advertising reduces schooling to a mere simulation of its educative potential. In essence, advertising copies and co-opts education and reduces it to an empty signifier when schools and schooling are used to endow consumerism with legitimacy. Many educational thinkers analyse schooling through a theory of reproduction, arguing that schools reproduce hegemonic social structures. This might match well with Baudrillard's idea of simulation as a copy of a copy. However, advertising construed as education changes the original, while presenting a facile facsimile of the educative experience. Echoing Naomi Klein's description of the town of Celebration, in its most extreme form the school itself becomes so thoroughly branded that a total enclosure within the brand is created.

Baudrillard's radical questioning of the character of signs, symbols, and simulation in our postmodern age points towards the necessity to reconsider education as a possible site of resistance to the code. The problem of school commercialism is currently being addressed by educators and concerned citizens in myriad ways, ranging from resistance campaigns and culture jamming (see Adbusters, Commercial Alert, the anti–Channel One campaign), to attempts to turn this debate into a learning opportunity where students are enabled to develop critical literacy in response to consumerism and discuss the implications of corporate influences on schooling. Where corporations are buying their way into schools, the need for critical discussion rather than a sponsored presence is required.

Conclusion

Consumerism has become the new real. What Baudrillard reveals is that consumption is not about buying or enjoying, needs or wants, fulfillment or affluence; it is a self-sustaining totalizing order of signification that obscures the real. Baudrillard's work demonstrates that we live and move and have our being in the realm of false things and artificial meanings yet continue to seek what lies behind the sign. He describes the increasing desperation with which we attempt to recapture the real or mourn its passing, even as this desperation parallels an apathetic and complacent acceptance of the prevalence of consumerism. Ironically, consumer dissatisfaction leads us to stronger beliefs in the promise of consumption and compels us to continue to participate in its endless cycle.

Baudrillard leaves us with this bleak picture, one increasingly nihilistic as he moved into the 1980s and 1990s. The originality and insightfulness of his critique of consumer society is tempered by his wariness about remedies or recommendations. Baudrillard's work is not a revolutionary call to arms (Marx), nor a practical, prudent, procedural way to realize a particular political order (Rawls). Instead he is a thinker whose contributions are more diagnostic and descriptive than directive or prescriptive. While it is not always appropriate to impose upon philosophy the demand that it be readily translatable into immediate practical relevance, nor that this is the most accurate measure of its value, I argue that education can function as a site for the critical engagement of these trends.

5 Resisting Consuming: Ruin or Renewal

Education is the point at which we decide whether we love the world enough to assume responsibility for it and by the same token save it from that ruin which, except for renewal, except for the coming of the new and young, would be inevitable.

– Hannah Arendt[1]

Should education reproduce a given social order or attempt to illuminate, critique, and alter it? Is education the acquisition of predetermined skills or a process of self-development and social transformation? In a consumer society, what often passes for education instead simply narrows horizons or undermines critical reflection. Teachers are often asked to compete with that other Great Educator, television, and become 'edutainers' or provide 'facts' and procedural ways of thinking that can be directly translated into relevant skills for commercial application. The critical and democratic aims of education are easily overlooked and forgotten as commercial inroads into schools invariably draw the next generation into the simulated discourse of consumption. Education is reduced to an empty signifier when schools are used to imbue products with legitimacy.

However, education need not acquiesce to these trends. As Arendt notes in the above quotation, education can help demonstrate our love for the world in the face of commercial forces. Children and their parents and teachers need a commercial-free refuge in which to develop the critical thinking skills required to participate fully within a democratic society. Without critical engagement, we're left vulnerable to an education system that omits a dialogue about consumer culture. My concern is that consumerism will narrow our political and pedagogical horizons by undermining the personally and politically transformative functions of education.

Consumption Promotion and Consumer Rights

While the previous chapter explored how Baudrillard fearfully suggested that consumerism displayed the capacity to integrate resistance and undermine political action, several key questions about consumerism remain limited to the 'consumer world view,' because they don't interrogate the ideological character of consumerism: Can consumption be ethical? Is it important that we become 'educated' consumers in order to shop more effectively? Is it important to increase consumer 'rights' and information? While consumer activism and the defence of consumer rights are certainly important – we all want to be sure that our food is safe and our brakes work – such approaches are limited in their ability to address the problematic consequences of consumerism. Many of these movements and organizations do not challenge the prevalence of consumerism but instead aim to ensure that the marketplace works efficiently to encourage consumption and satisfy consumers.

First, the manuals and handbooks of the business community and marketing experts are concerned with how to better meet consumer needs, more effectively reach a niche market, increase consumption, and better understand consumer behaviour and psychology.[2] Second, technical books for political economists, macroeconomists, policy-makers, and government economists consider how to enhance general consumer confidence, ease volatile fluctuations in consumer demand, ensure a stable governmental monetary policy, and prevent credit from disrupting national and international economic stability.[3] Third, many organizations intend to advance consumer rights and consumer empowerment. One of the better-known documents was a speech given by John F. Kennedy in 1962, his 'Special Message on Protecting the Consumer Interest,' in which he emphasized the important role for government in 'advancing consumer interests': 'The federal government – by nature the highest spokesman for all the people – has a special obligation to be alert to the consumer's needs and to advance the consumer's interests.'[4] In Ontario, the Consumer Protection branch of the Ministry of Government Services claims that 'smart consumers are good for business.'[5]

However, what's 'good for business' or 'improving the marketplace' is not equivalent to addressing the deeper implications of consumerism. Critical work on consumerism began to reach a popular audience in America through such figures as Ralph Nader and the 'consumer movement' of the 1960s. This movement focused on such issues as how to secure better deals and improve consumer 'safety, information, choice, and political representation.'[6] These reforms consider ways to better protect the health, safety, and legal rights of consumers, to demand consumer representation in price setting and economic decision-making, and to advocate for lower and fairer prices.

Much of the work on consumerism by these national and international, governmental and non-governmental organizations adopts the perspective of the individual consumer, consistent with the liberal emphasis on the importance of freedom, choice, rights, and fairness for the individual. For example, the literature written from the perspective of consumer 'empowerment' achieved through greater choice claims, 'In a democratic consumer society within a market economy, the consumer is king.'[7] The National Consumer League, America's oldest consumer advocacy group, asserts, 'To live means to buy, to buy means to have power, to have power means to have responsibility.'[8] Others ask such questions as 'Are consumers really in a position to decide which product or service to buy and how much to pay for it? Are we all, as consumers getting a fair deal?'[9]

While these movements and organizations may have important roles, they often facilitate the spread of consumerism rather than promote a critical engagement with it. It is problematic to suggest that buying brings power or that our identity as consumers determines our identity as such. These assumptions ultimately detract from a more sustained consideration of the nature of consumption and its problematic political and pedagogical implications, because they don't account for consumerism as an ideology. What happens when consumerism becomes a world view, a way of being in the world and relating to others, and a way of engaging in politics and pedagogy?

The Consumer Solution

Canadian philosophers and cultural theorists Joe Heath and Andrew Potter argue that there is in fact no need to resist consumerism: 'There never was any tension between the *values* of the counterculture and the functional requirements of the capitalist economic system,' because 'there *is* no such thing as "the culture" or "the system."'[10]

Heath and Potter criticize the argument that consumer society can assimilate resistance and create new forms of social control, by claiming that critical engagement is both ineffective and unnecessary, since the enormous success with which the market provides commodities demonstrates its merits. The critique of consumerism is invalid, because those who are critical of consumerism have consumer choices: 'The market obviously does an extremely good job at responding to consumer demand for anti-consumerist products and literature ... the critique of mass society has been one of the most powerful forces driving consumerism for more than forty years.'[11] Yet simply because it is possible to buy *Das Kapital* at Amazon.com or Che T-shirts at Walmart doesn't mean we needn't worry about consumerism.

Rather than express concern about the capacity of consumerism to incorporate resistance, Heath and Potter dismiss rebellion for its inability to sustain itself against consumerism, asking, 'If consumerism is so bad for us, why do we keep doing it?'[12] Yet simply because consumer culture has become even more pervasive does not mean that opposition is futile or unnecessary, but instead demonstrates the frightening and insidious capacity of consumerism to reincorporate alternative modes of resistance. That some protesters wore Nikes while protesting in Seattle is held up as evidence of the impotence of resistance. However, the use of similar strategies when criticizing one's opponent does not necessarily invalidate the critique. The use of a computer to write a critical essay about the social effects of modern technology, or of email to write critically about the effect of the Internet on society, or the burning of fossil fuels while researching or promoting environmental issues, does not demonstrate that there is no danger.

Similarly, business ethicists Guido Palazzo and Kunal Basu describe consumerism as a solution to rapid social change and resulting identity confusion and fragmentation. According to these ethicists, consumerism promotes trust and satisfies 'identity needs' by providing meaningful orientation in an often overwhelming world: 'Consumption decisions and the result of consumption have become significant contributors to redefining identity at a time of accelerated social change that emphasizes a rising individualization. Of particular relevance to our discussions is the proffered role of consumption in creating meaning.'[13] They assert that consumerism can in fact help reduce the challenge presented by change by satisfying 'growing identity needs.'

Yet Pallazzo and Basu don't notice that it is often the effect of consumerism itself that creates these 'identity needs' in the first place. They argue that the prevalence of commercial messages makes it even more pressing for marketers to devise increasingly effective ways to advertise by 'attracting their relevant audiences like a beacon in a fog,'[14] as if we're otherwise lost at sea. Many marketers claim that it is their task to simply meet our 'identity needs' in the context of identity fragmentation, destabilization, and disorientation, and serve society by helping consumers find meaning. 'Value-based corporate branding provides strong support to consumers' identity projects, serving "to structure our experiences" at a time of societal transformation. It successfully addresses the growing desire for orientation. [As] a generator of values and meaning, a sophisticated brand narrative helps to reconstruct identities damaged by social change.'[15]

We can recall that in the last chapter Baudrillard anticipated that resistance against consumerism would readily be reincorporated into the system. While for Baudrillard the reincorporation of resistance against consumerism revealed its totalitarian character, these approaches suggest it demonstrates that there is nothing wrong with consumerism, because it can gratify the demands of any market – even those resisting consumerism itself.

Consumer Choice or the Choice for a Better World?

Consumerism is often portrayed by the marketing industry as a way to improve our collective rights, because we become freer when presented with more choices. However, while we may have countless choices in our lives, there are many choices that we simply aren't offered. For example, globalization theorist Manfred Steger notes that the amount spent by the fast food industry on television advertising per year is $3 billion, while the amount spent promoting the National Cancer Institute's 5 A Day program encouraging the consumption of fruits and vegetables to prevent cancer and other diseases is three thousand times less, or $1 million. In 2001, the number of new models of cars available to suburban residents in the United States was 197, while the number of convenient alternatives to the car made available to most such residents was zero. In 2000, the number of U.S. daily newspapers was 1,483, while the number of companies that controlled the majority of those same newspapers was six.[16]

What's most unfortunate about this censorship is that the dominant mode of communication communicates only one message: to consume. As part of their Media Carta campaign, the Canadian group Adbusters has been trying for years to air their 'uncommercials,' or 'anti-ads,' which discourage shopping and over-consumption.[17] With the exception of CNN, television networks have declined airing these 'anti-ads.' Representatives from a variety of television stations explained that it 'wouldn't be in our best interests ... We would not want to abuse [advertising] or say anything derogatory' (CTV), and claimed they were 'not accepting commercials that discuss controversial issues ... We sell time for many many different things. But not controversial issues of public importance' (ABC), and perhaps most bluntly, 'I think it would be confusing to viewers.'[18] While it's true that we can individually choose to shop and consume less, we can't choose to live in a society with less consumerism. The choice to choose less is simply not on the radar of marketers, because there is little money to be made from such messages. Benjamin Barber points out the irony of consumerism when the consumer is 'permitted to choose from a menu of options offered by the world but not to alter or improve the menu or the world' (CN, 36).

Furthermore, the choices of others affect us each quite significantly, and the choices of a few people have wide-reaching effects around the world. Barber notes that there are significant public consequences of private choice – often choices that we would not agree to individually: 'Privatization turns the private, impulsive me lurking inside myself into an inadvertent enemy of the public, deliberative we that also is part of who I am. The private me screams "I want!" The privatization perspective legitimizes this scream, allowing it to trump the quiet "we need" that is the voice of the public me in which I participate and which is also an aspect of my interests as a human being. All the choices we make one by one thereby come to determine the social outcomes we must suffer together, but which we never directly choose in common.'[19] For those who don't participate in the dominant type of choices available, only a few options remain. Yet those options become less and less viable, sometimes even unsafe. For example, urban bicycle commuting becomes more and more dangerous as the number of cars – and the number of extremely large cars – increases, and cyclists must breathe the air polluted by those same cars around them.

While consumers may have rights, perhaps we also have a right to live in a less consumer-oriented society. Tremendous financial resources are invested into market research to better understand the desires, interests, and ideals of today's youth. While it is argued that this allows researchers to determine what choices young people will make, the true goal of market research is to determine which choices will bring the most profit. For example, if students choose to have less bullying in their school, they are less likely to be offered such a choice than if they wish to purchase sneakers associated with a celebrity whom they admire. While it is the job of marketers to research and present choices that will be financially profitable, it is in the interest of educators and parents to create choices for today's youth beyond the limited paradigm of commodities. This is why it is notable that marketers refer to youth as a 'market,' while teachers refer to them as 'students.'

Henry Giroux notes that as a result of consumerism 'the citizens' right to interfere in shaping the forces that govern his or her life is replaced by the individuals' liberty from interference.'[20] The myriad consumer choices that speak to the private self come disguised as liberating and democratic expressions of identity and independence, yet at the same time these choices often undermine legitimate democratic structures (such as schools) designed to serve the public by acknowledging our interdependence and interconnectedness. The latest development in video game technology from Nintendo is called 'Wii,' pronounced 'we.' Its ads show people of different ages and races bonding though gaming, as if Playstation were the UN of consumer cultures. Yet the 'we' in Wii is two separate and individual I's.

The discourse of choice is apparent in liberal political theory and classical political economy in which consumerism is construed as expressive – that is, how we express our identities through personal product choices and ways of life. These choices are rationally determined as a way to communicate a subjectivity that exists prior to consumption. However, it is more accurate to say that consumerism itself is a kind of production, because through our consumer choices we not only *express* ourselves but *produce* ourselves and our world. The expansion of choice is often simply an illusion, because more consumer choice doesn't reduce our problematic relationship with and attachment to commodities or contribute to the renewal of the public realm, but only offers particular types of choices.

Action and Natality: Schooling against 'the Social'

Arendt's account of natality, 'the faculty of interrupting [ruin] and beginning something new' (HC, 246), helps emphasize both the importance of education and the possibilities of critical engagement with consumerism in the classroom. The earlier discussion of Baudrillard ended with a consideration of the possibility of resisting consumer society, suggesting a fundamental difference between Arendt and Baudrillard. Just as Arendt's account of the ascent of the *oikos* and agora to a place of political dominance entailed the loss of reality and worldly alienation, so too in Baudrillard does the proliferation of signs entail the loss of reality. However, in contrast to Baudrillard's totalitarian character of consumer society, Arendt emphasizes the political possibilities that action and speech can provide: 'Needless to say, this does not mean that modern man has lost his capacities or is on the point of losing them … the capacity for action … is still with us' (HC, 323). Arendt takes this position because she links action with natality, the capacity to begin: 'Action has the closest connection with the human condition of natality; new beginning inherent in birth [which] can make itself felt in the world only because the newcomer possesses the capacity for beginning something anew, that is, of acting' (HC, 9).

It is through natality that we may address certain problems associated with the primacy of 'the social' by bringing newness into the world and interrupting the ruin that would otherwise overtake the public realm. This dynamic capacity is possessed by all newcomers to the world, as it is inherited by birth. Natality is the ability to initiate and set into motion something with 'startling unexpectedness,' because each unique human being is able to interrupt 'the inexorable automatic course of daily life' (HC, 246). This capacity to interrupt is of fundamental importance to preserving the public world from ruin: 'The miracle that saves the world, the realm of human affairs, from its normal, "natural" ruin is ultimately the fact of natality, in which the faculty of action is ontologically rooted. It is, in other words, the birth of new men and the new beginning, the action they are capable of by virtue of being born' (HC, 247).

Political philosopher Seyla Benhabib notes that natality has political implications, because it brings us into contact with others and the political world around us: '*Natality* is the condition through which we immerse ourselves into the world, at first through the good will and solidarity of those who nurture us and subsequently through our own deeds and words.'[21] Arendt argues that while this immersion into the political world is like a second birth, it is unlike work and labour, because it is not forced by necessity: 'Its impulse springs from the beginning which came into the world when we were born and to which we respond by beginning something new on our own initiative.'[22] We begin because we come new into the world. Indeed, we bring beginning itself into the world.

It is her emphasis on natality and openness to new things that makes Arendt more than merely nostalgic for the ancient Greek polis and motivates her passion for modern revolutionary politics. Revolutions, in her view, bear striking similarities to natality insofar as they are generated by the spontaneous efforts of political actors bound neither to the repetitiveness of *Animal laborans* nor the instrumentality of *Homo faber.* Arendt scholar Jerome Kohn argues that 'what for Arendt is perhaps most exemplary about the Greeks, and at the same time has the greatest relevance for the present, is that it was not just the memory of past actions but the possibility of new deeds, the novelty latent in newcomers, that made the laws that bound and secured the *polis.*'[23] By contributing to the renewal of the public realm, the introduction of the new ensures that politics does not succumb to either routinized processes or images of the artifice. Political philosopher George Kateb argues, 'Politics is all the more authentic when it is eruptive rather than when it is a regular and already institutionalized practice ... The reason is that eruptive politics is more clearly a politics of beginning and hence a manifestation of the peculiar human capacity to be free or spontaneous, to start something new and unexpected, to break with seemingly automatic or fated processes or continuities; in a word, to be creative. It is a burst of unfrightened, superabundant energy.'[24] In the same vein as Kateb's 'eruptive politics,' Arendt's account of natality points towards the resilience of the human spirit: the young are a constant source of the new, a 'miracle' through which the world is renewed, that rare burst of energy through which the world is preserved against decline and ruin. It is for this reason that education is so important.

Natality is a central theme of Arendt's essay 'The Crisis in Education,' in which she argues that natality is 'the essence of education,'[25] because it is among the 'most elementary and necessary activities of human society, which never remains as it is but continuously renews itself through birth, through the arrival of new human beings.'[26] Arendt's account of natality emphasizes the resilience of the human spirit as manifested in the young, a constant source of the new. If this wellspring of beginnings is eroded and absorbed into the endless cycle of consumption through the dominance of commercial discourse, it is our polis – and reality itself – that we stand to lose. There are indeed significant threats to the notion of natality in modern consumer society. We can recall Vandana Shiva's discussion of 'terminator technology' and the creation of a market of new consumers by manufacturing seeds that cannot reproduce and must be purchased anew each year. Shiva calls this 'the death of birth,'[27] a technology that is also a metaphor for the fate of newness in a consumer society.

It is possible to contrast Arendt's notion of natality with the obsession of consumer culture with novelty and designed obsolescence. Among a variety of monikers used to describe today's youth, ranging from Gen Y to Global Gen, Pepsi's marketing team once dubbed society's newest consumers as 'Generation Next.' Pepsi's notion of 'next' is strikingly different from the Arendtian notion of natality, because it is inextricably entwined with designed obsolescence, whereas natality is a form of renewal rooted in political life. Ironically, it is often our misguided evolutionary desire for the newness of natality that fuels our disposable culture of consumption.

Because the young bring new beginnings into the world, it is imperative they be sheltered from commercial forces, or this wellspring of beginnings will be fully drawn into consumerism. Natasha Levinson writes that because 'all newcomers bring with them the possibility that the world might be reinvigorated, natality is a source of social hope.'[28] It is through our capacity to create new things that we interrupt what would otherwise be inevitable or inexorable historical processes, and instead become actively engaged in political change. Levinson continues, 'Natality signals our transformation from being passive vectors of social processes to becoming social actors – which is to say, potential deflectors of these forces. Natality is manifest in the world whenever individuals and groups act in relation to the world in ways that suggest that seemingly intransigent social processes can be changed.'[29] If this wellspring of beginnings is eroded and absorbed into the endless cycle of consumption through the dominance of commercial discourse, it is our polis, and reality itself, that we stand to lose. It is the very newness of youth that is a resource harvested and threatened by commercial culture: harvested through market research, cool hunting, and consumer profiling, and threatened by school commercialism.

Arendt's work reveals that we can fall short in our responsibility for preserving the space of appearance when education becomes complicit in the erosion of a vibrant and robust public realm. In drawing from Arendt, I advocate not only the importance that education be funded *by* the public (the 'public sector'), but that education be *for* the public and public renewal, as described by Benjamin Barber: 'Education not only speaks to the public, it is the means by which a public is forged.'[30] Arendt emphasizes the conserving function of education to protect 'the child against the world,' by preserving its newness: 'Our hope always hangs on the new which every generation brings ... exactly for the sake of what is new and revolutionary in every child, education must be conservative; it must preserve this newness.'[31] Maxine Greene too shares this concern and asks, 'How can we educate for freedom? And, in educating for freedom, how can we create and maintain a common world?'[32]

Policy Improvements and Regulatory Practices

There are several impediments to addressing school commercialism. First, because the commercialization of education is relatively new, educational researcher Tamar Lewin notes that 'education officials say it is hard to know how to proceed.'[33] Second, Alex Molnar notes that the 'ubiquity of marketing helps frame attempts to question the status quo of schoolhouse commercialism as odd or quixotic.'[34] Commercialism is legitimized and normalized simply because it already so pervasive. Third, resistance against school commercialism is up against some well-funded organizations that provide substantial corporate money to sponsor research that will promote school–business partnerships. For example, Coca-Cola has founded the Council for Corporate and School Partnerships, which provides a 'How-To Guide for School–Business Partnerships,' and 'Guiding Principles for School Business Partnerships.' The guides are 'designed to help educators face the challenges' presented by 'competing points of view regarding commercialism in schools.'[35] These reports also have the support of university deans, PTA directors, health and education experts, and directors of many national educational organizations.[36]

However, successful attempts to address school commercialism at the level of public policy and school reform have occurred in some districts. For example, in 2004 the minister of education in Ontario announced that 'the province is banning junk foods from the machines in K–8 schools. The goal is to promote healthy choices and help battle childhood obesity.'[37] In 2005 California passed legislation banning the sale of junk food in high schools.[38] In December 2007 the province of Ontario announced that it would ban trans fats from school cafeterias.[39] While these mixed improvements in policy and regulations are important steps toward helping restrict the influence of consumerism on schools, their effect is quite limited. The Toronto District School Board provides some policy guidelines for advertising and sponsorship arrangements, but they are vague and often loosely enforced.[40] Cola companies easily find ways around such regulations, and many soft drink makers now sell sugary juices and 'sports drinks' instead of cola. The soft drink industry lobby group Refreshments Canada openly confirms that the decision to replace pop with juices and other drinks 'shouldn't affect how the companies work with the school boards ... there will still be revenue generated by school–business partnerships.'[41] Pepsi promotes Gatorade as 'good for you' because it claims to contain 40 per cent less sugar than most colas – yet Gatorade is sold in 600 ml containers – almost twice the amount found in the average 330 ml can! These drinks are marketed as 'sports drinks' and claim to maintain 'electrolyte balance,' yet most health professionals argue that 'the average student has no need for the "electrolytes" in Gatorade.'[42] Another example was a requirement of cola vendors that 'all vending machines be non-branded.'[43] Pepsi circumvented this requirement by dramatically increasing the size of the buttons used for product selection.

Many businesses restrict access to their contracts with schools through anti-disparagement clauses, an evasive strategy protecting information about the contracts out of concern that such details could be used in ways the company may not approve. Many companies threatened to revoke contracts and demand compensation by arguing that 'releasing the terms of the deals would put them at a competitive disadvantage in the marketplace.'[44] There are rare success stories, such as when a high school student fought and won a legal battle with the Ontario public schools, forcing Pepsi and Coke to reveal the details of their exclusive contracts with school boards. Yet in one startling case, attempts by three Toronto teachers to resist corporate incursions into schools by starting a group called People against Commercial Television in Schools were undermined by legal action taken by the Youth News Network to silence their opposition by suing the teachers for $900,000.[45] Support was not forthcoming from the school or the board, though the Ontario Secondary School Teachers' Federation stepped forward to cover their legal expenses.[46] Perhaps most dangerous for education, this case discourages opposition and critical dialogue, one of the main aims of education: 'The silence that the defamation suit has enforced teaches kids, by example, that getting involved, speaking out and expressing dissent will only lead to trouble. That's far more dangerous than making kids watch commercials in class.'[47]

This point leads into the final and perhaps most important limitation of regulations. Many of them convey the impression that school commercialism is only about health and diet rather than the larger questions of democracy and the public realm and the struggle over symbolic meaning – abstract notions often too difficult to convey in palatable sound bytes. Without directly questioning consumerism in schools, 'the overall legitimacy of marketing in schools remains largely unchallenged.'[48] Many thinkers discussed in this work emphasize the political importance of schools. Drawing from Michael Apple and critical pedagogy, Melissa Lickteig argues,

> To deny the power of corporate curriculum materials is a naïve blindness of the extent to which minds are influenced. Such materials intentionally provide levers to deconstruct the interconnections of economy, politics, and culture. They simultaneously depict representations of what powerful groups have defined as legitimate knowledge (Apple 1996). Those in positions of power attempt to define knowledge, how accessible it becomes, and the social relationships between the providers of knowledge and the consumers of knowledge (Apple 1990). As corporations supply increasing amounts of curriculum materials, their power to influence societal knowledge, values, and positions escalates. Through these tactics, corporations are escalating a hidden curriculum, which deserves scrutiny.[49]

While regulations and policy are a helpful first step in addressing consumerism and school commercialism, it is important to move beyond the incursions made by specific companies or the prevalence of particular products and examine the larger implications of commercial trends. It is necessary to go beyond regulations and policy in order to allow for direct engagement with pedagogical and political issues. In fact, schools may be sites where consumerism can be resisted, because advertising and marketing provide important 'teachable moments.'

Media Literacy and Culture Jamming

As mentioned above, one strategy to address these trends is through both adequate funding and appropriate policies and regulations regarding school–business partnerships. However, Alex Molnar is critical of educators' limited responses to these trends, because, 'with notable exceptions, educators' reactions range from tacit acceptance to outright embrace' (SC, 121). Maxine Greene laments that 'little is done to counter media manipulation of the young into credulous and ardent consumers. They are instructed daily, and with few exceptions, that human worth depends on the possession of commodities.'[50] In contrast, I suggest that commercialism can be explicitly addressed within the school environment. In this section I forefront existing strategies and how they can be more widely practised and more directly applied to consumerism. These are advanced not as a final solution to consumerism but as strategies of resistance that may open possibilities for critical dialogue aimed towards public renewal.

To overlook the transformative possibilities the classroom offers is to neglect the critical functions of schooling. Addressing consumerism in the classroom is a way to preserve natality and ensure that the world does not seem fixed. Levinson argues that to 'preserve newness is to teach in such a way that students acquire an understanding of themselves in relation to the world without regarding either the world or their positioning in it as fixed, determined, and unchangeable.'[51] Yet if education is increasingly dependent on funding from corporate sponsors, and if the values from consumer culture become integrated into the lessons presented, where in society can such a critical dialogue transpire? My concern is that without critical engagement, consumerism will narrow our political and pedagogical horizons by undermining the personally and politically transformative functions of education. For this reason I explore how media literacy and culture jamming help critically engage the meanings and messages of consumerism. Although the images of commercial culture are a significant part of the daily life of students, the classroom can be a site for analysis and critique of these images, and schools can function as sites for critical engagement rather than simply allowing the incorporation of consumerism. Baudrillard demonstrated the semiotic character of consumerism as a commercial discourse and system of signs and symbols. If the signs and symbols of commercial discourse have become as thoroughly integrated into society as the Branded Alphabet and the documentary *Super Size Me* demonstrate, it follows that the most effective way to engage consumerism is through critically investigating the language of consumerism among schoolchildren.

Some of the questions that arise for educators concerned with school commercialism include how media education can equip students and teachers to become more critical readers of the advertising messages that confront them, and how the 'marketization' of schools might provide teachable moments for media literacy. Groundbreaking consumer theorist and founder of the Media Education Foundation Sut Jhally shows that media literacy can enable students to critically evaluate the countless messages by which they are bombarded and find ways to think critically about what those messages are – and are often not – saying. According to Alison Cook-Sather, 'Education must be guided by metaphors that unsettle, that expect students to seek, find, and invent what we do not yet know, that lead us not only to imagine but also to create other possible worlds.'[52] In contrast to the notion that we are merely spectators who must accommodate ourselves to an unchanging and unchangeable political reality, critical pedagogical strategies allow reality to be seen as dynamic. Levinson notes that we 'educate in order to introduce the continual stream of newcomers into the world, but we have to take care to do so in a way that protects natality by preserving our students' capacities to act in ways that might renew the world.'[53] Critical media literacy and culture jamming can facilitate such a renewal.

Teachers willing and able to raise controversial issues in their classrooms can critique the constant images of commercial culture. However, educational theorist Allan Luke expresses concern about how 'teaching has increasingly been appropriated both by curriculum and instructional commodities and the extent to which teachers have moved towards consumer-like behavior.' Luke insists that there is a growing need for a 'new teacher' who will engage critical issues in the classroom: 'While new economic and geopolitical conditions are requiring a new teacher with critical capacities for dealing with the transnational and the global, current policies have turned the teacher into a generic consumer of multinational products.'[54] However, concrete pedagogical action such as critical media literacy and culture jamming in the classroom can allow students to engage in activities to decode and deconstruct the messages that dominate consumer society. These tools enable students to creatively express their daily experiences with the images of consumption and become active producers of meaning, contributing to culture rather than merely consuming it. The development of critical media literacy allows students to break out of the monologue of advertising and initiate a dialogical response based on their own creative appropriation and subversion of the messages of consumption.

Because literacy is always value-laden, reproducing hegemonic practices, conveying cultural norms, and shaping social and individual consciousness, it does not merely give passive 'access' to culture but instead allows cultural configurations of hegemony and power to be taken up and enacted by the subject. A commitment to a dynamic and vibrant democratic society requires forms of literacy that do not merely reproduce social problems or erode the possibilities of political change.

McLaren and Lankshear provocatively state that 'the ability to read and write may expose individuals and entire social groups to forms of domination and control by which their interests are subverted.'[55] Literacy is therefore the site of contestation insofar as 'it aims at understanding the ongoing social struggles over the signs of culture and over the definition of social reality – over what is considered a legitimate and preferred meaning at any given historical moment.'[56]

Yet the development of critical approaches to consumerism may have limited effect when structured according to rational and authoritarian norms while consumerism is construed as playful and pleasurable. Kenway and Bullen lament that 'schools generally lack enchantment for students,' and must 'rescue childhood from the enchantment of consumer culture by re-enchanting the classroom, because it allows the young both to participate in and negate the myths of the metropolis through their play' (CC, 151, 161). Because it is often the sterile and arid atmosphere of schools that may deepen students' absorption in the exciting world of consumerism, the aim is 'to rescue childhood from the enchantment of consumer culture by *re-enchanting the classroom*, because it allows the young both to participate in and negate the myths of the metropolis through their play' (CC, 161). As Kenway and Bullen explain, 'It is the responsibility of adults – teachers, parents, [and] policy makers – to ensure that school education is not absorbed into the "vortex of the commodity" and that it makes powerful connections with the young people of today who, in many ways, have "no choice" about their image-and commodity-drenched surroundings. At the very least, school could teach them to understand the differences between data, information, knowledge, education, entertainment and advertising. But can the marketized school tell the difference? Schools can play a role in alerting the young to matters of life politics in addition to matters of lifestyle. But if kids are to listen, we also need to re-enchant the school' (CC, 188).

There are significant challenges to critically engaging prevalent consumer images. Media theorist Geoff Pevere discusses the relationship between print and visual media and the unique challenges the latter presents in developing a critical perspective: 'If a basic principle of print literacy is based in the isolation of words and language for purposes of understanding and interpretation … the basic principle of contemporary image culture is unceasing and constant flow: the pictures must never stop, and the act of interpretation must always represent a struggle, an effort, against this tendency. By its nature, interpreting moving images goes against this flow. Reading images is work, while experiencing them is easy.'[57]

Cultural theorist Jennifer Sandlin also discusses the struggle of criticizing consumerism in schools, noting that 'the term *consumer education* conjures up images of teaching adult learners how to budget, calculate interest, get the most for their money, and know how to complain if they have problems with merchandise.'[58] This approach creates more knowledgeable consumers, helps consumers make better decisions, and accommodates the individual consumer to the present constellation of consumer choices. Sandlin suggests a more critical approach instead: 'Most of the consumer education happening in more formal arenas is based on a technical model and could be enlivened by an infusion of a more critical consumer education that grapples with issues of consumption and seeks to create learners who begin to view consumption as a cultural phenomenon that we can question and contest.'[59] Sandlin outlines several stages of reaction when addressing consumerism in the classroom while progressing from a benign approach towards one more critically oriented. First, 'embracing consumerism' involves learning the best routes to voice complaints about product quality and service, and 'criticalness is aimed at a producer within the system of capitalism, not at the system of capitalism itself.' Reaction two, 'individually questioning consumption,' responds to consumerism by recycling, using public transit, and reducing television usage. Such approaches have limited impact, because they 'view the responsibility for these negative impacts in an individualized way.' Sandlin advocates a third reaction, 'collectively politicizing and fighting consumption' by seeking to 'make consumerism appear less natural' and crafting 'anti-consumers' who 'see culture as a site of resistance.'[60] For example, students can do their own research on one of their favourite commodities, both before they own it (production) and after they own it (when they throw it away), and relate these discoveries to the image presented by marketers.

Sandlin's critical consumer education seeks not to create more knowledgeable consumers or ensure better consumer decisions – a concern promoted, for example, when marketers refer to young people as savvy because of their ability to recognize brands. Rather than accommodating the individual consumer to the present constellation of consumer values and products, the aim is to critique the underlying systemic features of consumerism. Critical consumer education aims to 'not only learn technical skills but investigate the naturalization of the consumer world [and] position learners to question the supposedly natural, taken-for-granted order of consumption and consumerism.'[61]

Resistance strategies such as culture jamming are educational approaches that turn this debate into a learning opportunity where students are enabled to develop critical literacy in response to consumerism. Toronto-based culture jammer Carly Stasko provides a helpful description of culture jamming:

> First, it means to improvise, to play off the environment, to play with what's already there, to create in a spontaneous and improvisational way, the same way jazz musicians might jam. Second, it means to stop something from working, to 'jam the gears,' to stop the machinery of consumerism and mass media from grinding us down. Culture jamming is a creative way to engage and respond to the messages of the mass media, and to become an active participant in our culture … It is taking media and advertisements and subverting their intended meaning – that's why it's sometimes called 'subvertising.' It's about creating a dialogue where there isn't one. It's against passive and mindless consumption, and instead becoming active producers in the kinds of messages and images that we're surrounded with every day. Its goal is empowerment, engagement, and dialogue not just consumption and consumerism.[62]

It might be argued that consumer relationships are in fact dialogical if, for example, a company listens to young consumers and changes their product according to the consumers' preferences. However, Stasko sees this as a form of market research or 'cool hunting,' which is more about 'finding out what's important to teenagers so that they can sell more things to them.'[63]

Culture jamming can be incorporated into several different classes, including English, civics, history, and art, from elementary school to high school. In a context where corporations are buying their way into textbooks, a need for critical discussion rather than a sponsored presence is required. For example, an online lesson plan for Grade 12 media studies provides instructional material for teaching culture jamming and creating 'anti-ads' based on print ads that students bring to class.[64] A Canadian civics textbook asks students to consider Pepsi's bid for exclusive sales rights in Toronto District schools, and students are encouraged to take the position of decision makers who weigh the issues and examine the controversy of such school–business contracts.[65] In both the Smarties and Pepsi cases, corporate products are being discussed in classrooms. However, in the latter, the learning is focused on developing a critical awareness of the role of corporations, while the former simply reinforces such presence without question.

Stasko describes a variety of in-class activities and how they can benefit teachers, including cutting up magazines and putting collages together in a new way that alters how the original message was intended to be interpreted, thereby expressing the development of their own critical attitude towards the media. 'Once they're finished, I invite them to talk about their work and share how their experience was. Teachers can keep their projects up on the walls for other classes to see … [These projects] can be great springboards for some really interesting and active class discussions and further assignments and classroom activities [and] can become a teaching aid: you can build up a resource library to showcase and share with other classes.'[66]

While these ideas are often taken up with great enthusiasm by students, 'some teachers are intimidated by the idea at first. Teachers are from a different generation than their students, and often they live in a different world. Sometimes students can seem like aliens from a different world. And these images are such a big part of their daily lives that often students are even more insightful than adults! This helps the two to bridge the gap, and gives them a chance to connect.'[67] While it is the goal of education to ensure the well-rounded development of our youth and the future they will inherit, the goal of advertising is unapologetically and narrowly focused on encouraging consumption and brand loyalty. Consumer choice is encouraged insofar as the choice is a product. Similarly, media literacy is often encouraged only if it will enable children to differentiate between brands. Media literacy educators are more interested in the ability of students to create new choices for themselves, in addition to making wise choices from the options made available to them. Yet true freedom comes when readers don't just choose but rather design and create their own story.

As students' lives become increasingly commercialized, Stasko asks, 'How are young people able to get their voices heard beyond voting with their dollars?' She points out that students increasingly 'are discovering their own powers as producers, turning their media saturated childhoods into media literate action. Growing up immersed in consumerism, many young people have shifted their relationship with commercial culture and have learned to deconstruct the commercial messages that dominate their environment as they explore new ways to co-opt and subvert such messages to express new alternatives.'[68] The spirit of do-it-yourself media has inspired many young activists, whose tactics range from culture jamming to indie-media production, global street parties, and protest. It has been described by zine publisher Liz Worth as 'an ever-expanding movement rooted in anti-consumerist ideals,' because it is 'a way for them to take a political stance, start up a scene, or accomplish something on their own terms.'[69] *Hey Kidz! Buy This Book*, a self-described 'radical primer on corporate and governmental propaganda and artistic activism for short people,'[70] is just one example of the kinds of resources that are made by youth for youth to challenge consumerism.

Consumerism has become perhaps the most important influence on socialization. Considering that the young will determine the character of our future, the commercialization of school space and curricula has significant long-term social implications. Even as we witness the acceleration and proliferation of consumerism, there are significant opportunities for its critical resistance in schools. While critical pedagogue Peter McLaren is concerned that the 'dominant culture tries to "fix" the meaning of signs, symbols, and representations to provide a "common" worldview,'[71] the aim of culture jamming and media literacy is to disrupt fixed meanings by opening space for new and alternative interpretations of commercial messages.

Empowering today's youth with media literacy skills allows them to express their perspectives beyond their consumer preferences held so dominant in consumer society. While the power and number of marketing messages can seem overwhelming, it is clearly still a challenge to successfully market to today's youth. It is also clear that while great amounts of money are spent to understand and influence them, much of that research provides data that cannot explain unpredictable and changing young people. Perhaps it is because the true desires of young people – or all people, for that matter – cannot be simply rewarded with commodities.

'What's Wrong with My Nikes?': Resistance and Refusal

It is important to recognize that emotional responses are central to engaging controversial issues in the classroom and must be a starting point for understanding the effect of consumerism. Students are more readily abandoned to the marketplace of constructed images and manufactured needs when educators don't see them as desiring subjects with wide-ranging emotions.

While natality helps preserve the world, its unpredictability means that one can never be sure how students in the classroom will take up critical issues. Arendt states that only the work of *Homo faber* and *Animal laborans* are predictable, while we as human actors are always unpredictable. Levinson argues that these unexpected developments by no means suggest that critical undertakings are a failure, but only that education is not subjected to the same linear demands as work or labour: 'Coming to grips with the paradox of natality reconfigures these supposed "failures" in ways that draw attention to the fitful and decidedly nonlinear nature of educational progress.'[72]

Perhaps one of the reasons consumerism has become so prevalent is because it is portrayed as fun and playful. It is therefore important to address consumerism in the classroom not by simply discrediting it or targeting particular students, nor by moralizing or using guilt and shame. Such approaches are likely to only alienate students rather than engage them. Australian philosophers of education Kenway and Bullen note that schools and teachers are limited in their effectiveness if they appear 'like finger waving moral authoritarians who turn kids off, rather than on, to commodity politics' (CC, 59), and instead must 'invite students to call into question their affective investments without devaluing them' (CC, 170).

Several philosophers of education have explored the complicated dynamics surrounding the challenges that arise when addressing controversial issues in the classroom. As mentioned in chapter 2, it is a testament to the seductive powers of consumerism that schools and teachers are portrayed as a negative 'Other' and resented as authority figures, even as the icons of consumption and entertainment are elevated as symbols of rebellion to identify with and emulate. Kenway and Bullen note that 'the danger with consumer-media education is its potential association in kids' minds with negative authority, with adult criticism of kids' pleasures and fantasies' (CC, 156). As a result, 'deconstruction may have an emotional fallout. It may also mean that students resist resistance ... teachers must work *with* and, just as importantly, *through* their pleasures, investments and identities' (CC, 153). Often legitimate critiques can be dangerously infused with personal and generational judgments, and sometimes it is the very novelty of ideas and perceiving brought forth by the natality of the young that provokes resistance from older generations. The key is to distinguish between the two, because critical opportunities can be lost when teachers discredit youth culture or claim that they know better than students.

The fallout Kenway and Bullen write about may occur because introducing students to critical issues in consumerism may not be entirely liberating but instead evoke what Jane Roland Martin called a 'narrative of loss.' In her essay 'Becoming Educated: A Journey of Alienation or Integration?' Martin describes the changes that a young Mexican-American student goes through as he excels in school and eventually completes a doctorate in English literature. Along the way he grows increasingly distant from his family and the Latino culture in which he was raised as he journeys 'from intimacy to isolation.'[73] As students engage in critical analysis of consumerism, they may mourn their lost identities as they grow alienated from friends and family and the dominant culture. This is why there may arise substantial resistance against critiques of consumerism.

Philosopher of education Deborah Kerdeman applies Hans-Georg Gadamer's concept of being 'pulled up short' to the classroom, arguing that 'being pulled up short is a particular experience of disorientation that poses unique pedagogical demands.'[74] Because 'every gain in self-understanding entails loss,'[75] Kerdeman insists that the experience of pain and disorientation that accompanies exposure to the unexpected and different must be done willingly and openly. She argues, 'Teachers cannot put students in the way of being pulled up short, structuring conditions such that self-exposure is likely. Unless a student already is disposed to acknowledge being pulled up short, she will miss or resist submitting to this experience.'[76] For this reason, the classroom may be not only a site for opposition and resistance but a place where critical perspectives themselves are actively opposed and resisted by any teacher who attempts to challenge deeply internalized consumer values. Not all students will be receptive to a critique of their way of life, and may resist discussing the extent to which they are caught up in consumerism.

In *Feeling Power*, Megan Boler explores the dynamics of resistance and refusal in her account of the 'pedagogy of discomfort.' Discomfort is likely to arise when 'educators and students engage in critical inquiry regarding values and cherished beliefs.'[77] Transformation can be 're-fused' and never materialize in what Boler calls 'Calvin's refusal,' after the cartoon character returned a book loaned by his mother, stating, 'It's complicating my life. Don't get me any more.' 'Calvin's refusal' is not simply an individual preference or personal choice, but rather an 'invisible conformity to the status quo.' Boler suggests that 'when new information is introduced that suggests a radical alternative to our accepted and/or common-sense ways of thinking and being, how do we react? Refusal is certainly one possible reaction.'[78]

The transformative possibilities of education are not exclusively private but aim towards public renewal, because whenever education stirs one's passions, it does so in a profoundly political manner. As Boler argues, emotions are not merely private or interior experiences but invariably political: 'Emotions are not simply located in the individual, are not simply biological or privately experienced phenomena, but rather reflect linguistically-embedded cultural values and rules and are thus a site of power and resistance.' She explores the complex terrain of our emotional investments in and attachments to particular world views, arguing that 'emotions are a primary medium through which we learn to internalize ideologies as commonsense truths.'[79] Such internalized ideological identifications are how we unknowingly – even unwillingly – identify with the dominant ideology. These investments, identifications, and attachments run deep and are not easily abandoned or altered. When some minimal changes do occur, intense emotions often follow, what Boler describes as 'defensive anger': 'a protection of beliefs, a protection of one's precarious sense of identity. To challenge a student's (or educator's) cherished assumptions may be felt as a threat to their very identity. This reaction of anger should be interpreted not so much as a righteous objection to one's honor, but more as a defense of one's investments in the values of the dominant culture. To respond in defensive anger is to defend one's stake ... the protection of precarious identities.'[80]

Along with the students' defensive anger, another significant challenge to teaching against consumerism is the notion that learning must be made easy, leisurely, and palatable. The growing self-understanding of student-as-consumers invariably obstructs the more difficult dimensions of learning. When facing what is new or contrary, students may express feelings of anger, aggression, or outright hostility. In such pedagogical circumstances, the students encounter something that isn't simply unfamiliar but downright offensive; not simply different but repugnant; not only incomprehensible but self-implicating. These encounters may lead students to become indignant and resentful and refuse the possibility of transformation. Gert Biesta suggests that, like this refusal to be disturbed, there is a risk and even violence inherent to pedagogical experiences, 'the risk that you will learn something that you rather didn't want to learn,' because 'there is a violent dimension to education ... in that it asks difficult questions and creates difficult situations.'[81]

For example, in a lesson on consumerism in a business ethics course I recently taught, we researched the Third World labour practices of the students' favourite shoemaker. At one point many students were fuming, attacking me with the question 'What's wrong with my Nikes?' Others in the class suggested that people enjoy working in sweatshops and are lucky to have jobs. This encounter with new and difficult knowledge provoked personal attacks, creating a palpable classroom tension. This only serves to confirm the level of self-identification with consumerism such that a critique of consumer choices is readily taken as a personal attack. Students have not only identified and personally 'invested' themselves with their Nikes but also with the entire social structure behind it.

Yet strangely this experience of anger and refusal also parallels a remarkable sense of apathy. What is perhaps most striking about many of these same students is their sense of the impossibility – even absurdity – of social transformation. How ironic that a society based on freedom apparently denies us the freedom to change that same society! How ironic that a society celebrating choice denies us the possibility to choose a better world! On those few occasions when students concede that all is not well with modern consumer society, they tend to retreat into apathy and indifference. 'What can you do? That's just the way it is.' It seems students deliberately retreat into passivity because they experience a collective impotence. Or perhaps such a fetishized posture of disaffected boredom or celebrated selfishness is more a mark of young people's limited sense of options beyond the sphere of consumerism, rather than an indication of their essentialized pessimism or true apathetic nature. Apathy is primarily a last resort when other options seem absent, when the only expression of power is the expression of disdain.

Apathy, Indifference, and Bad Marketing

The noise of commercial messages makes it increasingly difficult to distinguish the medium from the message, the public from the private, the real from the sign. While consumerism is increasingly portrayed as a method for the democratic expression of identity – and even as a means of bolstering national security – it is also credited with reducing civic participation, even as it is ironically presented as a potential strategy for increasing youth engagement in politics. Some marketers suggest that marketing might help increase political participation, because youth will become more demanding and empowered and therefore come to expect more of government. Present political apathy is said to result from 'bad marketing' by politicians because politics is not positioned as 'cool.' Marketing is thus construed as the new standard by which politics is measured. Voting is equated with buying, and citizenship with consumption, and politicians are packaged and sold as a consumer good. According to marketer Max Valliquette, 'Young people are being so engaged in every process right now *but* the political process. Your parents want to know what you think, your schools want to know what you think, marketers, for the love of God, always want to know what you think. Youth expect politics to be customized to them. This generation wants to be participatory because that's the way they've grown up; they expect it to be interactive.'[82]

Yet ironically many people are disengaged because politics is already so over-marketed and image-oriented as politicians provide slogans rather than genuine political speech. Society becomes so thoroughly saturated with marketing that there is little space left for politics, which itself becomes consumed; in Arendt's terms, the public realm is eclipsed by 'the social.' Perhaps people might be more likely to gain interest in politics, and be less cynical about their ability to influence the world around them in ways other than consuming, if politicians and issues seemed to be more 'real' and – in Baudrillard's terms – less of a 'sign.' While consumerism is concerned with individual gratification and private self-preoccupation, politics is based on the ability to think beyond one's own private needs. However, consumerism speaks to us only as private individuals, and problems are framed as purely individual issues that can be resolved only through individual acts of consumption. Ironically, marketing encourages us to think about the political world around us such that we engage in politics only to better protect our privacy.

Stasko points out that all too often 'the media paints a picture of today's youth as self-centered, apathetic, consumption-obsessed, tycoon-wannabees. Considering all the money put into market research, cool hunting and tailored marketing strategies, is anyone surprised that today's youth seem to care more about consuming than the possibilities of social change?'[83] Young people know they have power as a market, while in the political arena young people have considerably less power or influence. If they have things to say or questions to ask, who besides marketers are listening? Their teachers, families, and friends are overshadowed by the sheer size and slick packaging of commercial culture.

In spite of all this, many young people still believe that change is possible and are demanding to take part in creating a more just and sustainable world. Ironically, it is some of North America's most well-funded market researchers who are studying and exploiting this cultural trend towards civic agency among youth.[84] The new marketer's bible is a thirteen-country survey of over three thousand teens called 'GenWorld: The New Generation of Global Youth.'[85] This study calls today's teens 'Interactivist Gen' and describes the growing desire among youth to contribute to society, to make a positive difference in the world, and to 'do the right thing' both locally and globally. Yet marketers are interested in youth civic engagement only insofar as it can be packaged into a profitable marketing campaign rather than a genuine youth movement. In response to the complex desires of Interactivist Gen, marketers struggle to forge links between their products and social and environmental causes – often spending more money to promote an ethical and responsible image than on the issues about which they profess to care. Stasko notes that youth 'feel empowered when they are told that their opinion matters, but what kind of power is it when only their consumer interests or their ability to influence their family and friends is valued?'[86]

The divide between civic and financial interests in today's youth is most apparent when the issue of responsibility for the ethical or political implications of marketing arises – a contentious topic that most marketers prefer not to debate, using tactics such as evasion and deference to choice. The responsibility for problems associated with marketing is passed on to governments, consumers, or the corporations for which marketers work.[87] Consumers are said to have all the power while the marketers are helpless. By flattering the consumer for being savvy, marketers are able to evade responsibility and construe themselves as a part of a larger system over which they have little or no control. It is ironic that those who promote 'empowerment' claim they are powerless, and celebrate choice while they often defer to their own limited choices! The relationship between marketing and society is portrayed as one that is so complicated that it is virtually incomprehensible. Such a complicated system is best left untouched, and it is better to simply benefit from the way things are than try to imagine or initiate any alternative. Marketer Anne Sutherland explains that since parents often ask their kids what specific brands of household products they should buy, kids learn that it is important to pay attention to advertising, and advertisers have 'no choice' but to target young people in their advertising campaigns.

Many marketers argue that today's youth are savvy because they are more media literate than any generation before them. Marketer Debbie Gordon claims that 'children are doing a fabulous job now of understanding advertising, they have become so much more savvy.'[88] Yet often what marketers call 'savvy' among young consumers could be referred to as cynical, media saturated, able to differentiate between products, or simply hard to reach. It does not necessarily indicate critical understanding about consumerism. Sutherland argues that 'kids now have a chance to develop critical thinking skills that previous generations never had. They are neither gullible nor naïve ... They are so hyperaware of labels and brand names. They're very ready to talk about whether something measures up to its advertisers' claims. They're very ready to talk about when they think ads are phony or trying to manipulate them. Kids my daughter's age are media savvy and much more critical of their environment.'[89] These statements imply that since some youth are exposed to media literacy they are more savvy, which means that marketers must advertise even harder to reach them.

Max Valiquette describes to teachers and parents how difficult it is to sell to young people today because they've seen so much advertising: 'If an ad isn't smart and funny, then they will reject it.'[90] His challenge as a marketer is to keep the ever-shortening attention span of today's youth focused on his commercial message long enough for the desirable associations to register. In contrast, a parent or teacher has a different challenge: to promote a kind of literacy that moves beyond savvy and into the realm of creative and critical thinking. Youth marketer Shelly Reese describes the teen audience as a 'moving target' and explains that 'as teens age, their preferences rapidly change. That means companies have to be ready to shift their focus at a moment's notice – over, and over, and over again.'[91] This seems to suggest kids are to blame because marketing has become so pervasive, since they are such difficult 'moving targets.' Are we to pity the hard-working 'market hunters' in this metaphor? As Naomi Klein notes in *No Logo*, with 'so much competition, the agencies argue, clients must spend more than ever to make sure their pitch screeches so loud it can be heard over all the others.'[92] She quotes David Lubars, a senior ad executive in the Omnicom Group, who explains candidly that consumers are '"like roaches – you spray them and spray them and they get immune after a while."'[93] Marketers profess to have no choice but to continue to colonize new virgin territories with commercial messages, ranging from product placement and 'viral marketing' to school commercialism.

Young people who are critical of the excessive commercialization of their lives may present new challenges to marketers but are seen as a new demographic – as a market rather than a movement. Marketers imply that activism as a strategy of resistance is simply an 'identity project' equivalent to consumerism and assert that their task is to devise strategies to draw all identity projects into the realm of consumption. Palazzo and Basu contend that 'individuals associated with such forms of civic engagement are seen as deriving value and recognition from their actions, thereby reconstructing and reinforcing aspects of their identity.'[94] Resistance when seen through the lens of consumerism is not about political engagement or social transformation but merely self-expression – which often could in fact be better met by consumerism. This denies the possibility that resistance might be motivated by something other than 'self-identity needs': 'Individuals participating in acts of instant solidarity, linking their life stories to the narratives written by activist groups, often discover that consumption decisions are an efficient means to communicate moral and political statements. They shop for a better world.'[95] We can instead ask what kind of identities the market offers. Ironically, the 'we meet all your identity needs' approach to assisting 'identity projects' reveals that marketers market marketing as the solution to life in a consumer society. More marketing is held up as the solution to this very crisis of consumerism.

Yet an alternative to consumerism cannot be bought. Cultural theorist Joshua Gamson argues that what 'is truly disturbing is that it's hard for people to imagine alternative ways to make themselves known to each other [because] the symbolic tools in our society are largely about consuming.'[96] Perhaps our notion of media literacy needs to be expanded to include the ability to create meaning, identity, culture, and community, rather than simply buying products that communicate as well as shape our world views and sense of self. As Gamson puts it, 'The point is to create alternatives rather than just expose manipulation.'[97] In addition to encouraging critical literacy, we must also support creative literacy so that young people are empowered with the skills, opportunities, and mentors they need to engage in the project of being beyond buying.

In its most benign forms, advertising is framed as informing, educating, and empowering us for participation in our consumer world; many marketers imply that they are simply performing a public service. And yet this is not benign at all. Advertising merely simulates education, because it doesn't aim to educate critical thinkers and self-directed learners but to encourage consumers to develop life-long brand loyalties. This tendency invariably dilutes education in three ways. First, it undermines education as a project of inquiry oriented towards some sense of public good. For example, when a student observes an assembly on leadership presented by Coca-Cola, the lesson is inseparable from the brand identity of Coke. Second, rather than treating students as citizens, it serves up students as markets for advertisers, which ultimately encourages students to identify their locus of power in their role as consumers. Third, advertising simulates education only in its most entertaining and non-threatening forms, as 'edutainment,' never asking us to challenge our world views. This threat to education results in the expectation that learning be made easy, leisurely, and palatable. However, it will take more than savvy consumers to address the problems of consumerism, more than better marketing of politicians to address the decline of the public, and more than 'cool hunting' to address school commercialism.

Wonder, Hope, and the Possible

An account of political alternatives or new world views can inspire wonder as a possibility towards which we might strive. I am not speaking of mere utopianism or speculation about an unattainable and hypothetical promised land, but a concrete and tangible alternative to the present configuration of political life. Rather than cynicism, apathy, and indifference, wonder and hope might inspire such a possibility and help overcome the prevalent sense of collective impotence discussed in the last section, and aptly expressed by marketer Anne Sutherland who insists we can only passively accommodate to this new 'reality': consumerism 'is neither a good thing nor a bad thing. It is evolution.'[98] While wonder, hope, and optimism require vulnerability and risk, they are also ways that we have a concrete stake or interest in the world. Roger Simon distinguishes between hope and wish, arguing that while to wish or dream is a passive diversion, hope is an active imagining of an alternative, an openness and predisposition to action. He states that 'the hopeful person does not merely envisage this possibility as a wish; the hopeful person acts upon it now by loosening and refusing the hold that taken-for-granted realities and routines have over imagination. Thus hope is different from the wish in that it is a predisposition to action rather than merely a foretaste of pleasure. It grows from commitment to responsibility and not from a passive yearning for ultimate peace and resolution. As a particular crystallization of desire, hope is constituted in the need to imagine an alternative human world and to imagine it in a way that enables one to act in the present as if this alternative had already begun to emerge.'[99] Thus, perhaps we experience wonder not only before the incomprehensible but in the face of the possible. A classroom environment that encourages wonder must then always protect the possibility of possibilities. As Derrida puts it, 'We must do and think the impossible. If only the possible happened, nothing more would happen.'[100] To consider Socratic metaphors, we can recall that Socrates often described himself as a 'midwife' to new knowledge, alluding to the pain and even trauma in learning. Such suffering is a precursor to a new life, both literally for the child and symbolically for the learner.

Any teacher will attest to the profound influence of consumerism within the classroom and the deep grip that consumer values have on students. Considering alternatives will suggest ways to understand more fully what is otherwise seen as an innocuous and neutral undertaking. If education is a preparation for life within our modern democratic society, then it is essential to think – and practise – beyond the narrow confines of consumption.

There is no straightforward route to addressing the influence of consumerism, nor is there a singular approach. Consumer education, media literacy, culture jamming, and school board advertising regulations will not be sufficient on their own; critical engagement with consumerism requires many intersecting and complementary methods. Will the answer to these concerns about consumerism present itself as a consumer choice? Not likely. It is beyond the world of buying and selling and choosing that such solutions will be created.

However, there is hope: the very marketers responsible for promoting cynicism and insecurity among today's youth have learned through their own costly research that today's young people more than ever want to help to create a better world.[101] Stasko points out that 'they are hopeful, idealistic, multitalented and globally connected. They are all these things while at the same time struggling with their own apathy and superficiality. Many youth believe that they can be, do and have anything they want. What will happen when they realize that what they want most is not for sale?'[102] With the help of political action and a commitment to education, our next generation will have the support and skills they need to forge a brighter future for the generations that follow.

Conclusion

Consumption has become our primary language, literacy the interpretation of commercial symbols, and the act of consumption our primary mode of insertion into the world. We internalize the act of purchasing and translate this experience into all other human activities and aspects of our social existence, from political engagement to pedagogical practices. The effect of consumerism is thus not simply to gratify needs but legitimate capitalist societies by demonstrating their success at 'delivering the goods.' The economic achievements of our contemporary society are often reified as the natural and inevitable culmination of historical processes, thus implying that there is no alternative to capitalism and no point to its critique. Will today's youth accept unsustainable consumerism as a cooked lobster accepts the increasing temperature of the water in its cooking pot, or will they discover new ways of resisting consumerism? Perhaps we are too adaptive for our own good.

Yet we have seen that there is a paradox in this position: while the market is construed as a sphere of freedom, the rise of capitalism is seen as the historical outcome of a natural and inevitable process that operates without human influence, as articulated by Francis Fukuyama: 'Today we have trouble imagining a world that is radically better than our own, or a future that is not essentially democratic and capitalist ... We cannot picture to ourselves a world that is essentially different from the present one, and at the same time better.'[103] The prevalence of consumerism does not imply that it is beyond contestation, but rather that consumerism will require new forms of analysis, critique, and resistance.

Education must respond to the prevalent sense of the futility of resistance and impossibility of an alternative. Advertisers are interested in youth and schools for the same reason that educators are so determined to work with young people: they are energetic, open minded, and still forming their world views; the source of the new. The increasing influence of youth marketing is easy for kids and teens to accept if they have never known any other way.

Schools can neither create nor save the public realm, but can only support societies in which political action is a real possibility. Gert Biesta argues that otherwise 'schools therefore seem to be carrying all the responsibility for democracy ... It is not only not fair to burden schools with this task; it is also unrealistic to assume that schools can "make or break" democracy.'[104] However, the interest shown in schools by marketers demonstrates their profound political importance. There is much that schools can contribute to democracy and public renewal.

Conclusion: 'What Is to Come'

What does it mean to think forward into a future? To dream? To reach beyond? Few even dare to ponder what is to come.

– Maxine Greene[1]

It seems to be easier for us today to imagine the thoroughgoing deterioration of the earth and nature than the breakdown of late capitalism.

– Frederick Jameson[2]

Beyond Contestation

Writing a conclusion appears paradoxical in light of Baudrillard's statements about the interminable character of history and Arendt's account of the openness of action. Nevertheless, some final observations are in order after this long journey through these and other thinkers.

Consumerism has become our new ideology, the paradigm of postmodernity, the commodity and the brand our new idolatry. From Hannah Arendt through Jean Baudrillard, consumerism has been described as corrosive to political life, now an increasing challenge to education. When the public realm is eroded by the human preoccupation with consumption, we no longer experience ourselves as political beings but instead are caught up in consumption. And when schooling facilitates the incorporation of the next generation into consumer society, the critical and democratic possibilities of education are compromised. Maxine Greene describes how consumerism is readily linked to a passive acceptance of what is construed as objective reality: 'Rather than being challenged to attend to the actualities of their lived lives, students are urged to attend to what is given in the outside world … There is, in consequence, an implicit encouragement of the tendency to accede to the given, to view what exists around us as an objective reality, impervious to individual interpretation. Finding it difficult to stand forth from what is officially (or by means of media) defined as real, unable to perceive themselves in interpretive relation to it, the young (like their elders) are all too likely to remain immersed in the taken-for-granted and the everyday. For many, this means an unreflective consumerism; for others, it means a preoccupation with *having* more than *being* more.'[3]

Through consumption we attempt to insert ourselves into the world of human relations, to participate in our political world, and to experience ourselves as part of a larger whole. Arendt and Baudrillard reveal how these aims are illusory. Consumerism promotes a process by which the human being is depoliticized, students are reduced to passive spectators, and an active citizenry is transformed into complacent consumers. Consumerism has become our primary language, literacy experienced as the interpretation of commercial symbols, and the act of consumption our primary mode of insertion into the social world. Yet consumption is not action, and consumer society is not a public realm.

While this work began by quoting Bush calling upon Americans to go shopping, in fact it was the war – and even a particular sign of America itself – that he was selling to a consuming audience. Many of the war strategists were from the marketing industry, revealed by Naomi Klein in her article 'America Is Not a Hamburger.' Klein reports how the U.S. State Department under Bush hired brand manager Charlotte Beers, famous for her success in selling dog food and Uncle Ben's rice, to help 'rebrand America' and create a more positive image of America around the world. Klein observes, 'Now she was being asked to work her magic on the greatest branding challenge of all: to sell the US and its war on terrorism to an increasingly hostile world.'[4] The war – and even the nation itself – is construed as a commodity that can be sold like any other consumer product.

Consumerism advances a profound passivity under the illusion of political action and emphasizes individual gratification at the expense of collective engagement. The possibilities for political resistance are drained through the reorientation of the subject towards the commodity achieved by ever-advancing technologies of persuasion and control. This can be achieved without the necessity for explicit or violent methods, through the capacity for consumer society to incorporate resistance and reconcile oppositional forces. This narrowed vision of political life and contracted understanding of pedagogy profoundly changes our cultural landscape and radically alters modern democratic society. It could be said that consumer culture is the consumption of culture. But it is also the consumption of the next generation at the hands of schools. Ultimately, we must address the extent to which education is complicit in the reproduction of a society centred upon consumption and resist its relentless proliferation. This narrowed vision of political life and contracted understanding of pedagogy profoundly changes our cultural landscape. While Hollywood continues to produce apocalyptic blockbusters, it is up to teachers to respond to Jameson's fearful concerns.

There have been some recent positive developments regarding school commercialism. The Center for Science in the Public Interest and the Campaign for a Commercial-Free Childhood announced that some parents intend to sue Viacom and Kellogg for marketing junk food to young children.[5] Channel One has not been as successful as Chris Whittle initially hoped, partly because Kellogg and Kraft lost revenue: 'The concern by certain advertisers about the obesity issue in schools caused them to stop or reduce advertising in schools.'[6]

A more ambiguous development is the reopening of the outdoor education Frost Centre, discussed at the opening of chapter 2. Now under private ownership by a retired IBM executive, it will serve as a summer camp, research site for the University of Guelph, and conference centre. However, its website confirms that the new centre will be 'working with corporate sponsors,'[7] and the local newspaper notes that 'Aubry has always kept up his contacts in the business world and he soon had companies offering financial support for some of the projects, such as subsidizing the free weekends for school groups.'[8] Public schools must now compete with groups such as banks and other corporations looking for teambuilding weekend retreats, and, as a result, most school trips are from wealthy private schools. While opening the new Frost Centre is certainly preferable to leaving the site abandoned or developed for strictly private use, it allows private commercial sources to appear as benevolent saviours when they rescue the centre. Private interests acquire a favourable public image, even as they privatize school functions – yet this never would have happened if private market forces hadn't led to its closure for several years.

This book points towards several areas of future work: the increasing impact of consumerism on health and the environment, the links among consumerism and war and terrorism, and further contributions from other theorists such as John Dewey. Furthermore, there are many rapid technological changes that affect trends in school commercialism, such as the rapid emergence of the online social networking site Facebook, which may provide a more captive and targeted 'virtual' youth market than schools can,[9] and advertising within the virtual world of video games is booming.[10]

Political Prescriptions

Although I have offered suggestions regarding school policy and classroom strategies to address consumerism, it is not my intention to offer a comprehensive political program, pedagogical policy, or blueprint for political action. Indeed, that would run against Arendt's own concern about the influence of *Homo faber* and *Animal laborans*. The notion that we can 'make' politics or schooling according to predetermined or predictable patterns reflects the modern inclination – even imperative – to 'make' the world in our own image. Arendt shows that there is no way to control or predict how critical engagement with consumerism will be taken up in the classroom. Gert Biesta suggests that such an approach as advanced by Jurgen Habermas and John Rawls promotes an instrumental, individualistic, and homogeneous understanding of both education and democracy.[11] It could be argued that philosophy is not fully able to be prescriptive, because it can know the world and events only in hindsight; we will fully grasp the character and implications of our era of consumerism only in retrospect. As Hegel famously stated, 'Philosophy always comes late on the scene ... The owl of Minerva spreads its wings only with the falling of the dusk.'[12]

As mentioned in the introduction, the value of philosophical inquiry is not necessarily determined by the ease with which it can be translated into practical and concrete strategies. To construe philosophy in such a way would narrow the horizon of human thought and reduce its range of possibilities. I argue instead that the aim of philosophy is to push the boundaries of human understanding beyond the present constellations of political life in order to consider what could be, rather than reproduce what is. Without such 'thoughts out of season,' as Nietzsche described them, our own self-understanding would become increasingly limited to reinforcing our own particular ways of life. Such a position is radically different from that of Marx, who claimed that 'philosophy has hitherto only interpreted the world. The point is to change it.'[13]

In her last book, *The Life of the Mind*, Arendt stated that thinking 'gives no positive prescriptions' and 'does not create values,' but rather breaks down conventions and 'relentlessly dissolves and examines anew all accepted doctrines and rules.' Thought is 'equally dangerous to all creeds and, by itself, does not bring forth any new creed.' It 'belongs among those *energeia* which ... have their ends within themselves and leave no tangible outside end product,' a turning in circles, 'that never reaches an end or results in an end product.'[14] Hence, it was not Arendt's intention to offer readily applicable political prescriptions. Political philosopher Ronald Beiner claims that this reflects the contrast between a civic commitment among citizens to a particular normative political order, and the philosophical quest to challenge and expand that order: 'Radically different existential demands are made by civic life on the one hand and by the life of theory on the other [because] the purpose of the theorist is not to offer sensible guidance on the conduct of social life, but rather to probe the normative adequacy of a given vision of social order ... The practice of citizenship should be sober, sensible, prudential, moderate, and (in the best sense of the word), "liberal," whereas theory should be radical, extravagant, probing, biting and immoderate.'[15] It is within this vein of thought that this analysis of consumerism has been offered.

In closing, it is inadequate to simply argue that we should stop spending, never go shopping, live without money, or have no possessions. A critique of consumerism is about more than the question whether to buy a specific commodity or not, but rather about whether to buy into a particular way of life or let the seductive power of consumerism drive political values and educational aims. My aim in pointing out key political and pedagogical problems of consumerism is to encourage rethinking and resistance to the extent to which education is complicit in the reproduction of a society centred upon consumption, in hopes that our era is not remembered as one so frighteningly described by Arendt as 'the most mundane society the west has ever known' (HC, 321).

Notes

Introduction

1 Solon, fifth-century-BC Athenian legislator and poet. Qtd in Aristotle, *The Politics*, trans. Carnes Lord (Chicago: University of Chicago Press, 1980), 1256b33.

2 'America Strikes Back: Bush's Press Conference Runs on Themes,' aired 12 Oct. 2001, CNN.com, http://archives.cnn.com/TRANSCRIPTS/0110/12/se.04.html.

3 The complete text is available at 'June 4, 1940, Winston Churchill, "We Shall Fight on the Beaches,"' Fifties Web, http://www.fiftiesweb.com/usa/winston-churchill-fight-beaches.htm.

4 Willie L. Brown, Jr, 'A Message from the Mayor, San Francisco Chamber of Commerce, 11–17 Nov. 2000,' http://www.sfvirtualshop.com/mayor_brown.htm.

5 'Patriotic Shopping Tote,' American Promotions, 2008, http://www.ameripromo.com/patriotic-shopping-tote-p-3493.html.

6 Garnet Fraser, 'Up Front,' *See Magazine*, 8 Nov. 2001, http://www.seemagazine.com/Issues/2001/1108/front1.htm.

7 *Los Angeles Times*, 17 Sept. 2001. Article unavailable without subscription; however, the quotation can be found at Janine Jackson, 'Media Define Citizenship as Consumerism,' familyresource.com, http://www.familyresource.com/lifestyles/10/322/.

8 See 'The Text of President George W. Bush's Address to America before Representatives of Firemen, Law Enforcement Officers, and Postal Workers,' Atlanta, Georgia, 8 Nov. 2001, Archives of Global Change in the 21st Century, http://www.september11news.com/PresidentBushAtlanta.htm.

9 'No, We Don't Lost War in Iraq: Bush,' 20 Dec. 2006, CBCNews, http://www.cbc.ca/world/story/2006/12/20/bush-presser.html.

10 Tavia Grant, 'Canadians Not Saving Enough,' *Globe and Mail*, 13 Sept. 2005.

11 Robert E. Lane, *The Loss of Happiness in Market Democracies* (New Haven: Yale University Press, 2000), 183.

12 Marcos Chamon and Eswar Prasad, 'Why Are Savings Rates of Urban Households in China Rising?' 2008, http://prasad.aem.cornell.edu/doc/ChamonPrasad.AEJMacro.pdf, 4.

13 Doug Saunders, 'Top Central Bankers Play Down Threat of Global Economic Crisis,' *Globe and Mail*, 5 Feb. 2005.

14 Will Smale, 'China's Growth Looks Set to Continue,' 27 Dec. 2006, BBC Online, http://news.bbc.co.uk/2/hi/business/4528514.stm.

15 Marcus Gee, 'China's Thrift Is No Saving Grace,' *Globe and Mail*, 24 Jan. 2009.

16 'Power at Last,' *Economist*, 2 Apr. 2005, 11.

17 See Lauren Wiseberger: *The Devil Wears Prada: A Novel* (New York: Broadway Books, 2004). See the series by Sophie Kinsella titled *Confessions of a Shopaholic: Shopaholic Ties the Knot; Shopaholic Takes Manhattan; Shopaholic and Sister*. The back of the novel describes the plotline: 'If you've ever paid off one credit card with another, thrown out a bill before opening it, or convinced yourself that buying at a two-for-one sale is like making money, then this silly, appealing novel is for you.' See entry on Amazon.com at http://www.amazon.com/gp/product/0385335482/104-6276754-0030309?v=glance&n=283155.

18 Matthew Creamer, 'Ad Agency of the Year: The Consumer,' *Advertising Age*, 8 Jan. 2007, http://adage.com/article?article_id=114132.

19 Robert Goldman and Stephen Papson. 'Capital's Brandscapes.' *Journal of Consumer Culture* 6, no. 3 (2006): 351.

20 Manuel Castells, *The Rise of the Network Society* (Oxford: Blackwell, 1996), 1:3.

21 None of these three terms are my own. I borrow *McDonaldization* from G. Ritzer, *The McDonaldization of Society* (Thousand Oaks: Pine Forge Press, 2001); and D. Boyles, *American Education and Corporations: The Free Market Goes to Schools* (New York: Garland, 1998), 43–4. I borrow *Disneyification* from Henry Giroux, *The Mouse That Roared: Disney and the End of Innocence* (New York: Rowman and Littlefield, 1999); and more recently Ian E. Bryman, *The Disneyization of Society* (Thousand Oaks: Sage, 2004). It has also been called *McDisneyification*.

22 Daniel R. White and Gert Hellerick. 'Nietzsche at the Mall: Deconstructing the Consumer,' *CTHEORY*, 2007, http://www.ctheory.net/articles.aspx?id=50.

23 'Loose Change: The Spending Addict Forum,' http://www.loose-change

.org/ (accessed 9 Sept. 2007). Now renamed 'Debtor's Anonymous,' http://www.debtorsanonymous.org.

24 A psychiatric study concluded that 'Citalopram appears to be a safe and effective treatment for compulsive shopping.' See L.M. Koran, K.D. Bullock, H.J. Hartston, M.A. Elliott, and V. D'Andrea, 'Citalopram Treatment of Compulsive Shopping: An Open-Label Study,' *Journal of Clinical Psychiatry* 63, no. 8 (2002): 704–8.

25 See, for example, Stephen H. Baird, 'The Malling of America: The Selling of America's Public Parks and Streets – The Economic Censorship and Suppression of First Amendment Rights,' http://www.buskersadvocates .org/saamall.html; William Severini Kowinski, *The Malling of America: Travels in the United States of Shopping* (New York: Xlibris, 2002).

26 Ashish Kumar Sen, 'The Malling of America,' *Span* (Mar./Apr. 2005): 3–70.

27 See http://www.deadmalls.com/.

28 Frank Trentmann. 'Beyond Consumerism: New Historical Perspectives on Consumption,' *Journal of Contemporary History* 39, no. 3 (2002): 382.

29 John Dewey, *Democracy and Education: An Introduction to the Philosophy of Education* (1916; New York: Free Press, 1944), 35, 57.

30 Benjamin Barber, *An Aristocracy of Everyone: The Politics of Education and the Future of America* (New York: Random House, 1992), 9.

1 The Origins and Nature of Consumerism

1 The Persian king Xerxes (5th century BC), qtd in Colin Campbell, *The Romantic Ethic and the Spirit of Modern Consumerism* (Oxford: Blackwell, 1987), 58.

2 John Lukacs, *The End of the Twentieth Century and the End of the Modern Age* (New York: Ticknor & Fields, 1993), 64.

3 Sut Jhally, 'Image-Based Culture: Advertising and Popular Culture,' in *Gender, Race and Class in Media*, ed. Gail Dines and Jean Humez (London: Sage, 2003), 249.

4 Ad Creep, http://adcreep.co.uk/.

5 Tijn Touber, 'A Real Revolution in Advertising,' Ode (Sept. 2004), http://www.odemagazine.com/doc/16/a_real_revolution_in_advertising.

6 See, for example, Seven Shugan, 'Editorial: Who Is Afraid to Give Freedom of Speech to Marketing Folks?' *Marketing Science* 25, no. 5 (2006): 403–10; Ann Sutherland and Betty Thompson, *Kidfluence: Why Kids Today Mean Business* (Toronto: McGraw-Hill Ryerson, 2001).

7 David B. Clarke, Marcus A. Doel, and Kate M. L. Housiaux, *The Consumption Reader* (New York: Routledge, 2003), 1.

8 'Consume,' in *Oxford English Dictionary* (1989).
9 'Phthisis,' in *Oxford English Dictionary* (1989). *Phthisis* is Greek for 'consumption.' Cancer has increasingly emerged as the dominant disease today, one that 'consumes' the body and the body politic with equal intensity and aggressiveness, often promoted by the very way of life upon which consumerism is based. See Susan Sontag, *Illness as Metaphor* (New York: Farrar, Straus and Giroux, 1988).
10 Raymond Williams, *Keywords* (Oxford: Oxford University Press, 1976).
11 *Oxford English Dictionary*, 1989.
12 Clarke, Doel, and Housiaux, *Consumption Reader*, 1.
13 Jean-Christopher Agnew, 'The Consuming Vision of Henry James,' in *The Culture of Consumption: Critical Essays in American History 1880–1980*, ed. Richard Wightman Fox and T.J. Jackson Lears (New York: Pantheon, 1983), 102.
14 Anthony Giddens, *Beyond Left and Right: The Future of Radical Politics* (Cambridge: Polity, 2004).
15 Svi Shapiro, *Between Capitalism and Democracy: Educational Policy and the Crisis of the Welfare State* (New York: Bergin and Garvey, 1990), 32.
16 Ibid., x.
17 Alan Aldridge, *Consumption* (Cambridge: Polity, 2003); Robert Bocock, *Consumption* (London: Routledge, 1993); David B. Clarke, *The Consumer Society and the Postmodern City* (London: Routledge, 2003).
18 Steve Best and Douglas Kellner, 'Debord, Cybersituations, and the Interactive Spectacle,' Illuminations, 2002, http://www.uta.edu/huma/illuminations/best6.htm.
19 Naomi Klein, *No Logo: Taking Aim at the Brand Bullies* (Toronto: Vintage, 2000).
20 Henry Giroux, *The Abandoned Generation* (New York: Palgrave, 2003), 46.
21 Robert E. Lane, *The Loss of Happiness in Market Democracies* (New Haven: Yale University Press, 2000), 178.
22 Edward Bernays cited in Stuart Ewen, *Captains of Consciousness: Advertising and the Social Roots of the Consumer Culture* (Toronto: McGraw-Hill, 1976), 83. See also the documentary *The Century of the Self*, BBC Online notice, 2002, http://www.bbc.co.uk/bbcfour/documentaries/features/century_of_the_self.shtml.
23 Clarke, Doel, and Housiaux, *Consumption Reader*, 18.
24 Daniel Bell, *The Cultural Contradictions of Capitalism* (New York: Basic Books, 1976).
25 Ralph W. Larkin, *Suburban Youth in Cultural Crisis* (Oxford: Oxford University Press, 1979).

26 John Kenneth Galbraith, *The Affluent Society* (New York: Penguin, 1968); Bocock, *Consumption*.

27 Frank Trentmann, 'Bread, Milk and Democracy: Consumption and Citizenship in Twentieth-Century Britain,' in *The Politics of Consumption*, ed. Martin Daunton and Matthew Hilton (New York: Bergin and Garvey, 2001), 132.

28 Hannah Arendt, *Totalitarianism*, vol. 2, *The Origins of Totalitarianism* (New York: Harcourt, Brace and World, 1951), 468.

29 Francis Fukuyama, *The End of History and the Last Man* (Toronto: Free Press, 1992). The notion of an 'end of history' in fact originates in the work of Alexander Kojeve, particularly his reading of Hegelian dialectics and anticipation of the arrival of a 'universal and homogeneous state.' See Alexandre Kojeve. *Introduction to the Reading of Hegel: Lectures on the Phenomenology of Spirit* (Ithaca: Cornell University Press, 1980).

30 Ibid., 48, xi, 46.

31 As will become apparent in chapter 4, Baudrillard echoes this aspect of consumerism. See Jean Baudrillard, 'The Global and the Universal,' in *Screened Out* (New York: Verso, 2000), 155–9.

32 Thomas L. Friedman, *The Lexus and the Olive Tree* (New York: Farrar, Straus and Giroux, 2000), 68. The thesis was disproved by such events as the American bombing of Serbia and Bosnia in 1999 and the 2006 conflict between Israel and Lebanon. See also Kenneth Saltman and Robin Truth Goodman, *Strange Love: Or How We Learn to Stop Worrying and Love the Market* (New York: Rowman and Littlefield, 2002).

33 Ibid., 79. It is noteworthy that Thomas Friedman married into the billionaire Bucksbaum family, owners of the commercial real estate giant General Growth Properties, instrumental in the early development of shopping malls in the United States. See 'Over 50 Years of Experience,' GGP, 2010, http://www.ggp.com/company/CompanyHistory.aspx.

34 Lizabeth Cohen, *The Consumers Republic: The Politics of Mass Consumption in Postwar America* (New York: Vintage, 2003), 127.

35 Gary Cross, *An All-Consuming Century: Why Commercialism Won in Modern America* (New York: Columbia University Press, 2000).

36 Richard Wightman Fox and T.J. Jackson Lears, *The Culture of Consumption: Critical Essays in American History 1880–1980* (New York: Pantheon, 1983).

37 The full text of the debate is available on the educational division of the CNN website: http://teachingamericanhistory.org/library/index.asp?document=176.

38 Ibid. Khrushchev said, 'You're a lawyer for capitalism, I'm a lawyer for communism. Let's kiss.'

39 David Reisman, *Abundance for What? and Other Essays* (New York: Doubleday, 1964), 67.

40 Ibid., 68.

41 Barbara Ehrenreich, 'Laden with Lard,' *ZETA* (July/Aug. 1990): 46.

42 See You Tube, 2006, http://www.youtube.com/watch?v=C9lvzzH0STw.

43 See The Intangible Economy website, http://www.intangibleeconomy .org/.

44 Clarke, Doel, and Housiaux, *Consumption Reader*, 17.

45 Ernst Vollrath, 'Hannah Arendt and the Method of Political Thinking,' *Social Research* 44 (1977): 174. As Vollrath summarizes Arendt, 'The loss of the ability [to distinguish] leads to notorious generalizations which paralyze the perception of reality; nothing new and nothing distinctive can be discerned any longer.'

46 Adam Smith, *An Inquiry into the Nature and Causes of the Wealth of Nations* (1776; New York: Modern Library, 1937), v.

47 Ibid., viii.

48 Clarke, Doel, and Housiaux, *Consumption Reader*, 3.

49 Smith, *Wealth of Nations*, 625.

50 See, for example, Aldridge, *Consumption*.

51 Joachim Israel, *Alienation: From Marx to Modern Sociology*, ed. Amitai Etzioni (New Jersey: Humanities, 1971), 287.

52 Ibid., 280.

53 Max Weber, *The Protestant Work Ethic and the Spirit of Capitalism*, trans. Talcott Parsons (1905; New York: Scribner, 1958).

54 Ibid., 51, 53.

55 C.B. Macpherson, *The Political Theory of Possessive Individualism* (Oxford: Oxford University Press, 1962).

56 Ibid., 3.

57 Ibid., 194.

58 Thomas Hobbes, *Leviathan*, ed. C.B. Macpherson (1651; New York: Penguin Books, 1982), 119–30.

59 John Locke, 'Second Treatise on Civil Government,' in *Political and Social Philosophy: Traditional and Contemporary Readings*, ed. J.C. King and J.A. McGilvray (1689; Toronto: McGraw-Hill, 1972), chap. 2: 4.

60 Ibid., chap. 5: 25.

61 John Stuart Mill, *Utilitarianism, on Liberty, Essay on Bentham* (New York: New American Library, 1962).

62 C.B. Macpherson, *The Life and Times of Liberal Democracy* (Oxford: Oxford University Press, 1977), 179.

63 Ruth Jonathan, *Illusory Freedoms: Liberalism, Education and the Market* (Oxford: Blackwell, 1997), 6. Her italics.

64 Qtd in Campbell, *Romantic Ethic*, 58.

65 See, for example, Aldridge, *Consumption*.

66 Daniel Bell, *The Cultural Contradictions of Capitalism* (New York: Basic Books, 1976).

67 Thorsten Veblen, *The Theory of the Leisure Class* (1899; New York: Modern Library, 1931), 28.

68 Harry Hodder, 'Thorstein Veblen,' in *Architects of Modern Thought: Twelve Talks for CBC Radio*, ed. John A. Irving (Toronto: CBC Publishing Branch, 1959), 49.

69 Veblen, *Theory of the Leisure Class*, 75.

70 Ibid., 32.

71 Clive Hamilton, *Growth Fetish* (Chicago: Pluto, 2004), 145.

72 Robert L. Heilbroner, *The Worldly Philosophers: The Lives, Times, and Ideas of the Great Economic Thinkers* (New York: Simon and Shuster, 1953), 221.

73 Clarke, Doel, and Housiaux, *Consumption Reader*, 19.

74 Walter Benjamin, *The Arcades Project* (Cambridge: Belknap, 2002), 178.

75 Ibid., 195.

76 Pasi Falk, 'The Benetton-Toscani Effect: Testing the Limits of Conventional Advertising,' in *Buy This Book: Studies in Advertising and Consumption*, ed. Blake Mica, Andrew Nava, Iain MacRury, and Barry Richards (London: Routledge, 1997), 66.

77 Bocock, *Consumption*.

78 Ibid., 191.

79 Ibid., 46.

80 Paul Virillo, *The Information Bomb* (London: Verso, 2000); Paul Virillo, *Speed and Politics: An Essay on Dromology* (1977; New York: Semiotext(e), 1986), 117.

81 Ibid., 125.

82 David Harvey, *The Condition of Postmodernity: An Enquiry into the Origins of Cultural Change* (Cambridge, MA: Blackwell, 1990).

83 Ibid., 241.

84 Zygmunt Bauman, *Liquid Modernity* (London: Polity, 1990), 41, 43, 44.

85 Samuel P. Huntington, *The Clash of Civilizations and the Remaking of World Order* (New York: Touchstone Books, 1996).

86 Ali Shariati, 'Reflections of Humanity,' Iran Chamber Society, http://www.iranchamber.com/personalities/ashariati/works/reflections_of_humanity.php.

87 Ibid.
88 Ibid.
89 Ibid.
90 Vandana Shiva, *Monocultures of the Mind: Perspectives on Biodiversity and Biotechnology* (London: Zed Books, 1993).
91 Vandana Shiva, *Earth Democracy* (Boston: South End, 2005), 67.
92 *Thano* is derived from the Greek *thanatos* or 'death.' See Nathan B. Batalion, *Fifty Harmful Effects of Genetically Modified Foods* (Oneonta, NY: Americans for Safe Food, 2000).
93 Vandana Shiva, 'The Suicide Economy of Corporate Globalization,' *Znet* (19 Feb. 2004).
94 Vandana Shiva, *Biopiracy: The Plunder of Nature and Knowledge* (Boston: South End, 1997).
95 Matthew Forney, 'How Nike Figured Out China,' *Time*, 1 Nov. 2004.
96 Galbraith, *Affluent Society*; John Kenneth Galbraith, *The New Industrial Society* (London: Hamish Hamilton, 1967).
97 Israel, *Alienation*, 273.
98 Joel Bakan, *The Corporation: The Pathological Pursuit of Profit and Power* (Toronto: Viking Canada, 2004). See the compelling documentary by the same title, directed by Mark Achbar, Jennifer Abbott, and Joel Bakan, Zeitgeist Production, 2004.
99 George Lodge and Craig Wilson, *A Corporate Solution to Global Poverty: How Multinationals Can Help the Poor and Invigorate Their Own Legitimacy* (New Jersey: Princeton University Press, 2006).
100 Sweden's GDP in 2005 was $283.2 billion and in 2009 was $288.3 billion; see Organisation for Economic Cooperation and Development, OECD. StatExtracts, 'Gross Domestic Product,' http://stats.oecd.org/Index. aspx?datasetcode=SNA_TABLE1.
       By comparison, WalMart revenue in 2005 was $288.2 billion and in 2009 was $405.6 billion; see CNNMoney.com, http://money.cnn.com/ magazines/fortune/fortune500_archive/snapshots/2005/1551.html, and http://money.cnn.com/magazines/fortune/fortune500/2009/ snapshots/2255.html.
101 Wesley Cragg, 'Ethics and Business in the New Age of Globalization: Creating a Collaborative Business Ethics Research Network,' SSHRC research proposal, York University (2005), 5. See also 'Building a Canadian Business Ethics Research Network,' CBERN, http://www.cbern.ca/ about_us/grants/SKC_grant/skc_proposal/.
102 Ibid., 3. See also Lodge and Wilson, *Corporate Solution*.
103 John Dewey, 'Individualism Old and New,' in *Intelligence in the Modern*

World: John Dewey's Philosophy, ed. John Ratner (New York: Modern Library, 1930), 405–6.

104 George Ritzer, *The McDonaldization of Society* (Thousand Oaks, CA: Pine Forge, 2000), 1.

105 Ibid., 11.

106 Ibid., 16.

107 Ibid., 11.

108 Daniel Bell, *The Cultural Contradictions of Capitalism* (New York: Basic Books, 1976), 25.

109 'The *Economist's* Big Mac Index,' http://www.economist.com/markets/bigmac/.

2 Consuming Schooling: Whose Schools Are They?

1 Raymond Callahan, *Education and the Cult of Efficiency* (Chicago: University of Chicago Press, 1962), 261.

2 Neil Postman, *Education as a Subversive Activity* (New York: Dell, 1969), 42.

3 David Gabbard, *Knowledge and Power in the Global Economy: Politics and the Rhetoric of School Reform* (New York: Erlbaum, 1999), xi, xvii. Italics his.

4 Pierre Bourdieu, 'Cultural Reproduction and Social Reproduction,' in *Knowledge, Education, and Cultural Change: Papers in the Sociology of Education*, ed. Richard Brown (London: Tavistock, 1973), 72.

5 Samuel Bowles and Herbert Gintis, *Schooling in Capitalist America: Educational Reform and the Contradictions of Economic Life* (New York: Basic Books, 1976).

6 Ibid., 11, 129, 56.

7 Raymond E. Callahan, *Education and the Cult of Efficiency* (Chicago: University of Chicago Press, 1962), 1.

8 Ibid., 115.

9 Ibid., 6.

10 Lawrence A. Cremin, *The Transformation of the School: Progressivism in American Education 1876–1957* (New York: Vantage Books, 1961).

11 Ibid., 34, 38.

12 Emery Hyslop-Margison, 'Alternative Curriculum Evaluation: A Critical Approach to Assess Social Engineering Programs,' *Center for the Study of Curriculum and Instruction* 6 (2000); Emery Hyslop-Margison, 'Career Education and Labour Market Conditions: The Skills Gap Myth,' *Journal of Educational Thought* 37, no. 1 (2003): 5–21; Emery Hyslop-Margison, 'The Market Economy Discourse on Education: Interpretation, Impact and Resistance,' *Journal of Educational Research* 46, no. 3 (2000): 203–13.

13 Heather-Jane Robertson, *No More Teachers, No More Books: The Commercialization of Canada's Schools* (Toronto: McClelland & Stewart, 1998), 297.

14 Ivan Illich, *Deschooling Society* (New York: Harrow Books, 1970).

15 Ibid., 21, 67, 89, 57.

16 David Ramsay, minister of natural resources, 15 Oct. 2004, Ontario Fisheries Society, http://www.afs-oc.org/frost.htm.

17 Friends of the Frost Centre, http://www.friendsofthefrostcentre.ca/frame1.asp (accessed 5 Sept. 2007).

18 Field Trip Factory, homepage, http://www.fieldtripfactory.com/home.php?sid=&ts=e63b87614897582d5e1e6c1609bee79d (accessed 5 Sept. 2007).

19 Field Trip Factory, 'Vision Statement,' http://www.fieldtripfactory.com/pto.php?sid=f88ae7fbb8222d70b9bc45ac2bcc6894 (accessed 5 Sept. 2007).

20 'Field Trips,' Commercial Alert, http://www.commercialalert.org/issues/education/field-trips.

21 Field Trip Factory, 'Places to Visit,' http://www.fieldtripfactory.com/trips/walmart.php?sid=70277f7ca65e3aca75942e19bb858d09 (accessed 5 Sept. 2007).

22 Jan Nespor, 'School Fieldtrips and the Curriculum of Public Spaces,' *Journal of Curriculum Studies* 32, no. 1 (2000): 39.

23 Ibid., 28.

24 'Brand-Name Field Trips – A Total Sellout,' Commercial Alert, 29 May 2004, http://www.commercialalert.org/issues/education/field-trips/brand-name-field-trips-a-total-sellout.

25 Bernie Froese-Germain, Colleen Hawkey, Alec Larose, Patricia McAdie, and Erika Shaker, *Commercialism in Canadian Schools: Who's Calling the Shots?* (Ottawa: Canadian Teachers Federation, 2006), 4.

26 Ruth Jonathan, *Illusory Freedoms: Liberalism, Education and the Market* (Oxford: Blackwell, 1997), 4.

27 Larry Kuehn, 'What's Wrong with Commercialization of Public Education?' *Teacher Newsmagazine* 15, no. 4 (2003): 1.

28 Alex Molnar, *The Ninth Annual Report on Schoolhouse Commercialism Trends: 2005–2006* (Tempe: Arizona State University, 2006), 45.

29 Caroline E. Mayer, 'A Growing Marketing Strategy,' Commercial Alert, 3 June 2003, http://www.commercialalert.org/issues/education/field-trips/a-growing-marketing-strategy-get-em-while-theyre-young.

30 Deborah Stead, 'Corporate Classrooms and Commercialism,' *New York Times*, 5 Jan. 1997.

31 Kerry T. Burch, *Eros as the Educational Principle of Democracy* (New York: Lang, 2000), 197.

32 This remark was made before the Senate Armed Services Committee.

Wilson went on to become Eisenhower's secretary of defense. 'Business and Commerce,' *Oxford Dictionary of Phrase, Saying, and Quotation* (Oxford: Oxford University Press, 1997), 52.

33 Council for Corporate and School Partnerships, 'Council Led by Former US Education Secretaries Provides Guidelines for Model School Business Relationships,' news release, 25 Sept. 2002.

34 Kristen A. Graham. 'Is This Any Way to Pay for Public Education?' *Philadelphia Inquirer*, 22 Feb. 2004.

35 Erika Shaker, 'Youth New Network and the Commercial Carpet-Bombing of the Classroom,' *Education, Ltd.* 5 (Ottawa: Canadian Centre for Policy Alternatives, 1999), 1; Sarah Elton, 'Parental Discretion Advised,' *This Magazine*, July/August 2001, 19–23. More about Channel One and YNN will be said below.

36 Michael J. Sandel, 'Are We Still a Commonwealth? Markets, Morals, and Civic Life,' 2004, http://www.vote-auction.net/legal/Markets_Morals_and_Civic_Life.pdf.

37 Melissa K. Lickteig, 'Brand-Name Schools: The Deceptive Lure of Corporate–School Partnerships,' *Educational Forum* 68 (Fall 2003): 46.

38 Tara Kuczykowski, 'Good Student Report Card Freebies,' Deal Seeking Mom, 1 June 2010, http://dealseekingmom.com/good-student-report-card-freebies/.

39 Alex Molnar, 'The Commercial Transformation of American Public Education,' 1999 Phil Smith Lecture, Ohio Valley Philosophy of Education Society, http://epsl.asu.edu/ceru/Documents/1999phil.html.

40 See, for example, Henry Giroux, *The Mouse That Roared: Disney and the End of Innocence* (New York: Rowman and Littlefield, 1999); Henry Giroux, *Stealing Innocence: Youth, Corporate Power, and the Politics of Culture* (New York: Palgrave, 2000); Joe Kincheloe and Shirley Steinberg, eds., *Kinder Culture: The Corporate Construction of Childhood* (Boulder, CO: Westview, 1997); Naomi Klein, *No Logo: Taking Aim at the Brand Bullies* (Toronto: Vintage Canada, 2000); Alex Molnar, *Giving Kids the Business* (Boulder, CO: Westview, 1996); and Phyllis Sides, 'Captive Kids: Teaching Students to Be Consumers,' in *Selling Out Our Schools: Vouchers, Markets, and the Future of Public Education* (Milwaukee: Rethinking Schools Publication, 1996).

41 Chris Berdik, 'Your All-Mall Mater,' *Boston Globe*, 30 May 2004.

42 Matthew D. Taylor and Lisa Snell, 'Innovative School Facility Partnerships: Downtown, Airport, and Retail Space,' *Policy Study* 276 (2000): 1–21.

43 'Turn Everyday Shopping into Effortless Fundraising,' Shop and Support, 2004, http://www.shopandsupport.ca/newsas/info/Article_Dec04.

44 Steve Manning. 'The Corporate Curriculum,' *Nation*, 27 September, 1999, 17.
45 Ibid.
46 http://www.ed.arizona.edu/rimes2000/ComputerSoftware.htm (accessed 5 July 2007).
47 Personal report from Derek vanderMolen, Halifax School Board, 2004.
48 Caroline E. Mayer, 'A Growing Marketing Strategy: Get 'Em While They're Young,' Commercial Alert, 3 June 2003, http://www.commercialalert.org/ issues/education/field-trips/a-growing-marketing-strategy-get-em-while-theyre-young.
49 Coca-Cola, 'Council for Corporate & School Partnerships,' http://www.corpschoolpartners.org/.
50 Qtd in Alex Molnar, *Virtually Everywhere: Marketing to Children in America's Schools – The Seventh Annual Report on Schoolhouse Commercialism Trends, 2003–2004* (Tempe: Commercialism in Education Research Unit, Education Policy Studies Laboratory, Arizona State University, 2004).
51 Klein, *No Logo*, 95; Kenneth Saltman, *Collateral Damage: Corporatizing Public Schools – A Threat to Democracy* (New York: Rowman and Littlefield, 2000), 61, 69; Kenneth Saltman, 'Coca-Cola's Global Lessons: From Education for Corporate Globalization to Education for Global Justice,' *Teacher Education Quarterly* (Winter 2004): 155–72.
52 Erika Shaker, 'Youth New Network and the Commercial Carpet-Bombing of the Classroom,' *Education, Ltd.* 5 (Ottawa: Canadian Centre for Policy Alternatives, 1999), 8.
53 Ibid.
54 Erica Weintraub Austin, Yi-Chun 'Yvonnes' Chen, Bruce E. Pinkleton, and Jessie Quintero Johnson, 'Benefits and Costs of Channel One in a Middle School Setting and the Role of Media-Literacy Training.' *Pediatrics* 117, no. 3 (Mar. 2006), doi:10.1542/peds.2005-0953.
55 Ibid., e424, e431.
56 'Children's Advocates Ask Companies Not to Advertise on Bus Radio and Channel One,' Commercial Alert, news release, 14 Sept. 2006, http://www.commercialalert.org/news/news-releases/2006/09/childrens-advocates-ask-companies-not-to-advertise-on-busradio-and-channel-one.
57 *Super Size Me*, Free Documentaries, http://freedocumentaries.org/teatro.php?filmID=98.
58 Steven Greenhouse, 'The Rise and Rise of McDonald's,' *New York Times*, 8 June 1986.
59 'Quick Facts 2007–08 about the Pattonville School District,' http://www.psdr3.org/aboutPSD/pdf%20files/QuickFacts0708.pdf; 'East Hartford

School/Business Partnerships, Inc.,' http://www.easthartford.org/page .cfm?p=96.

60 D.M. Jacobsen and J.V. Lock, 'Technology and Teacher Education for a Knowledge Era: Mentoring for Student Futures, Not Our Past,' *Journal of Technology and Teacher Education* 12, no. 1 (2004): 75–100.

61 Brenda Gladstone and Michele Jacobsen, 'Educational Partnerships in Rocky View School Division, Part I,' *International Electronic Journal for Leadership in Learning* 3, no. 1 (1999): 1.

62 Ibid.

63 Ibid., 8.

64 'Is Junk Foot Marketing Making Kids Sick?' *Edmonton Journal*, 21 Nov. 2006, http://www.canada.com/edmontonjournal/news/bodyandhealth/ story.html?id=ab57c930-99dc-4647-a8b9-9c0b33e16770.

65 Andrew Clarke, 'How Teens Got the Power: Gen Y Has the Cash, the Cool – and a Burgeoning Consumer Culture,' *Maclean's*, 22 Mar. 1999.

66 Calvin Curran, 'Misplaced Marketing,' *Journal of Consumer Marketing* 16, no. 6 (1999): 534.

67 Youthography. 'If It's Big with You,' 2004, http://www.youthography. com/aboutus/press/news/25.html (accessed 4 May 2006).

68 Erika Shaker, 'Corporate Content: Inside and Outside the Classroom,' *Education, Limited: CCPA Education Project* 1, no. 2 (1998): 4.

69 Robyn Greenspan. 'The Kids Are Alright with Spending,' Internetnews.com, 16 Sept. 2003, http://www.internetnews.com/stats/article. php/3077581.

70 See Joel Bakan, *The Corporation: The Pathological Pursuit of Power* (Toronto: Viking, 2004), 119–22; Ann Sutherland and Betty Thompson, *Kidfluence: Why Kids Today Mean Business* (Toronto: McGraw-Hill Ryerson, 2001).

71 Jonathan Rowe and Gary Ruskin, 'The Parent's Bill of Rights: Helping Moms and Dads Fight Commercialism,' *Mothering* 116 (Jan./Feb. 2003), http://www.mothering.com/green-living/parents-bill-of-rights. See also Kim Campbell and Kent Davis-Packard, 'How Ads Get Kids to Say, I Want It!' *Christan Science Monitor*, 18 Sept. 2000, http://www.csmonitor .com/2000/0918/p1s1.html.

72 Sutherland and Thompson. *Kidfluence*, 119.

73 This is a term widely used by marketers. See the discussion by Erika Shaker of the Canadian Centre for Policy Alternatives in her article 'Individuality.com: Empowering Youth through Consumption?' in *Our Schools/ Ourselves*, July 2001, http://www.media-awareness.ca/english/resources/ articles/advertising_marketing/empowering_youth.cfm.

74 Sut Jhally interviewed by William O'Barr, 'Advertising, Cultural Criticism

& Pedagogy: An Interview with Sut Jhally,' http://www.sutjhally.com/articles/advertisingcultura.

75 Al Urbanski, 'The Branded Generation.' *Promo Magazine*, 1 July 1998, http://promomagazine.com/mag/marketing_branded_generation/index.html.

76 Michele Jacobsen and Louise Mazur, *Marketing Madness: A Survival Guide for a Consumer Society* (Boulder, CO: Westview, 1995), 21.

77 J.C. Hoekstra and E.K.R.E. Huizingh, 'The Lifetime Value Concept in Customer-Based Marketing,' *Journal of Market Focused Management* 3, no. 3 (1999): 257–74.

78 Tamar Lewin, 'In Public Schools, the Name Game as a Donor Lure,' *New York Times*, 26 Jan. 2006.

79 Erika Shaker, 'Corporate Content: Inside and Outside the Classroom,' *Education, Limited: CCPA Education Project* 1, no. 2 (1998): 4.

80 Lewin, 'Public Schools.'

81 Dianne Dunsmore, 'Losses Often Outweigh Gains: 12 Reasons to Say "No" to Corporate Partnerships,' *Canadian Centre for Policy Alternatives Education Monitor* (Ottawa: CCPA, 2000): 2.

82 Heather-Jane Robertson. 'Shall We Dance?' *Kappan* 80 (1999): 731.

83 Justin Pope, 'Textbooks: Your Ad Here? To Help Keep Costs Down, Some Say Advertising Is the Answer,' *CBS News*, 23 Aug. 2006. Articles defending this trend can be found on Textbook\Media, http://www.textbookmedia.com/OurMission.aspx.

84 Kenneth Saltman, 'Book Review: A Brief History of Neoliberalism, by David Harvey,' *Policy Futures in Education* 5, no. 2 (2007): 5.

85 Peter Cowley, 'Should Schools Accept Corporate Funding?' *Fraser Forum*, Sept. 2007, http://www.fraserinstitute.org/commerce.web/product_files/Sept07ffCorpfund.pdf.

86 Milton Friedman, 'The Social Responsibility of Business Is to Increase Its Profits,' *New York Times Magazine*, 13 Sept. 1970.

87 Robertson, *No More Teachers, No More Books*, 28.

88 Dale Duncan, 'A Big Swoosh of a Schoolyard: Is Letting Private Companies Build Public Spaces Really Our Best Hope?' *Eye Magazine*, 25 May 2006.

89 Bernie Froese-Germain, 'Getting a Read on Education Privatization,' *Perspectives* 4, no. 1 (2004): 3.

90 Robertson, *No More Teachers, No More Books*, 125.

91 Duncan, 'Big Swoosh.'

92 See, for example, Henry Giroux, *Disturbing Pleasures: Learning Popular Culture* (New York: Routledge, 1994); Joe Kincheloe and Shirley Steinberg,

eds., *Kinder Culture: The Corporate Construction of Childhood* (Boulder, CO: Westview, 1997); and Klein, *No Logo*.

93 See several works that explore this dynamic: Giroux, *Disturbing Pleasures*; Kincheloe and Steinberg, *Kinder Culture*; and Klein, *No Logo*.

94 Sarah Elton, 'Parental Discretion Advised,' *This Magazine*, July/August 2001, 19–23.

95 Ibid., 20.

96 Ibid., 23.

97 Mark Evans, 'Canadian Advertisers Must "Wake Up" to Internet,' *National Post*, 27 Oct. 2005.

98 'The Global Entertainment and Media Industry in Its Strongest Position since 2000, Will Grow 7.3 Percent Annually to $1.8 Trillion in 2009,' BNET, 19 Oct. 2005, http://findarticles.com/p/articles/mi_m0EIN/is_2005_Oct_19/ai_n15699363/.

99 Gary Ruskin, 'Why They Whine: How Corporations Prey on Our Children,' *Mothering*, http://www.mothering.com/green-living/why-they-whine-how-corporations-prey-our-children.

100 Alissa Quart, *Branded: The Buying and Selling of Teenagers* (Cambridge: Perseus Publishers, 2003); Al Urbanski, 'The Branded Generation,' Promo, 1 July 1998, http://promomagazine.com/mag/marketing_branded_generation/index.html.

101 Sutherland and Thompson, *Kidfluence*, 77.

102 Melanie Wells, 'Kid Nabbing,' *Forbes*, 2 Feb. 2004, http://www.forbes.com/free_forbes/2004/0202/084.html.

103 Ibid.

104 Keith McArthur, 'Ronald McDonald Recruits New Posse,' *Globe and Mail*, 29 Mar. 2005.

105 Tessa Wegert, 'Advertisers Playing Video Game Card,' *Globe and Mail*, 17 Dec. 2004.

106 Sutherland and Thompson, *Kidfluence*.

107 Ibid., 18.

108 Rowe and Ruskin. 'Parent's Bill of Rights.'

109 Wells, 'Kid Nabbing.'

110 Henry Giroux and Roger I. Simon, 'Schooling, Popular Culture, and a Pedagogy of Possibility,' in *Popular Culture, Schooling, and Everyday Life* (Boston, MA: Bergin and Garvey, 1989), 221.

111 'What We Do,' Mindshare, http://www.mindshareworld.com/what-we-do.

112 Melanie Wells, 'In Search of the Buy Button,' *Forbes*, 31 Aug. 2003.

113 '"Troubling Science" Worries Some,' CBC Marketplace (2002), http://

www.cbc.ca/marketplace/pre-2007/files/money/science_shopping/
index2.html.

114 Giroux, *Stealing Innocence*, 174.

115 Hal Niedzviecki, 'Can We Save These Kids?' *Globe and Mail*, 5 June 2004.

116 Melissa Lickteig, 'Brand Name Schools: The Deceptive Lure of Corporate-School Partnerships,' *Educational Forum* 68 (2003): 46.

117 Ruskin, 'Why They Whine.'

118 Juliet Schor, 'Those Ads Are Enough to Make Your Kids Sick,' *Washington Post*, 12 Sept. 2004, http://www.washingtonpost.com/wp-dyn/articles/A13374-2004Sep11.html.

119 Juliet Schor, *Born to Buy: The Commercialized Child and the New Consumer Culture* (New York: Scribner, 2004), 9.

120 Jonathan, *Illusory Freedoms*. Jonathan describes the impact of 'liberal neutrality' on education.

121 Giroux, *Stealing Innocence*, 173.

122 Deron Boyles, *American Education and Corporations: The Free Market Goes to Schools* (New York: Garland Publishing, 1998), xv.

123 Svi Shapiro, *Between Capitalism and Democracy: Educational Policy and the Crisis of the Welfare State* (New York: Bergin and Garvey, 1990), 52–3.

124 World Bank Group, 'Facilitating Investment in the Global Education Market,' International Finance Corporation, http://www2.ifc.org/edinvest/newsletter.htm.

125 Claudia R. Hepburn, 'The Canadian Educational Freedom Index,' *Studies in Educational Policy*, 2003, http://www.fraserinstitute.org/COMMERCE.WEB/product_files/freedom(scans).pdf.

126 Ibid., 7.

127 Kenneth Saltman, *The Edison Schools: Corporate Schooling and the Assault on Public Education* (New York: Routledge, 2005), 2.

128 Ibid., 76.

129 Ibid., 17.

130 Jonathan, *Illusory Freedoms*, 103.

131 Saltman, *Edison Schools*, 43.

132 Ibid., 59.

133 Ibid., 4.

134 Jonathan, *Illusory Freedoms*, 117.

135 Gordon Bigelow, 'Let There Be Markets: The Evangelical Roots of Economics,' *Harper's Magazine*, May 2005, 1.

136 Jonathan, *Illusory Freedoms*, 6.

137 Commercialism in Education Research Unit, http://www.epicpolicy.org/ceru-home.

138 'Consulting Services for Education Industry Suppliers,' Eduventures, http://www.eduventures.com/services/supplier-services.
139 M.T. Moe, K. Bailry, and R. Lau, *The Book of Knowledge: Investing in the Growing Education and Training Industry*. Report no. 1268 (Merrill Lynch & Co. Global Securities Research and Economics Group, Global Fundamental Equity Research Department, 1999).
140 Bernie Froese-Germain, Colleen Hawkey, Alec Larose, Patricia McAdie, and Erika Shaker, *Commercialism in Canadian Schools: Who's Calling the Shots?* (Ottawa: CCPA, 2006), http://www.ctf-fce.ca/documents/ Resources/en/commercialism_in_school/en/FullReport.pdf, 6.
141 Ibid., 36.
142 Ibid., 18.
143 Robertson, *No More Teachers, No More Books*, 206.
144 Paulo Freire, *Pedagogy of the Oppressed* (New York: Continuum, 1970), 133.
145 Ibid., 133, 134.
146 Ruth Davenport, 'Muir: Mcdonald's Promotion Ok If Students Benefit,' *Daily News*, 23 Jan. 2005.
147 Froese-Germain et al., *Commercialism in Canadian Schools*, 20.
148 Kuehn, 'What's Wrong with Commercialization of Public Education?' 1.
149 Alan Luke, 'Teaching after the Market: From Commodity to Cosmopolitan,' *Teachers College Record* 106, no. 7 (2004): 1427–8.
150 Michael Sandel, 'Are We Still a Commonwealth? Markets, Morals, and Civic Life,' Massachusetts Foundation for the Humanities. http://www.masshumanities.org/?p=f04_awsc&searchlight=commonwealth.
151 Giroux, *Stealing Innocence*, 173.
152 Ibid.
153 Ibid.
154 Lewin, 'Public Schools.'
155 Froese-Germain et al., *Commercialism in Canadian Schools*, 16.
156 'Children's Advocates.'
157 Qtd in Kathleen Deveny, 'Consumer-Products Firms Hit the Books, Trying to Teach Brand Loyalty in School,' *Wall Street Journal*, 17 July 1990.
158 Keith Leslie, 'Province to Ban Trans Fats from School Cafeterias,' *Toronto Star*, 4 Dec. 2007, http://www.thestar.com/News/article/282562.
159 Stephen Petrina, 'Book Review: School Commercialism: From Democratic Ideal to Market Commodity,' *Teachers College Record*, 26 May 2006.
160 Ibid.
161 Alan Luke, 'Teaching after the Market: From Commodity to Cosmopolitan,' *Teachers College Record* 106, no. 7 (2004): 1427.

162 Kerry T. Burch, *Eros as the Educational Principle of Democracy* (New York: Lang, 2000), 197.
163 Walter Parker, 'Public Schools Hotbeds of Democracy?' *Our Schools, Our Selves* 16, no. 1 (2006): 152.

3 Hannah Arendt: Consuming the Polis

1 Aristotle, *The Politics*, trans. Carnes Lord (Chicago: University of Chicago Press, 1980), 1253a1–29.
2 Hannah Arendt, *The Origins of Totalitarianism*, vol. 2, *Imperialism* (New York: Harcourt, Brace and World, 1951), 297.
3 Maxine Greene, *The Dialectic of Freedom* (New York: Teachers College Press, 1988), 2, 114.
4 Ibid., 2.
5 Ibid., 7.
6 Joe Heath, 'The Structure of Hip Consumerism,' *Philosophy and Social Criticism* 27, no. 6 (2001): 4.
7 'Job Postings,' The Yonge-Dundas Square, http://ydsquare.ca/gm_position.htm (accessed 7 Sept. 2005).
8 'March 2005 Newsletter,' Toronto Publicspace Committee, http://publicspace.ca/newsletter_mar05.htm. The takeover of public space is also occurring on public transit systems, as new technology allows for constantly changing televised ads to replace outmoded print and photo ads. Keith McArthur of the *Globe and Mail* notes, 'Television is going underground in Canada as commuter train systems look for new ways to entertain customers and boost advertising revenue.' See Keith McArthur, 'TV Ads Go Underground: Canada's Commuter-Advertising Business Looks to Increase Revenue, Entertain Riders,' *Globe and Mail*, 29 Mar. 2005. See also Matt Hartley, 'Tunnel Visionaries,' *Globe and Mail*, 30 Jan. 2008, http://www.theglobeandmail.com/archives/article664325.ece.
9 Richard Sennett, *The Fall of Public Man: On the Social Psychology of Capitalism* (New York: Vintage Books, 1974), 3.
10 Hannah Arendt, 'What Remains? The Language Remains: A Conversation with Gunter Gaus,' in *Essays in Understanding: 1930–1954* (New York: Shocken Books, 1994).
11 Hannah Arendt, *Men in Dark Times* (New York: Harvest Books, 1970).
12 See, for example, Charles Larmore, 'Political Liberalism,' in *The Morals of Modernity*, ed. Charles Larmore, 121–44 (New York: Cambridge University Press, 1996); John Rawls, *Political Liberalism* (New York: Columbia University Press, 1993).

13 Hannah Arendt, 'The Crisis in Education,' in *Between Past and Future: Eight Exercises in Political Thought* (New York: Penguin, 1968), 196.

14 Noel O'Sullivan, 'Hannah Arendt: Hellenic Nostalgia and Industrial Society,' in *Contemporary Political Philosophers*, ed. B. de Crespigny and K. Minogue (New York: Metheun, 1975), 228–9.

15 Margaret Canovan, 'Introduction,' in Hannah Arendt, *The Human Condition* (Chicago: University of Chicago Press, 1958), viii.

16 Ibid.

17 Hannah Arendt, *The Origins of Totalitarianism*, vol. 2, *Totalitarianism* (New York: Harcourt, Brace and World, 1951), xxxi.

18 Kimberly Curtis, *Our Sense of the Real: Aesthetic Experience and Arendtian Politics* (Ithaca: Cornell University Press, 1999), 84.

19 Benjamin Barber, *Strong Democracy: Participatory Politics for a New Age* (1984; Los Angeles: University of California Press, 2003), 122.

20 Hannah Arendt, 'A Reply to Eric Voegelin's Review of the Origins of Totalitarianism,' *Review of Politics* 6 (1953): 83.

21 Ibid., 79–80.

22 Hannah Arendt, *Between Past and Future* (New York, Penguin, 1961), 15.

23 Jacques Taminiaux, *The Tracian Maid and the Professional Thinker: Arendt and Heidegger* (New York: State University of New York Press, 1977), 122.

24 Hannah Arendt, 'Concern with Politics,' in *Essays in Understanding: 1930–1954* (New York: Shocken Books, 1994), 432.

25 Curtis, *Our Sense of the Real*, 63.

26 I used quotations here for the same reasons as outlined above: because the public seems to be a highly and intangible concept, one of the reasons why it is difficult for us to understand or experience the 'public realm.'

27 Alastair Hannay, *On the Public* (London: Routledge, 2005), 20.

28 Ibid., 7.

29 Curtis, *Our Sense of the Real*, 81.

30 Ibid., 176.

31 Ibid., 43.

32 Michel Foucault, *The History of Sexuality* (London: Penguin, 1990).

33 Georgio Agamben, *Homo Sacer: Sovereign Power and Bare Life* (1995; Stanford, CA: Stanford University Press, 1998), 4.

34 Ibid., 8.

35 Carl Schmitt, *The Concept of the Political* (New Brunswick: Rutgers University, 1976), 70–1.

36 For example, this assumption can be found in the first sentence for the entry 'public sphere' in what would seem to be that most public of spheres,

Wikipedia: 'The concept of Public Sphere was first introduced by Jürgen Habermas, in his book, *The Structural Transformation of the Public Sphere: An Inquiry into a Category of Bourgeois Society*,' http://en.wikipedia.org/wiki/Public_sphere (accessed September 2007).

37 Jurgen Habermas, *The Structural Transformation of the Public Sphere: An Inquiry into a Category of Bourgeois Society* (1962; Cambridge, MA: MIT Press, 1988), 46, 48.

38 Jurgen Habermas, 'Hannah Arendt's Communicative Conception of Power,' *Social Research* 144 (1977): 8–9.

39 Habermas, *Structural Transformation of the Public Sphere*.

40 Hannay, *On the Public*, xi.

41 Habermas, *Structural Transformation of the Public Sphere*, 33.

42 This concept occurs on several occasions in both *The Politics* and *The Nicomachean Ethics*.

43 Hannah Arendt, 'The Crisis in Culture,' in *Between Past and Future*, ed. Hannah Arendt (New York: Penguin, 1960), 211.

44 David Riesman, *The Lonely Crowd* (New Haven: Yale University Press, 1950).

45 Lizabeth Cohen, *The Consumers Republic: The Politics of Mass Consumption in Postwar America* (New York: Vintage, 2003).

46 H.K. Nixon, *Principles of Selling* (New York: McGraw-Hill Book, 1942), 145.

47 Ashish Kumar Sen, 'The Malling of America,' *Span* (March/April 2005): 3–7.

48 Ibid.

49 Zygmunt Bauman, *Society under Siege* (London: Polity, 2002), 167, 179.

50 Ibid., 168.

51 Ibid., 170.

52 Arendt, 'Crisis in Culture,' 207, 212.

53 Ibid., 208.

54 Curtis, *Our Sense of the Real*, 19.

55 Ibid., 7.

4 Jean Baudrillard: Consuming Signs

1 Søren Kierkegaard, *The Present Age*, trans. Alexander Du (London: Collins, 1962), 36, as qtd in Jean Baudrillard, *The Intelligence of Evil, or, the Lucidity Pact*, trans. Chris Turner (New York: Berg, 2005), 1.

2 Jean Baudrillard, *The System of Objects* (1968; London: Verso, 1996), 25.

3 Bradley Levinson, *Schooling the Symbolic Animal: Social and Cultural Dimensions of Education* (New York: Rowman and Littlefield, 2000), 2, 15.
4 'Stay Free! High School Media Literacy Curriculum,' Stayfree Magazine, http://www.stayfreemagazine.org/ml/index.html.

American Alphabet by Heidi Cody

There is also a similar alphabet available at MIT Laboratory for Branding Cultures: http://web.mit.edu/cms/bcc/2005/03/retail-alphabet-game. html.

5 E.D. Hirsch Jr, *Cultural Literacy: What Every American Needs to Know* (Boston: Houghton Mifflin, 1987).
6 Trevor Norris, 'Cultivating Sweet Things: An Interview with Culture Jammer Carly Stasko,' *Orbit Magazine* (Spring 2005): 22–5.
7 Michael Peters, 'Introduction,' in *Naming the Multiple: Poststructuralism and Education*, ed. Michael Peters (Westport, CT: Bergin and Garvey, 1998), 4.
8 Jean-Francois Lyotard, *The Postmodern Condition: A Report on Knowledge* (Minneapolis: University of Minnesota Press, 1984).

9 Friedrich Nietzsche, *The Gay Science*, trans. Walter Kaufman (1882, 1887; New York: Vintage, 1974), sec. 125, 181–2. The full description reads,

> 'Whither are we moving? Away from all suns? Are we not plunging continually? Backward, sideward, forward, in all directions? Is there still any up or down?' ... Here the madman fell silent and looked again at his listeners; and they, too, were silent and stared at him in astonishment. At last he threw his lantern on the ground, and it broke into pieces and went out. 'I have come too early,' he said then; 'my time is not yet. This tremendous event is still on its way, still wandering; it has not yet reached the ears of men. Lightning and thunder require time; the light of the stars requires time; deeds, though done, still require time to be seen and heard. This deed is still more distant from them than most distant stars – *and yet they have done it themselves.*'

10 Jean Baudrillard, *The Gulf War Did Not Take Place* (Bloomington: Indiana University Press, 1995).
11 Jean Baudrillard, 'The Spirit of Terrorism,' *Le Monde*, 2 Nov. 2001.
12 Doug Kellner, 'Introduction,' in *Baudrillard: A Critical Reader*, ed. Doug Kellner (Oxford: Blackwell, 1994), 19.
13 Charles Levin, *Jean Baudrillard: A Study in Cultural Metaphysics* (New York: Prentice Hall, 1996), 88.
14 Doug Kellner, 'Remembering Baudrillard: A Good Long Run,' *International Journal of Baudrillard Studies*, 11 Mar. 2007, http://www.ubishops.ca/BaudrillardStudies/obituaries_dkellner.html.
15 Robert Fulford, 'A French Intellectual – in the Worst Sense of the Term Jean Baudrillard Could Make Any Subject More Obscure Just by Briefly Visiting It,' *National Post*, 10 Mar. 2007.
16 Steven Poole, 'Jean Baudrillard: Philosopher and Sociologist Who Blurred the Boundaries between Reality and Simulation,' *Guardian Unlimited*, 7 Mar. 2007, http://www.guardian.co.uk/obituaries/story/0,,2028464,00.html.
17 Jean Baudrillard, *Cool Memories IV* (New York: Verso, 2003), 65.
18 Gerry Coulter, 'Passings – Jean Baudrillard: Remembering a Writer ... a Photographer ... and a Friend.' *International Journal of Baudrillard*, http://www.ubishops.ca/BaudrillardStudies/obituaries_gcoulter.html#32.
19 Douglas Kellner, 'Baudrillard: A New McLuhan?' Illuminations: The Critical Theory Project, http://www.gseis.ucla.edu/faculty/kellner/Illumina%20Folder/kell26.htm.
20 Eric Voegelin, *The New Science of Politics: An Introduction* (1952; Chicago: University of Chicago Press, 1987), 27.

21 See Don Delillo's extraordinary novel on this theme, *White Noise* (New York: Penguin, 1999).

22 Jean Baudrillard, 'The Violence of the Image,' The European Gradual School, http://www.egs.edu/faculty/baudrillard/baudrillard-the-violence-of-the-image.html.

23 Steven Shugan, 'Editorial: Who Is Afraid to Give Freedom of Speech to Marketing Folks?' *Marketing Science* 25, no. 5 (2006): 403.

24 Roger A. Shiner, *Freedom of Commercial Expression* (Oxford: Clarendon, 2004), 2.

25 Kellner, 'Remembering Baudrillard.'

26 Peter McLaren and Zeus Leonardo, 'Jean Baudrillard: From Marxism to Terrorist Pedagogy,' in *Naming the Multiple: Poststructuralism and Education*, ed. Michael Peters (Westport: CT: Bergin and Garvey, 1998), 222.

27 Ibid., 222–3.

28 Jean Baudrillard, *Symbolic Exchange and Death* (London: Sage, 1993), 20.

29 Mark Gottdiener, 'The System of Objects and the Commodification of Everyday Life: The Early Baudrillard,' in *Baudrillard: A Critical Reader*, ed. Doug Kellner (Oxford: Blackwell, 1994), 29.

30 Ibid., 32.

31 George Ritzer, *The McDonalidization of Society* (Thousand Oaks, CA: Pine Forge, 2000), 190.

32 Sut Jhally, 'Advertising as Religion: The Dialectic of Technology and Magic,' in *Cultural Politics in Contemporary America*, ed. Ian Angus and Sut Jhally (New York: Routledge, 1989), 221–2.

33 Jean Baudrillard, *The Mirror of Production* (St Louis: Telos, 1975), 126–9.

34 Ibid., 22.

35 Jean Baudrillard, *For a Critique of the Political Economy of the Sign* (St Louis: Telos, 1981), 5.

36 Sut Jhally, 'Image-Based Culture: Advertising and Popular Culture,' in *Gender, Race and Class in Media*, ed. Gail Dines and Jean Humez (London: Sage, 2003), 253.

37 Quoteworld.com, http://www.quoteworld.org/category/age/author/herbert__marshall__mcluhan.

38 Jim Munro, *Everyone in Silico* (Toronto: Insomniac, 2002), 46.

39 Baudrillard, 'Violence of the Image.'

40 Ibid.

41 Kenneth Wain, *The Learning Society in a Postmodern World: The Education Crisis* (New York: Lang, 2004), 290.

42 Baudrillard, 'Violence of the Image.'

43 Ibid.

44 Baudrillard, *Intelligence of Evil*.
45 Ibid., 23.
46 Audrey Gillan, 'US Will Shoot Down Hijacked Jets,' *Guardian*, 28 Sept. 2001, http://www.guardian.co.uk/world/2001/sep/28/terrorismandtravel. september11.
47 Jean Baudrillard, 'Disneyworld Company,' trans. François Debrix, *Liberation*, 4 Mar. 1996, http://www.egs.edu/faculty/baudrillard/baudrillard-disneyworld-company.html.
48 Naomi Klein, 'No Logo: Brands, Globalization & Resistance,' transcript, Media Education Foundation, http://www.mediaed.org/handouts/pdfs/NO-LOGO.pdf.
49 Ibid.
50 Naomi Klein, *No Logo: Taking Aim at the Brand Bullies* (Toronto: Vintage Canada, 2000), 155.
51 Ibid.
52 Newfoundland and Labrador, http://www.newfoundlandlabrador.com/. Available on You Tube at http://www.youtube.com/watch?v=k7B19bzRHEA.
53 It may be contentious to call money 'real,' especially after the liquidation of hundreds of billions in fall 2008 – money that in fact may never have been 'real' in the first place, though it certainly feels real to those who lose it, either in Vegas or on Wall Street.
54 Place Branding, http://www.placebrands.net/placebranding/placebranding.html.
55 Nation Branding, http://www.nation-branding.info/.
56 Robert Goldman and Stephen Papson, 'Capital's Brandscapes,' *Journal of Consumer Culture* 6, no. 3 (2006): 337.
57 Ibid., 327, 330.
58 Ibid., 344–5.
59 Tom Peters, 'The Brand Called You,' *Fast Company*, 31 Aug. 2007. The tagline reads, 'Big companies understand the importance of brands. Today, in the Age of the Individual, you have to be your own brand. Here's what it takes to be the CEO of Me Inc.,' http://www.fastcompany.com/magazine/10/brandyou.html.
60 Carly Stasko and Trevor Norris, 'AML Panel on Youth Marketing: Transcript of Event,' Association for Media Literacy, 2 Nov. 2005, http://www.aml.ca/articles/articles.php?articleID=349.
61 'If It Works, It's Obsolete: Marshall McLuhanisms,' http://www.marshallmcluhan.com/poster.html.
62 Robert Goldman and Stephen Papson, 'Capital's Brandscapes,' *Journal of Consumer Culture* 6, no. 3 (2006): 332.

63 Ibid., 350.
64 Ibid.
65 Ibid., 351.
66 Baudrillard, ' Violence of the Image.'
67 Wain, *Learning Society*, 288.
68 Ibid., 22.
69 Jean Baudrillard, *The Vital Illusion* (New York: Columbia University Press, 2000), 15–16.
70 Francis Fukuyama, *The End of History and the Last Man* (1992; Toronto: Free Press, 2006).
71 Jean Baudrillard, *The Illusion of the End*, trans. Chris Turner (1992; Stanford, CA: Stanford University Press, 1994), 5.
72 Wain, *Learning Society*, 292.
73 Baudrillard, *Illusion of the End*, 91.
74 Ibid., 7.
75 Ibid., 116.
76 See Maurizio Passerin d'Entreves and Seyla Benhabib, eds., *Habermas and the Unfinished Project of Modernity* (Cambridge: MIT Press, 1997). The title of this book makes reference to a now-famous speech given by Habermas in September 1980 entitled 'Modernity: An Unfinished Project' at the College de France, and later became the first chapter of his *Philosophical Discourses of Modernity: Twelve Lectures*, trans. Frederick Lawrence (Cambridge: MIT Press, 1987).
77 Jean Baudrillard. *In the Shadow of the Silent Majorities* (New York: Semiotext[e], 1983), 2.
78 See Paul Hegarty, *Jean Baudrillard: Live Theory* (London: Continuum International, 2004), 85.
79 See Mike Gane, *Jean Baudrillard: In Radical Uncertainty* (London: Pluto, 2000), 19ff.
80 Jean Baudrillard, *Fatal Strategies* (1982; New York: Semiotext[e], 1990).
81 Jean Baudrillard, interview with N. Czechowski, in Mike Gane, *Baudrillard Live: Selected Interviews* (London: Routledge, 1993), 195–6.
82 Qtd in Douglas Kellner, 'Baudrillard, Globalization and Terrorism: Some Comments on Recent Adventures of the Image and Spectacle on the Occasion of Baudrillard's 75th Birthday,' *International Journal of Baudrillard Studies* 2, no. 1 (2005).

5 Resisting Consuming: Ruin or Renewal

1 Hannah Arendt, *Between Past and Future: Eight Exercises in Political Thought* (New York: Penguin, 1968), 196.

2 See, for example, *On Knowing the Consumer*, ed. Joseph W. Newman (New York: Wiley, 1966).

3 See, for example, the works of Davide Gualerzi, *Consumption and Growth: Recovery and Structural Change in the US Economy* (Northampton, UK: Elgar, 2001).

4 John F. Kennedy, 'Special Message to the Congress on Protecting the Consumer Interest,' 15 Mar. 1962, JFK Link, http://www.jfklink.com/speeches/jfk/publicpapers/1962/jfk93_62.html.

5 'McGuinty Government Offers Advice to Holiday-Season Travellers,' news release, 18 Nov. 2004, http://www.gov.on.ca/MGS/en/ConsProt/050451.html.

6 Robert N. Mayer, *The Consumer Movement: Guardians of the Marketplace* (Boston: Twayne Publishers, 1989), 7.

7 Russell W. Belk, *Collecting in a Consumer Society* (New York: Routledge, 1995).

8 Florence Kelley, first executive secretary, National Consumers League. 'A Brief Look Back on 100+ Years, of Advocacy,' National Consumer League, http://www.nclnet.org/about-ncl/history.

9 David Asch and Brian Wolfe, *New Economy, New Competition: The Rise of the Consumer* (New York: Palgrave, 2001), 1.

10 Joseph Heath and Andrew Potter, *Rebel Sell: Why the Culture Can't Be Jammed* (Toronto: Harper Collins, 2004), 3, 8.

11 Joseph Heath and Andrew Potter, 'The Rebel Sell: If We All Hate Consumerism, How Come We Can't Stop Shopping?' *This Magazine* 11 (2002): 48.

12 Ibid., 101.

13 Guido Palazzo and Kunal Basu, 'The Ethical Backlash of Corporate Branding,' *Journal of Business Ethics* 73 (2007): 335.

14 Ibid., 337.

15 Ibid.

16 Manfred B. Steger, *Globalization: A Very Short Introduction* (Oxford: Oxford University Press, 2003), 72.

17 'Media Carta,' Adbusters, https://www.adbusters.org/campaigns/mediacarta. See also these Adbusters video clips and their accompanying audio rejections by major broadcasters: https://www.adbusters.org/campaigns/bnd.

18 'TV Spots,' Adbusters, https://www.adbusters.org/campaigns/bnd.

19 Ibid., 128–9.

20 Henry Giroux, *The Abandoned Generation* (New York: Palgrave, 2003), 106.

21 Seyla Benhabib, 'Arendt's Eichmann in Jerusalem,' in *The Cambridge Com-*

panion to Hannah Arendt, ed. Dana Villa (Cambridge: Cambridge University Press, 2000), 81. Italics hers.

22 Ibid., 177.

23 Jerome Kohn, 'Freedom: The Priority of the Political,' in *Cambridge Companion*, 126.

24 George Kateb, 'Political Action: Its Nature and Advantages,' in *Cambridge Companion*, 135.

25 Hannah Arendt, 'The Crisis in Education,' in *Between Past and Future* (New York: Penguin, 1960), 174.

26 Ibid., 185.

27 Vandana Shiva, *Earth Democracy* (Boston: South End, 2005), 67.

28 Natasha Levinson, 'The Paradox of Natality: Teaching in the Midst of Belatedness,' in *Hannah Arendt and Education: Renewing Our Common World*, ed. Mordechai Gordon (Boulder, CO: Westview, 2001), 13.

29 Ibid., 16.

30 Benjamin Barber, 'Taking the Public out of Education,' *School Administrator* 61, nos. 5–10 (May 2004): 1.

31 Arendt, 'Crisis in Education,' 192, 196.

32 Maxine Greene, *The Dialectic of Freedom* (New York: Teachers College Press, 1988), 116.

33 Tamar Lewin, 'In Public Schools, the Name Game as a Donor Lure,' *New York Times*, 26 Jan. 2006.

34 Alex Molnar, *The Ninth Annual Report on Schoolhouse Commercialism Trends: 2005–2006* (Tempe: Arizona State University Press, 2006), 48.

35 'About the Council,' The Council for Corporate & School Partnerships, http://www.corpschoolpartners.org/about.shtml.

36 Including among others: Susan Fuhrman, dean, Graduate School of Education, University of Pennsylvania; Warlene Gary, executive director, National PTA; Paul D. Houston, executive director, American Association of School Administrators; Judith C. Young, vice-president, American Alliance for Health, Physical Education, Recreation & Dance. 'Members of the Council for Corporate & School Partnerships,' The Council for Corporate & School Partnerships, http://www.corpschoolpartners.org/members .shtml (accessed 23 Sept. 2004).

37 D. Yourk, 'Ontario Introduces Healthy Menu to Elementary Schools.' *Globe and Mail*, 20 Oct. 2004.

38 'California Bans School Junk Food,' BBC News, 16 Sept. 2005, http://news .bbc.co.uk/2/hi/americas/4251928.stm.

39 Canadian Press, 'Ontario to Ban Trans Fats from School Cafeterias,' *Globe and Mail*, 4 Dec. 2007.

40 'Advertising Policy,' Toronto District School Board, 2005, http://www
    .tdsb.on.ca/wwwdocuments/parents/fundraising_guide/docs/
    fundraisingguide2.pdf; 'External Partnerships,' 2009, Toronto District
    School Board, 1999, http://www.pssp.on.ca/documents/TDSB%
    20PR-578%20SCS%20Exec%20Summary.pdf.
41 G. Livingston, 'Taking Soft Drinks out of Schools Only First Step to Deal
    with Youth Health,' CP Wire, 6 Jan. 2004.
42 'Ont. Minister Wants to Rid Schools of Junk Food,' CTV.ca, 26 Nov.
    2003, http://montreal.ctv.ca/servlet/an/local/CTVNews/20031126/
    cola_deals031126?hub=MontrealSports. See also 'Should Drinks Like
    Gatorade Sport the "Junk Food" Label?' Washington Post, 26 Sept. 2007,
    http://www.washingtonpost.com/wp-dyn/content/article/2007/09/25/
    AR2007092502281.html?nav=rss_health.
43 Caroline Alphonso, 'Taking the Brand to the Classroom: Call It Market-
    ing or Call It Goodwill, Companies Are Donating to Schools Like Never
    Before,' Globe and Mail, 30 Apr. 2005.
44 Sarah Schmidt, 'Aurora Boy Forces Cola Deals into Open,' CanWest News
    Service, 12 Nov. 2003, 1.
45 Sarah Elton, 'Parental Discretion Advised,' This Magazine 35, no. 1 (2001):
    19–23.
46 Ibid., 22.
47 Ibid., 23.
48 Molnar, Ninth Annual Report, 5.
49 Melissa Lickteig, 'Brand-Name Schools: The Deceptive Lure of Corporate-
    School Partnerships,' Educational Forum 68 (Fall 2003): 48. Qtd in Michael
    W. Apple, Ideology and Curriculum (1979; London: Routledge and Kegan
    Paul, 1990).
50 Maxine Greene, The Dialectic of Freedom (New York: Teachers College Press,
    1988), 12.
51 Levinson, 'Paradox of Natality,' 19.
52 Alison Cook-Sather, 'Movements of Mind: The Matrix, Metaphors, and
    Re-imagining Education,' Teachers College Record 105, no. 6 (2004): 14.
53 Levinson, 'Paradox of Natality,' 18.
54 Alan Luke, 'Teaching after the Market: From Commodity to Cosmopoli-
    tan,' Teachers College Record 106, no. 7 (2004): 1427, 1438.
55 Peter McLaren and Colin Lankshear, 'Critical Literacy and the Postmodern
    Turn,' in Critical Literacy: Politics, Praxis and the Postmodern (Albany: SUNY
    Press, 1993), 379. See also C. Luke and J. Gore, eds., Feminism and Critical
    Pedagogy (New York: Routledge, 1993).
56 Ibid., 382.

57 Geoff Pevere, 'Against the Flow: The Limits of Image Literacy,' in *Light Onwords / Light Onwards: Living Literacies* (text of the Conference at York University, Toronto, 14–16 Nov. 2002), http://www.nald.ca/fulltext/ltonword/complete.pdf, 120.

58 Jennifer Sandlin, 'Consumerism, Consumption, and a Critical Consumer Education for Adults,' *New Directions for Adult and Continuing Education* 102 (2004): 26.

59 Ibid.

60 Ibid., 29–30.

61 Ibid., 30.

62 Trevor Norris, 'Cultivating Sweet Things: An Interview with Culture Jammer Carly Stasko,' *Orbit Magazine* 35, no. 2 (2005): 22.

63 Ibid., 23.

64 'Marketing to Teens: Parody Ads,' Media Awareness Network, http://www.media-awareness.ca/english/resources/educational/lessons/secondary/advertising_marketing/mtt_parody_ads.cfm.

65 Mark Evans, Michael Slodovnick, Terezia Zoric, and Rosemary Evans, *Citizenship: Issues and Action* (Toronto: Pearson Education Canada, 2000).

66 Norris, 'Cultivating Sweet Things,' 22–5.

67 Ibid., 24.

68 Carly Stasko, '(R)Evolutionary Healing: Jamming with Culture and Shifting the Power,' in *Next Wave Cultures: Feminism, Subcultures, Activism*, ed. Anita Harris (New York: Routledge, 2007), 199.

69 Liz Worth, 'Just Do It – Yourself,' *Toronto Star*, 15 Aug. 2006.

70 Anne Elizabeth Moore, *Hey Kidz! Buy This Book: A Radical Primer on Corporate and Governmental Propaganda and Artistic Activism for Short People* (Chicago: Soft Skull, 2004).

71 Peter McLaren, *Life in Schools: An Introduction to Critical Pedagogy in the Foundations of Education* (New York: Longman, 1998), 116.

72 Levinson, 'Paradox of Natality,' 13.

73 Jane Roland Martin, 'Becoming Educated: A Journey of Alienation or Integration?' in *Philosophy of Education: Introductory Readings*, ed. John Portelli and William Hare (1985; Calgary: Detselig Enterprises, 2001), 73.

74 Deborah Kerdeman. 'Pulled up Short: Challenges for Education,' *Philosophy of Education Society Yearbook* (2003), 208.

75 Ibid., 211.

76 Ibid., 215.

77 Megan Boler, *Feeling Power: Emotions and Education* (New York: Routledge, 1999), 176.

78 Ibid., 2.

79 Ibid., 6, 32.
80 Ibid., 191.
81 Gert Biesta, 'Against Learning: Reclaiming a Language for Education in an Age of Learning,' *Nordisk Pedagogik* 23 (2004): 77, 79.
82 Carly Stasko and Trevor Norris, 'AML Panel on Youth Marketing: Transcript of Event,' Association for Media Literacy, 2 Nov. 2005, http://www.aml.ca/articles/articles.php?articleID=349.
83 Carly Stasko, 'More Than a Target Market: Active Youth,' *Clamor Magazine*, 20 (2002): 62.
84 Carly Stasko and Trevor Norris, 'Packaging Youth and Selling Tomorrow: Deconstructing the Myths of Marketalkracy,' in *The Corporate Assault on Youth: Commercialism, Exploitation, and the End of Innocence*, ed. Deron Boyles, 126–55 (New York: Lang, 2008).
85 Gia Medeiros and Chip Walker, 'GenWorld: The New Generation of Global Youth,' Energy BBDO Report, 2005, http://www.energybbdo.com/uploads/GenWorld%20Overview.pdf.
86 Stasko, '(R)Evolutionary Healing,' 196.
87 Stasko and Norris, 'Packaging Youth.'
88 Medeiros and Walker, 'GenWorld.'
89 Ann Sutherland and Betty Thompson, *Kidfluence: Why Kids Today Mean Business* (Toronto: McGraw-Hill Ryerson, 2001), 72.
90 Stasko and Norris, 'AML Panel.'
91 Shelly Reese, 'The Quality of Cool,' *Marketing Tools* 3, no. 6 (1997): 27.
92 Naomi Klein, *No Logo: Taking Aim at the Brand Bullies* (London: Harper Perennial, 2000), 9.
93 Ibid.
94 Guido Palazzo and Kunal Basu, 'The Ethical Backlash of Corporate Branding,' *Journal of Business Ethics* 73 (2007): 338.
95 Ibid.
96 Carrie McLaren, 'Celebs, Freaks, Media Lit: Interview with Joshua Gamson.' *Stay Free!* 15 (1998), http://ibiblio.org/pub/electronic-publications/stay-free/archives/15/josh.html.
97 Ibid.
98 Sutherland and Thompson, *Kidfluence*, 176.
99 Roger Simon, *Against the Grain: Texts for a Pedagogy of Possibility* (Toronto: OISE Press, 1992), 4.
100 Geoffrey Bennington, 'Politics and Friendship: A Discussion with Jacques Derrida' (Center for Modern French Thought, University of Sussex, 1 December 1997). http://www.sussex.ac.uk/Units/frenchthought/derrida.htm (accessed 24 Oct. 2007).

101 Medeiros and Walker, 'GenWorld.'
102 Stasko, '(R)Evolutionary Healing,' 193–220.
103 Francis Fukuyama, *The End of History and the Last Man* (1992; Toronto: Free Press, 2006), 46.
104 Gert Biesta, 'Education and the Democratic Person: Towards a Political Conception of Democratic Education,' *TCRecord* 109, no. 3 (2007): 2.

Conclusion

1 Maxine Greene, *The Dialectic of Freedom* (New York: Teachers College Press, 1988), 3.
2 Frederic Jameson, *The Seeds of Time* (New York: Columbia University Press, 1994).
3 Greene, *Dialectic of Freedom*, 7.
4 Naomi Klein, 'America Is Not a Hamburger: President Bush's Attempts to Rebrand the United States Are Doomed,' *Guardian*, 14 Mar. 2002, http://www.guardian.co.uk/media/2002/mar/14/marketingandpr.comment.
5 'Parents and Advocates Will Sue Viacom & Kellogg,' Campaign for a Commercial-Free Childhood, http://www.commercialfreechildhood.org/pressreleases/nickkellogglawsuit.htm.
6 Claire Atkinson, 'Channel One Hits Bump, Losing Ads and Top Executive,' *Advertising Age*, 14 Mar. 2005.
7 'Services,' Frost Centre Institute, http://www.frostcentreinstitute.com/seminars.html (accessed December 2007).
8 Martha Perkins, 'Retired IBM Executive Wins Bid for Frost Centre,' *Haliburton Echo*, 5 Dec. 2006.
9 Tom Hodgkinson, 'With Friends Like These ...,' *Guardian*, 14 Jan. 2008, http://www.guardian.co.uk/technology/2008/jan/14/facebook.
10 Tessa Wegert, 'Advertisers Playing Video Game Card,' *Globe and Mail*, 15 Dec. 2004. For consideration of the commercialization of the digital and online environment, see Henry Jenkins, *Fans, Bloggers, and Gamers: Media Consumers in a Digital Age* (New York: NYU Press, 2006).
11 Gert Biesta, 'Education and the Democratic Person: Towards a Political Conception of Democratic Education,' *TCRecord* 109, no. 3 (2007): 740–69.
12 Georg Wilhelm Hegel, *Elements of the Philosophy of Right*, ed. Allen W. Wood, trans. H.B. Nisbet (1820; Cambridge: Cambridge University Press, 1990), 23.
13 Karl Marx, 'The Thesis on Feurbach,' in *The Marx-Engels Reader*, ed. Robert C. Tucker (1845; New York: Norton, 1978), 145.

14 Hannah Arendt, *The Life of the Mind: Thinking* (New York: Harcourt Brace Jovanovich, 1978), 190, 129, 124.
15 Ronald Beiner, *Philosophy in a Time of Lost Spirit: Essays on Contemporary Theory* (Toronto: University of Toronto Press, 1997), x–xi.

Index